SPANISH BLUECOATS

Spanish Bluecoats

THE CATALONIAN VOLUNTEERS IN NORTHWESTERN
NEW SPAIN 1767–1810

Joseph P. Sánchez

PUBLISHED IN OBSERVATION OF THE 500TH ANNIVERSARY
OF SPAIN'S DISCOVERY OF THE NEW WORLD

University of New Mexico Press / Albuquerque

Library of Congress Cataloging-in-Publication Data

Sánchez, Joseph P.
Spanish bluecoats : the Catalonian Volunteers in northwestern
New Spain, 1767–1810 / Joseph P. Sánchez.—1st ed.
p.   cm.
"Published in observation of the 500th anniversary of Spain's
discovery of the New World."
Includes bibliographical references (p.
ISBN 0-8263-1195-4
ISBN 0-8263-1207-1 (pbk)
1. Catalans—California—History. 2. Catalans—Northwest,
Pacific—History. 3. California—History—To 1846. 4. Northwest,
Pacific—History. 5. New Spain—History. I. Title.
F864.S227   1990
979.4'00449—dc20
90-10709
CIP

Illustration for the stamping on the cloth edition is by David Siegel.

FIRST EDITION

For my wife, Clara Joyce, and my sons, Joseph and Paul

Contents

Contents

Figures

Maps

Maps

Foreword

The history of the Free Company of Catalonian Volunteers begins with the Spanish crown's last efforts to consolidate its empire following the Seven Years War (1756–1763). Spain's pride had been wounded by embarrassing concessions forced on both the French and Spanish Bourbons by England, principally, in the Treaty of Paris of 1763. For Carlos III, the empire's salvation lay in a body of reforms that came to be called the Bourbon Reforms. There were four notable features of the reforms introduced into the New World: the widespread reorganization of professional troops and the enlistment of colonial militia units for the defense of the empire; the adoption of free trade for Spanish ships most any place in the empire, a policy that reversed the colonial commercial practice of nearly three centuries; the expulsion of the Company of Jesus (the Jesuits) from all the Spanish colonies as well as Spain in the interest of discouraging an *imperium in imperio,* which had allegedly threatened the integrity of the empire; and the reorganization of New World provinces into intendancies in order to reform the fiscal system and increase revenues toward the betterment of colonial administration. The Bourbon Reforms almost worked, but in the end, an independence movement that began in New Spain and spread to the rest of the overseas dominions spoiled all hope of restoring a dying empire. The story of the Catalonian Volunteers begins with the inspiration of the Bourbon Reforms and ends on the battlefields of the provinces southwest of Mexico City where insurgents brought the king's army to its knees.

The rise and fall of the Spanish Empire is a history of institutional control of natural and cultural resources. Indeed, for 328 years, exploration, pacification, settlement, and missionization constituted the dynamics of Hispanic frontier cultures throughout the Spanish empire from northern Africa to the Americas and the Philippines. Continuity and change characterized the process of the developing Spanish frontier cultures, which imitated their European parent culture and modified it until a diluted representation resulted. Yet, at the heart of the process were Spanish institutions that controlled social, religious, economic, military, and political behavior within colonial societies. From 1492 to 1821, Hispanic frontiersmen moved from valley to valley, planting the Spanish flag on an ever expanding imperial claim.

The historical development of Spanish colonialism is well known. However, not unlike England, France, Portugal, and other colonial powers, Spanish colonialism was predicated on the exploitation of natural resources and cheap labor. In order to control its far-flung empire, the Spanish crown at first employed exclusivistic policies that precluded foreigners from participating in its imperial economy so that Spanish penisulars could reap the profits of the resources within the Spanish claim. Additionally, a dual Indian policy, one for sedentary tribes that were readily exploitable and the other for nomadic or warlike tribes, followed Spanish expansion each step of the way across the Americas. Spanish colonialism molded and reshaped the face of most of the New World.

Colonial administration depended on intelligence gathering and reporting. Like their English, French, and Portuguese counterparts, Spanish explorers recorded on maps the locations of sedentary and nomadic tribes, topographical features such as rivers, mountains, and vegetation, and to the extent that colonial technology revealed them, minerals such as gold, silver, tin, iron, copper, and other metals. European cartographers also plotted the best hardwood and softwood forests, salt beds, dyestuffs, tarpits, soils, wildlife, fisheries, and other exploitable resources. Reports, correspondence, and cartographical sources on such matters filled the king's archives throughout Spain and the empire.

Continual exploration, control of cheap native labor, and widespread Hispanic settlement patterns were the mechanisms through which exploitation of resources took place. Colonial-native relationships that resulted from European domination of the Americas were, in part, aimed at the methodical exploitation of resources. Given the intense rivalry between English, French, Portuguese, Spanish, and other European colonial powers, competition for strategic and resource-rich lands led to wars among them.

It is little wonder that in 1786, Carlos III declared in his *Ordinance of Intendants for New Spain,* "It is my royal will that the intendants in their provinces shall take care of everything pertaining to war which may be connected with my royal treasury." A copy of the document was sent to all officials in the empire and deposited in their archives for future reference. Already, the Free Company of Catalonian Volunteers had been hard at work performing the king's will.

The imperial context under which Spain assumed sovereignty over the Americas, placed the Catalonian Volunteers in a unique situation. As troubleshooting military units, the First and Second Companies of Catalonian Volunteers participated in the age-old colonial plan aimed at controlling and defending the Spanish claim to the New World. They took part in the pacification and settlement of Sonora (which included present-day southern Arizona) and parts of Sinaloa and Nayarit in western Mexico and in the exploration and settlement of Alta California from San Diego to San Francisco. Indeed, the Catalonian Volunteers participated in the discoveries of San Francisco Bay and the Great Central Valley; the exploration of the Pacific Northwest as well as the reestablishment of the Spanish claim to Alaska, 1790–1792; the defense of Veracruz, Guadalajara, and the Minas Reales de Pachuca; and, the crown's ill-fated attempt to quell an independence movement in New Spain. Between 1767 and 1815, the Catalonian Volunteers militarily reinforced Spain's claim to the northwestern portion of her American empire, assisted in the imposition of Spanish sovereignty over native groups, and defended Spain's right to exploit natural resources and cheap native labor in North America.

Without doubt, the history of the Catalonian Volunteers is as much a part of our national story as the American Westward Movement. Joseph P. Sánchez, director of the Spanish Colonial Research Center, National Park Service, at the University of New Mexico, demonstrates that Hispanic frontiersmen had much in common with their Anglo-American counterparts. Furthermore, the Christopher Columbus Quincentennial in 1992 will evermore serve as a milestone to our Pan-American heritage that began as an encounter between two worlds:

Indian America and Europe. The present study examines a part of our Indo-European heritage as it stood 300 years after Columbus's landing. It is a heritage which not only forms part of our national history but ascribes to it our common history with Latin America.

Manuel Lujan, Jr.
Secretary,
Department of the Interior

Preface

For nearly five decades, from 1767 to 1815, the Free Company of Catalonian Volunteers participated in Spain's last great effort to secure the northwestern portion of its vast empire in the Western Hemisphere. During those years, the Catalonian Volunteers served in a number of assignments that represented a renewed defensive expansion into Sonora, California, and Alaska. The Sonora expedition (1767–1771), led by Domingo Elizondo, introduced the Catalonian Volunteers to New Spain's northwestern frontier. In Sonora, the unit formed part of an eleven-hundred-man army sent to crush Indian resistance to European settlement. The four-year war, a testimony to the indomitable spirit of Indian America, nevertheless represented one of Spain's major efforts to pacify the area for colonial investors and settlers. As the war in Sonora raged, a detachment of Catalonian Volunteers was reassigned to the California expedition (1769–1774) under the command of Governor Gaspar de Portolá. During that period, the coast and interior of California were explored by land for the first time. The Catalonian Volunteers participated in the establishment of San Diego and the discovery of San Francisco Bay in 1769, and, later, in the sighting of the immense Central Valley of California from the headwaters of the San Francisco River in the north to the San Joaquin Valley in the south. The Catalonian Volunteers returned for service in Sonora, ultimately pursuing Yuma rebels into the Arizona wastelands in what came to be called the Colorado River campaign of 1781–82.

In the early 1790s, the Catalonian Volunteers served with the *Expedición de los Límites,* which reestablished Spain's claim to the Pacific Northwest. Establishment of fortifications at Nootka Sound on the west coast of Vancouver Island was accomplished by the Catalonian Volunteers, many of whom were concurrently assigned to ships that sailed north past present-day Sitka, Mount St. Elias, Cordova, Valdez, the Kenai Fjords, Cook Inlet, and beyond Katmai on the Alaska Peninsula.

The last great adventure of the Catalonian Volunteers is linked to the demise of the Spanish empire as it had been known in the Americas. Caught up in the military events of Mexican Independence (1810–1821), the Catalonian Volunteers were absorbed into the royalist armies fighting the insurgents of Mexico. At the Battle of Cuautla (1812) in southern Mexico, the unit was badly mauled by the desperate rebel army led by Father José María Morelos y Pavón. The unit survived to fight the rebels at Tuxpango (1813), Tlacotepe (1814), and Ajuchitlan (1815), whereupon the Catalonian Volunteers disappear from the historical record.

The historical significance of the Catalonian Volunteers in their assignment to New Spain lies chiefly in their military accomplishments as well as in their activities as colonizers. Although their historical significance has been widely recognized for nearly a century, precisely who served in the company, how it was organized, and how fully the Catalonian Volunteers influenced the course of regional history has been hinted at more than revealed. This book attempts to bring the Catalonian Volunteers into sharper focus, and to explore in a broader sense their contributions in an imperial context extending beyond the realm of regional history.

Historians of Spanish colonial history have known of the Catalonian Volunteers, especially with reference to the 1769 establishment of California. Hubert Howe Bancroft's *History of California* (1884–1890)[1] makes passing references to the Catalonian Volunteers and to some of their officers. Details in Herbert I. Priestly's *José de Gálvez, Visitor-General of New Spain, 1765–1771* (1916) first reveal the use of Catalonian Volunteers in Sonora.[2] Later, Donald W. Rowland's dissertation, "The Elizondo Expedition against the Indian Rebels of Sonora, 1765–1771" (1930), supplied more details concerning the use of Spanish troops in the Sonora campaign, in which the Catalonian Volunteers played a part.[3] Although Rowland's study closed the gap somewhat, the broad interpretive perspective of the Catalonian Volunteers was still wanting. The first significant study with respect to the Catalonian Volunteers was accomplished in Donald A. Nuttall's dissertation, "Pedro Fages and the Advance of the Northern Frontier of New Spain, 1767–1782" (1964).[4] Predating Nuttall's study was Oakah L. Jones's thesis, "The Spanish Occupation of Nootka Sound, 1790–1795" (1960);[5] and Donald C. Cutter's unpublished essay "Pedro de Alberni and the First Scientific Agricultural Experiments in the Northwest" (1973)[6] revealed still other glimpses of the Catalonian Volunteers and the Spanish claim to the Pacific Northwest. Finally, Ronald Ives's *José Velasquez: Saga of a Borderland Soldier* (1984) offered another brief view of the Catalonian Volunteers in Sonora.[7] As each study complemented its predecessors, none placed the Catalonian Volunteers within the greater picture of the Bourbon Reforms and the defense of the Spanish empire, nor linked them with events that stretched across the continent from Veracruz to Alaska.

Before acknowledging the professional archivists and historians who assisted me in the research for this book, I express my love and appreciation to my wife Clara and to my sons Joseph Max and Paul Adrian for accompanying me throughout every step of this endeavor; and to my parents, Bersabe Martínez Sánchez and the late José Patricio Sánchez, for teaching me about our colonial forefathers. My sister-in-law, the late Rosemary Castillo Timmons, read the manuscript and offered invaluable criticism as it was being written.

This study began as a dissertation under the able direction of Donald C. Cutter at the University of New Mexico. Moreover, a Ford Foundation fellowship generously funded my travel to Spain and Mexico. The product of such work is often accomplished with the support of legions of people whose kindness and expertise encouraged me to its conclusion. In the United States, I extend my appreciation to Edwina Abreu of the National Park Service's Spanish Colonial Research Center; Dr. Alex Sánchez, Vice President for Community and International Affairs at the University of New Mexico, Albuquerque; Mary Isabel Fry and the staff at the Huntington Library; Nettie Lee Benson, Jane Garner, and Laura Gutierrez-Witt of the University of Texas Library, Austin; and three fine gentlemen, now deceased: France V. Scholes, Manuel Servin, and George Eckhardt. In Mexico, the staff of the Archivo General de la Nación, Salvador Victoria Hernández in particular, greatly facilitated my search for materials related to Sonora and Sinaloa. In Spain, I am indebted to the staff of the Archivo General de Indias, especially Directora Rosario Parra Cala and María Antonia Colomar; Dr. Luis Navarro García of the Universidad de Sevilla; the staff of the Archivo General de Simancas near Valladolid; the staff of the Museo Naval (Madrid); the staff of the Archivo Histórico Militar (Madrid); and the staff of the Archivo Histórico Nacional (Madrid). Dr. Jaime Salas of the Fundación Xavier de Salas and Lic. José María Caller Celestino of the Universidad Complutense de Madrid, also gave invaluable research assistance. Finally, a special note of appreciation for Dr. David Holtby, Associate Director, University of New Mexico Press.

Joseph P. Sánchez
Director, Spanish Colonial Research Center
National Park Service
Albuquerque, New Mexico

SPANISH   BLUECOATS

1 / The Catalonian Volunteers Come to New Spain

Turning his gaze toward Spain's international affairs, the middle-aged Carlos III, king of Spain, perceived England as his most dangerous enemy. Partly because of his attitude toward the English and also due to close family ties, the Spanish Bourbon patriarch entered into an alliance, the Family Compact, with his French cousin Louis XV. Soon after, in 1761, Spain belatedly entered the Seven Years War (1756–1763) waged by France against England. Although the war was rooted in an earlier Franco–Prussian dispute over possession of Silesia along the Oder River, by midcentury the struggle had reached proportions approximating a world conflict. In Europe, France, Spain, Austria, and Russia pitted their armies against the forces of Great Britain and Prussia, while on several other fronts Spanish and French colonials clashed with Englishmen for control of Canada and the trans-Appalachian West to the Mississippi River Valley in North America, the Caribbean, and India. In the end, however, Prussia and England emerged victorious; the former content with its repossession of Silesia and the latter triumphant as supreme mistress of the seas. In the wake of defeat, Carlos III ordered a reassessment of England's victory.

Indeed, the outcome of the Seven Years War proved to be significant for the later history of Europe. For the moment, however, Carlos III was concerned about his American empire. Although his diplomats were able to negotiate for the return of British-held Havana by conceding the loss of western Florida, the hapless French representatives at Paris in 1763 made important strategic concessions to their British counterparts. Of her American possessions, France lost all but a few islands off the coast of Newfoundland and others in the Lesser Antilles, as well as surrendering part of Guiana in South America. The meaning of such concessions was evident to Spanish officials who realized that England had gained strategic bases and an abundance of raw materials. Doubtless, the British victory caused widespread alarm among the Spanish colonial authorities.

The Peace of Paris in 1763 had given North America a new map. Inasmuch as Spain had gained sovereignty in 1762 over a portion of the Mississippi River possessions extending from St. Louis to New Orleans, wary Spanish sentinels later kept their watchful eyes on the woodlands to the East for British activity. Beyond the Appalachian Mountains lay thirteen English colonies, all eager to expand westward toward the weakly held Spanish frontier. After 1763, English parliamentarians debated on how to use to their advantage the waterways of the St. Lawrence River and the Great Lakes as well as the lands of the trans-Appalachian West and their newly acquired West Indies possessions. They realized that the treaty had given Great Britain an advantage she had never before enjoyed.

In an effort to shut the Pandora's Box opened by defeat, Spain and France planned to avenge their losses. Carlos III formed a secret committee which met once a week in Madrid to discuss a program of defense for the Spanish Indies. Composed of the principal ministers of the crown, the committee, early in 1764, presented their king with a general plan.[1] Thereafter, defense of empire became the Spanish watchwords for their new policies, and an intensive Bourbon reform program was inaugurated.

The Bourbon Reforms called for greater efficiency in key administrative institutions of the empire as well as a defense plan which stimulated recruitment of new military units. In charge of the defense program for New Spain was Lieutenant General Juan de Villalba y Angulo,[2] captain general of Andalusia. As one of the most important officers in Spain, Villalba received the post of "Comandante General and Inspector General of the Army of New Spain." At his command was the Regimiento de America, comprised of Spanish troops and foreign mercenaries who were to serve as training cadres in the armies of New Spain. Villalba had formed the Regimiento by recruiting troops from Naples, Brabante, Flanders, Lisbon, and the North African post of Oran, all within the Spanish sphere of influence. The greater number of troops, however, came from within the Spanish provinces and principalities such as Sevilla, Granada, Corona, Castilla, Navarra, Toledo and others.[3]

Departing from Cádiz, Villalba, his staff, and a contingent of troops arrived in Veracruz on November 10, 1764.[4] In beginning their work, they reassessed New Spain's defense firsthand and debated, once again, proposed solutions to an age-old dilemma. Villalba saw the obvious. Aside from different enemy challenges, there were two corresponding parts to the defense problem, each one extremely complex in nature. The first part concerned the coastal defenses of New Spain, especially those at Veracruz, whose primary function was to defend against invasion from the sea by Spain's European rivals. The second part of the defense problem involved the northern frontier of New Spain. Stretching from the Gulf of Mexico to the Pacific Coast of the Californias lay a hostile Indian frontier which had never been pacified. Villalba realized that he must not only reorganize the interior defenses but regenerate them through the cadres of professional soldiers in the Regimiento de America. In their assessment of the defenses, Villalba and his staff also reviewed defense proposals submitted by military advisors in New Spain.

Although the reassessment was military in scope, it was not without its political complications. As the *comandante general* went about his business, he inadvertently offended the Viceroy Marqués de Cruillas, whom he failed to consult on military affairs.[5] The rift between Villalba and the viceroy, who by dint of his office was indeed captain general of New Spain, became an unnecessary affliction to the much-needed cooperation affecting a program of defense. Notwithstanding Villalba's failure to acknowledge the viceroy, he still had his mission to accomplish.

In the midst of the commotion, however, Viceroy Cruillas did issue instructions to the Marqués de Rubí, a *mariscal de campo* attached to the Villalba mission, to begin a general inspection of the north.[6] Bidding farewell to their superiors, Rubí and a small escort left Mexico City in May 1766. For two years the dutiful field marshal and his staff inspected the entire presidio system of the Provincias Internas from Guanajuato to New Mexico and from Sonora to Texas. During Rubí's inspection tour, Villalba returned to Spain, and Cruillas was replaced by the Marqués de Croix. Neither Villalba nor Cruillas realized the significance of Rubí's *visita*. Ironically, the two rivals had agreed to order an inspection that resulted in a series of military policies affecting the defense of New Spain's northern frontier.

Returning to Mexico City in February 1768, Rubí made his report to Viceroy Marqués de Croix, who, with a military council, had been left to struggle with the problem of defense. Rubí's return was not only timely but invaluable to Croix's planning. Realizing that Rubí's report added nothing new about the deplorable defenses of the north except detail, Croix found it exploitable as a selling point for his defense proposals to the king. Croix and his round table of military advisors in Mexico City could now substantiate the understatement that the Provincias Internas lacked an adequate defense program. Important to the report was a series of recommendations that Rubí had included. Moreover, in his correspondence to the king and to the viceroy, Rubí expanded upon his suggested remedies for the defense problem. His most famous recommendations included the repositioning of presidios to form a strategic line of defense against Indian raiders and to upgrade the morale of soldiers through the regulation of discipline, training, and salaries. He even suggested that a new Indian policy based on alliances would secure the frontier against rebel warriors. Although some of his recommendations had been tried before, Rubí's enthusiasm seemed to add a new perspective to an age-old problem. Given Rubí's practical insights and the need to act quickly, the crown issued the Reglamento de 1772,[7] a set of military regulations that provided a plan of defense as well as rules governing the deportment of military personnel while on duty. To that end, the 1772 regulations served to set the tone and pattern for soldiering on New Spain's frontier.

In the meantime, Spanish officials had to contend with a military structure in transition. Even as Rubí was making his inspection of the north, a full-scale Indian war broke out in Sonora and Nueva Vizcaya. Despite the lack of military preparedness, Spanish provincial governors had to be content with whatever military forces they possessed. For years, Governor Juan de Pineda of Sonora had petitioned authorities in Mexico City for permission to lead a punitive expedition against rebel Seri, Pima, Suaqui, and Sibubapa warriors.[8] Finally, upon taking the matter to the newly arrived Marqués de Croix, his petition was placed on the agenda of the next scheduled *Junta de Guerra de Generales*. Among those present at the junta of January 4, 1767, was José de Gálvez, the politically powerful Visitador General of New Spain.[9] Gálvez, a favorite of Carlos III, regarded Pineda's petition favorably. Lis-

Map of Northern New Spain by Manuel Mascaró, 1779.
(Biblioteca National, Madrid)

tening politely while glancing at a copy of the governor's request, Gálvez was probably thinking about the relationship between the pacification of Sonora and the settlement of Alta California, a project he had been planning. Certainly, Pineda asked for military aid at a most propitious moment. Upon termination of the order of business, the Council of War was adjourned to meet again four days hence.

Meeting again on January 8, the viceroy, the visitador, and their military advisors quickly moved to order a punitive expedition to Sonora.[10] Also present at that meeting were Colonel Domingo Elizondo, of the Dragones de España, and his staff. Elizondo delivered a status report on the availability of troops in New Spain for the campaign. After a lengthy discussion, the council members agreed that the ex-

7

peditionary forces be composed of 1,110 men and ordered Colonel Elizondo to begin mobilization of troops for the Sonora expedition.

Recruitment of 1,110 men for his army would not be an easy task, as Elizondo soon learned when he spoke to company commanders about releasing some of their men for voluntary duty in Sonora. Even Governor Antonio María de Bucareli of Cuba declined to send the one hundred troops he had promised earlier because he needed them to guard the port at Havana. Determined to fill the ranks of his army, Elizondo at once began the search for a company of riflemen. Slowly, the persistent colonel created his expeditionary force.

Luck favored Elizondo, for at that very moment in the northeastern Spanish province of Catalonia, a company of one hundred riflemen had recently been formed. Organized throughout April 1767 as part of the ongoing Villalba project, the Compañía de Fusileros de Montaña de Cataluña had orders to serve as harbor guards at Havana.[11] Having discovered the existence of that much-needed unit, the wily Elizondo began to pull at the political strings of Viceroy Marqués de Croix to get the orders of the Catalan company of mountain fusiliers changed for duty in Sonora. Before long, the viceroy received a letter from Julián de Arriaga, Spanish minister of Marine Affairs and the Indies.[12] Writing from Madrid, Arriaga informed him that the governor of Cuba could not spare the troops originally promised to Elizondo. Coincidentally, Governor Bucareli had already decided to keep his riflemen in Havana. And so the Company of Mountain Fusiliers of Catalonia, which meanwhile had begun its march from Barcelona to Cádiz, was informed of the change en route to Sevilla in early May.

A week or so after they received the change in orders, Agustín Callis, their captain, announced a response to his petition for a name change of his new unit. In response to Callis's request, Señor Don Juan Gregorio Muniain, a royal counselor at Aranjuez explained that

> Instead of mountain fusiliers, His Majesty grants that in its assignment these troops be called Compañía Franca de Voluntarios as they have petitioned, in order that they may depart from the vulgar terms of Miñones or Migueletes which Catalonians are called.[13]

The miguelete, part of the firing mechanism of the fusil, had somehow inspired a derogatory name given to mountain fusiliers from Catalonia. Although Callis had his reasons for the request, the new name, Free Company of Catalonian Volunteers, certainly hinted that the unit would be used as a trouble-shooting reserve outfit in New Spain's Provincias Internas.

Marching through the narrow, cobbled streets of Sevilla, the Volunteers, stepping in cadence to the drummers' beat, attracted the attention of shopkeepers, vendors, and other interested passersby. In advance of the unit strode Callis and his three junior officers, smartly attired in the traditional uniform of the Second Regiment of Light Infantry of Barcelona. Dressed in blue breeches, white stockings, black shoes, a yellow waistcoat with white buttons and a black cravat, Callis cut a dashing figure. His large gallooned hat of silver silk thread with a flowing cockade and his long blue overcoat with yellow collar and yellow stitchings added to his striking appearance.[14]

Presenting his officers and men to Señor Don Alonso Cavallero, comisario de Sevilla, Callis began the review. Don Alonso listened to the roll call while he observed that the noncommissioned officers and men wore a slightly similar uniform to that of Callis, except that their shirts had high collars with yellow stitching, and instead of the long great coat the men wore a short blue cloak with sleeves. Their hat was different, too; it was a small, blue woolen cap. As they stood in the mid-May sun, their muskets and bayonets reflected in the bright Andalusian sunlight. Armed with light infantry fusils with Catalan stocks,[15] the blue-cloaked troopers responded to the roll call.

Up to that time little was known about the Catalonian Volunteers aside from their availability for service in Mexico. Numbering one hundred men, the unit was recruited from the Segundo Regimiento de Infantería Ligera de Cataluña stationed in Barcelona. Besides Captain Callis, Cavallero met Lieutenant Pedro Fages and the two sublieutenants, Estévan de Vilaseca and Pedro de Alberni, the three junior officers of the company. In descending order, the other members of intermediate rank who responded to the roll call were the four sergeants, Joseph Casas, Juan Puig, Juan Puyol, and Ramón Conejo; two drummers, Joseph Demeus and Melchor Leoni; and four corporals, Jaime Joven, Juan Recio, Mauricio Faulia, and Miguel Pericas. Signing the review, Comisario Cavallero noted that the company comprised four officers, four sergeants, two drummers, four corporals, and ninety soldiers.[16]

Of them all, the most experienced and dedicated to the call of arms

Uniform of the Catalonian Volunteers. (Rendering by David Siegel, U.S. Fish and Wildlife Service)

was Captain Callis. Born some time in 1718 to Francisco and Josepha Callis of Vich in the Principality of Catalonia,[17] seventeen-year-old Agustín enlisted in the Regimiento de Fusileros de Barcelona.[18] Rising through the ranks from soldier to corporal, Callis made sergeant in 1741. Five years later, the stalwart Catalan musketeer received promotion to lieutenant, a rank he held until 1748 when his company was extinguished during a peacetime cutback of the military. As he packed his bags to return to civilian life, Callis and his comrades probably reminisced about their thirteen years of army life. Doubtless, the regiment meant much to Callis, for he was one of the original foot soldiers of the unit, which had been organized in 1735.[19]

Thinking back to this early combat experiences, Callis recalled his first two expeditions, both against Italy in the War of the Austrian Succession. In the first expedition (1736–1738), an inexperienced eighteen-year-old Callis caught a glimpse of warfare at the successful siege of Mantua in northern Italy. Soon after, Spanish and Italian officials negotiated a peace which lasted until 1742. In the second expedition (1743–1748), an experienced Callis, now a sergeant, faced a more serious and determined enemy. At Campo Santo the Barcelona troopers tasted a short-lived victory, but later they were repulsed and nearly routed at Pesaro. Retreating from Pesaro to Naples, Sergeant Callis deployed his men in rear-guard action. Quickly rebounding from defeat, the Fusileros de Barcelona attacked Italian musketeers in the mountains of Veletri, and moved forcibly against Montalfonso, where they captured its castle. Next, they advanced against the Italians at Voltagio. There, in hand-to-hand combat, Callis and his men fought victoriously for the tower of the Genovesado. Advancing, the hard-fighting Barcelona troops marched against Marsailles in the kingdom of Naples, and after that they marched against Fortuna, Monferrato, and Pavia. To Callis, the battle of Pavia was unforgettable. In the ensuing successful surprise attack, both the city and citadel fell to rejoicing Spanish forces.[20] Callis was there, and he had seen it all. Throughout the two campaigns in Italy, Callis's conduct, valor, and selflessness were commended by his commander, Miguel Boix.[21]

Returning to Vich, thirty-one-year-old Callis determined to establish a new life for himself. Winning the hand of Doña Rosa Casañas Maso, the daughter of Dr. José and María Maso, Callis married on March 6, 1750. It was Doña Rosa's second marriage, as she was the widow of José Casañas.[22] Two children were born to Callis and Doña Rosa, and both progeny later became historically notable in New Spain. The eldest, Eulalia Francisca y Josepha Callis, was born sometime in 1751, and her brother, Antonio, was born in 1760.[23] Although little is known in regard to Callis's thirteen years at Vich, he undoubtedly tried his hand at farming, for that was the main occupation of that region. Had it not been for a call for troops, this time against Portugal, the restless Catalan might never again have donned a uniform. In the summer of 1762, Callis joined the Second Regiment of Light Infantry of Catalonia as a lieutenant, the rank he had formerly held as Fusilero de Barcelona. Obviously, Don Agustín preferred the thrill of military life to the pastoral existence at Vich.

April 1767 was a decisive month for the forty-nine-year-old Catalonian officer. During that month, Callis committed himself to the organization and leadership of the Catalonian Volunteers. Much was on his mind during that time, for he had to negotiate that his men be paid three months in advance to cover the period of transit from Barcelona to Havana; in addition, he recruited officers and men for his new command. Aside from the business of mobilizing a military unit, Callis made arrangements for his family. Doña Rosa was not pleased about the prospect of being left behind with two children while her husband sailed off to a new assignment, possibly never to return. Nonetheless, Callis arranged for his wife and children to remain in Barcelona and to receive part of his salary for living expenses.[24] Organization of the Catalonian Volunteers had indeed been quick, requiring only a few short weeks, and other members of the company had to make similar decisions. Soon enough, amidst emotional farewells, the Volunteers began their march from Barcelona to Cádiz by way of Madrid and Sevilla.

At Sevilla they were reviewed and presented with orders. Instead of serving as guards at Havana, they were assigned to New Spain as combat troops in the Sonora campaign. Contemplating their mission in the Americas, some of the men, especially two *armeros,* or gunsmiths, changed their minds and asked to be relieved of duty.[25] For the moment, Captain Callis calmed his men, but he was unable to persuade the two gunsmiths to return to the unit. Realizing that his fusiliers would be virtually useless without the much needed *armeros,* Callis quickly advertised the vacancies in Sevilla. Pressed for time and having failed to find such replacements, Callis and his staff decided to march to Cádiz and set sail without them, hoping they could be replaced upon arriving in New Spain.[26]

Meanwhile, at the port of Cádiz, fidgety Don Juan Antonio de la Colina, *Jefe de Escuadra,* paced on his ship, the frigate *Juno,* impatiently awaiting the arrival of the Catalonian Volunteers. Upon meeting Callis, Don Juan Antonio hurriedly advised him to get underway while sailing conditions were still favorable.[27] Boarding the *Juno* and the storeship *San Juan,*[28] the blue-cloaked Catalan troopers prepared themselves for the nauseating voyage across the rough water of the Atlantic Ocean. After ordering his crewmen to raise the sails and weigh anchor, Don Juan noted the first entry in his logbook, dated May 27, 1767.[29] As for Callis and his men, their first assignment with an unknown destiny would soon begin.

Disembarking at the humid port of Veracruz in August 1767,[30] Callis ordered his men to begin the long march to Mexico City. After a month of marching along winding mountain roads over a mile above sea level, the volunteers entered the ancient Mexican capital.[31] Because of unexpected problems that had developed in the transport of troops to Sonora, the exhausted Catalan soldiers were given a few extra days to recuperate from their traveling. In the meantime, Agustín Callis reported on the condition of his command. In his review, Don Agustín indicated that twenty-five soldiers were ill, one was dead, and one had deserted.[32] Accounting for ninety-six men (less the casualty and the deserter) and four officers, Callis submitted a copy of his report to Viceroy Marqués de Croix, who was interested in the condition of the Volunteers.

Once rested in Mexico City, the Catalans marched westward, to the green mountainous country of Nayarit. Meanwhile, on the western Mexican coast, the transport of troops to Sonora by sea had bogged down, and Elizondo petitioned the viceroy to detain the Volunteers in Mexico City until he could find a ship to take them to Guaymas. Furthermore, wrote Elizondo, the Catalonian troops probably would not be transported until mid-November.[33] But the Volunteers were on their way, and by October they camped outside the mountain village of Tepic, not far from Matanchel, the proposed port of departure.

At Tepic, Callis and his men observed Jesuits under guard. Removal of the Jesuits from their Sonora and Baja California missions had required the use of the ships that Elizondo had requested for the transport of his troops. As they watched the haggard priests and their military escorts, the Catalan troops witnessed the historical expulsion of the Jesuits from the Spanish empire. Although stunned by the events that had befallen them, the Jesuits would later defend themselves against the charges. Antagonistic royal officials had insisted that the Jesuits were disloyal to the crown, had conspired to establish a theocratic state within the empire, and had comprised too many foreigners. Simultaneous with the arrest and removal of the Jesuits, Franciscan missionaries in the area were being escorted northward by soldiers to assume their duties.[34] Thus the operation had involved the use of Elizondo's troops[35] and ships, considerably delaying the campaign. Concurrently, Tepic appeared to be a crossroads for the two events.

Assembly of troops for the Sonora expedition took place in Tepic.[36] Reviews of troops there show that the Catalan Volunteers had regained full strength of four officers and one hundred men. Because the weather had changed drastically, making navigation by sea virtually impossible,[37] Tepic became the temporary barracks for Callis and his men, and they remained there through December. They were now part of the expedition.

As the Christmas holidays passed and the new year approached, Elizondo's mind began to "vacillate incessantly" under pressure from the viceroy, who demanded to know why the expeditionary forces had not been moved to Guaymas, the next point of assembly.[38] Elizondo met with naval personnel, who advised him that under conditions of contrary winds transportation from San Blas, the newly established port north of Matanchel, to Guaymas would take fifty days.[39] For the moment, Don Domingo was caught between his naval advisor's counsel and his viceroy's orders. Reflecting upon the *junta de guerra* held the previous year, Elizondo recalled the viceroy's mandate "to cover the Province of Sonora as quickly as possible with so many troops that conditions for Indian raids would be eliminated."[40] Realizing the importance of the strategy, Elizondo decided to gamble despite the weather.

Announcing that the expeditionary force would be divided, Elizondo ordered his men to break camp. Part of his command would go by land and the rest would go by sea. Ordering his men to march to San Blas, Callis told them that they were part of the seagoing contingent. On January 20, 1768, the Volunteers boarded the packetboat *Laurentana,* a 54-ton vessel confiscated from the Jesuits, and the remaining troops boarded the brigantine *San Carlos,* a 193-ton ship built in 1767.

Hoping to get all of the troops to Sonora at about the same time, Elizondo ordered his land forces to begin their march northward.[41]

Suffering strong contrary winds, both ships bobbed back and forth in the Gulf of California without making much headway. After two weeks of sailing, the *San Carlos* was forced to return to San Blas, and her captain reported that he had sighted Culiacán. On February 24, the *Laurentana* attempted to enter the Port of Culiacán, but it returned to Mazatlán after a furious wind forced the ship out. Determined to accomplish its mission, the *Laurentana* left Mazatlán on April 1, and a month later it entered the Port of Guaymas. The next day Callis and his seafaring Volunteers left the ship, and after trudging along the beach they arrived at the Guaymas barracks. A few days later, the *San Carlos* anchored in the bay where the rest of the seagoing troops landed. After 105 days the sea wing of the expeditionary force established itself at the Sonoran post.[42] In contrast, the land phase of the expedition had arrived in Guaymas after marching for 58 days.

Once settled at Guaymas, Callis, Fages, Vilaseca, and Alberni looked back and took stock: it had taken them over a year to travel from Barcelona to Guaymas. Remarkably, in all of that time, they had lost only two men. Callis reviewed his troops once again as they prepared to adjust to a new environment and a different style of warfare.

2 / Campaigning in Sonora, 1767–1771

Captain Agustín Callis and his men caught their first glimpse of the Sonoran malpaís from their Guaymas barracks. Despite the cool December air and the captivating rhythm of the swaying tide along the Gulf of California, they were aware of the desert behind them. Looking inland, they saw the dry and craggy landscape of the barren terrain of Sonora. Already Callis and his men knew of the aridity of the hinterland, for they had been ordered to remain at Guaymas until potable water for the campaign could be found.[1] Soon, they would go with scouting parties and learn more about the interior.

Looking through their telescopes, Domingo Elizondo's scouts gathered information about the terrain. Before long, Elizondo's sketchy field maps were marked with locations of *ojos,* or waterholes, mountain ranges, river valleys, and Indian strongholds. From his maps, the commander and his staff discovered that the *"tierra de guerra"* was a tremendously large area. Nevertheless, they planned to concentrate their efforts with the land stretching from the western seacoast to the Sierra Madre Occidental that formed the eastern limits of Sonora and, from two immediate points, Guaymas in the south and Pitic near Hermosillo in the north. Between those points lay a long mountain range called Cerro Prieto, which rebel Indians used as their stronghold.

Cerro Prieto, also known as Sierra de Santa Rosa, stretches across the desert north of Guaymas for about a hundred miles. It comprises many canyons, some of which the Spaniards named Cajón de Ana María,

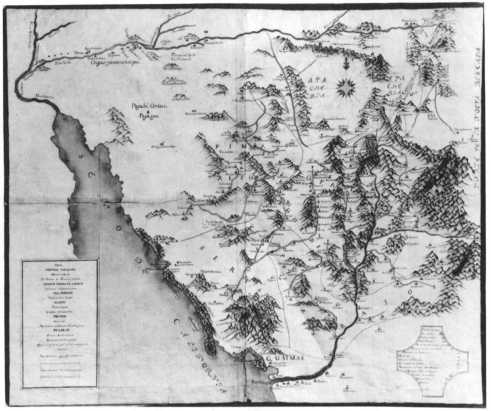

Map of Sonora, c. 1776. (Biblioteca National, Madrid)

Cajón de Loreto, and Cajón de la Palma. Earlier, when Father Tomás Ignacio Lizasoin, a Jesuit chaplain, saw it, he wrote that the range was "covered with brier and undergrowth."[2] Later, Agustín Callis, who led his Catalan soldiers through Cajón de la Palma, described the land as "craggy, full of brambles, of bad footing, *de mal piso,* and loose rock."[3] And, Captain Matías de Armona, who scouted the area, explained that

> Cerro Prieto is not a loaf of sugar, *no es pilon de azucar,* as some have thought, but a place composed of elevations and stretching mountains, which is 40 to 50 leagues in circumference, and in the heart of it are heights or peaks superior to all the others . . .

Plano del Corazón de Cerro Prieto (Campaign Map, 1768).
(Archivo General de Indias, Sevilla)

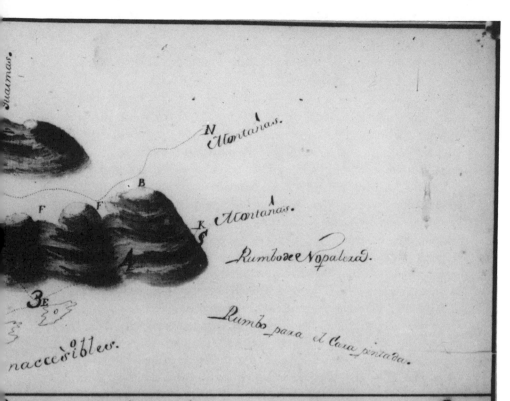

Juamas.

N Montañas.

B

F   F

K Montañas.

Rumbo de Nopalera.

Rumbo para el Casa pintada.

3 E

inaccesibles.

Dijose que en Cerro Prieto, no harra sino tales quales Tinajas, ó Calderas de ?
...ia; que harra muy poco Mezcal, de que se pudieran mantener los Enemigos
...estos andavan por Naciones en distintos Cañones, ó Barrancas, hasta
abismos del Infierno; y todo hera mentira: pues ay Agua, para to-
los Siglos; Mezcal para otro tanto tiempo; y los Enemigos, viven aqui,
, quando son perseguidos en los llanos, y en las entradas de los Cañones
mismo modo, que en los Campos: Esto es, en pequeñas tropillas, y en
a una de ellas, se encuentran Seris, Suaquis, y Pimas: yo vivi quin-
ó diez, y veas rancherias de ellas, que no son otra cosa, que un mal en-
rejido delos ramales, delas matas, vajo las quales viven

252

19

and, outside are other rugged ridges and boggy lakes covered
with undergrowth where the enemy hides when vigorously pursued.[4]

The rebel Indians used it because it was formidable. The undergrowth,
the stony ground, and the many labyrinths and elevations made it
difficult for Spanish foot soldiers and cavalrymen to pursue them.
Looking purplish and forbidding in the distance, the Sierra de Santa
Rosa became one of the best known battle sites of the Sonora campaign.

In mid-August 1768, Elizondo convened a council of war to plan
the invasion of Cerro Prieto. Gathered around him and his maps were
Governor Juan de Pineda; Juan Bautista de Anza, the legendary Indian
fighter from Fronteras; and Captains Lorenzo de Cancio and Joseph
Bergosa, who were familiar with the Cerro Prieto range.[5] After reviewing and discussing the scouting reports, they agreed to order troops
to attack rebel warriors wherever they might be found.[6] Their plan,
to force the Indians into their Cerro Prieto strongholds, was designed
to render them incapable of maneuvering freely in the open desert. At
that point, the soldiers could surround the strongholds or at least close
off escape passages, thus forcing the enemy to surrender. In practice,
the plan operated by using small patrols to press the offensive against
the enemy. Once the patrols located the rebels, they held them under
observation until reinforcements arrived. As soon as the troops were in
position, the soldiers began their assault on the strongholds. Throughout the Cerro Prieto campaign, such tactics were used time and again.

In early September, Elizondo's command was spread about camps
at Pitic, Guaymas, and San José de Pimas. Starting with a series of
forays against the Sonoran warriors, the troops from Pitic probed the
northern side of the mountain range at Cerro de Tonuco, Pilar de
Ibarburu, and the Sierra del Bacuachi. Meanwhile, at Guaymas, Agustín Callis and his Catalonian Volunteers readied themselves for whatever
orders would be forthcoming from the Council of War.[7] They did not
have long to wait, for at that very moment a skirmish was taking place
near Cerro Prieto, a fight that would prompt Elizondo to commit the
Guaymas detachments to action.

In the vicinity of Cajón de la Nopalera, Captain Anza and fifty soldiers
shot it out with a band of Indians. Moving quickly, Anza's men killed
five warriors and captured a fifteen-year-old youth. The young man, it
turned out, was Spanish. He had been held captive for nine months,
before Anza's attack had given him an opportunity to escape. Eagerly,

Anza questioned him. Giving the captain the information he needed, the youth explained that the rebels planned to ambush his men at Cajón de la Nopalera. Because, the youth continued, "the warriors could see that Anza's soldiers were not wearing their leather armor, they were not afraid to attack them."[8] Despite the threat, Anza must have allowed himself a moment of glee, as he looked toward the canyon. For the moment, he declined the challenge. Riding away from Cerro Prieto, the astute Anza had a better plan, one which would involve the troops from Guaymas and Pitic.

Meeting with the Council of War at San José de Pimas, Anza presented his report and recommendations to Elizondo and his staff. Captain Anza speculated that the rebels were disposed to run into the canyons whenever the soldiers were nearby. Relying on that information, Elizondo proposed a plan. In order to force the Indians into their Cerro Prieto strongholds, the Guaymas and Pitic troops would sweep the coastline from two directions.[9] Hoping that each encounter would create a major confrontation at Cerro Prieto, Elizondo ordered the commencement of an operation which would take a month to complete.

Cooperating with their counterparts from Pitic, the Guaymas-based Catalonian Volunteers began their sweep from the south. In the north, meanwhile, Pitic scouts reported that the drive was forcing the rebels into the densely forested Monte del Tenuage. Marching hard for six straight days, the troops from Guaymas headed north to reinforce the Pitic movement. Exhausted from heat and lack of water, the sweat-soaked soldiers abruptly stopped their march. It appeared that they could proceed no farther. Even their horses and mules, which had climbed each grade with difficulty, whinnied and brayed in objection to the forced march. Undaunted, the strong-willed Elizondo was determined that they should reach their objective in three more days. After a short rest period, Don Domingo pushed them forward to Monte del Tenuage. Finally on September 9, his scouts found tracks of the enemy.[10] Pursuing their trail despite his fatigued troops, the commander smelled a battle in the offing. The sweep seemed to be forcing the rebels to take a stand.

Wise in the ways of war, however, the rebel warriors planned an ambush. Picking the heavily wooded Monte del Tenuage was no accident on their part. Lying in wait, the Indians could see the green- and blue-uniformed soldiers advancing. As they approached a clump of trees, the warriors let out their war cries and stopped the Spaniards with a tremendous volley of arrows. Quickly, the surprised soldiers pulled back and set up a line of musket fire. Moving his horsemen away from the trees, Elizondo tried to maneuver them to a more advantageous position. Terrain proved important in this battle. The Indians not only held the high ground; the forest allowed them enough cover so that other warriors in the vicinity could join them. For almost an hour, Spanish troops traded musket shots with zinging arrows from the woods. In an effort to dislodge the enemy, Elizondo ordered that a heavy line of fire be concentrated on the woods.[11] But the warriors still held the upper hand, for they had stopped the Spanish advance, at least momentarily.

As the action tapered off, the troops pushed through the woods. Counting thirteen dead rebels, the soldiers saw much blood on the ground along a trail leading deeper into Monte del Tenuage. Unable to defeat the Indians in their first major skirmish, Elizondo explained that his troops were inhibited by a forest that was eight leagues long. That, he believed, had saved the rebels. Still, the Indians had managed to attack his rear in an attempt to capture Spanish horses. Moreover, the valiant desert warriors had taught the soldiers a lesson in respect. One officer wrote that the Indians were "not as cowardly as they have been made out to be by those who have not seen them."[12] While the rebels retreated, mounted soldiers patrolled the area. In the calm that followed the battle, Elizondo ordered a roll call, and wounded soldiers were taken to Pitic because Guaymas was too far away.

Planning a general attack on Monte del Tenuage, Elizondo ordered more patrols to scout the area. In one such sortie, the Guaymas troops attacked a war party, killing seven Indians at Cerro del Tambor.[13] Other, similar missions denied the enemy an opportunity to regroup and attack Elizondo's main troop. Each encounter was a step toward the major offensive they planned against the fearless warriors in the forest.

The tension in Elizondo's camp was electrifying. Dramatically, the stalwart commander issued orders that no one was to leave camp without permission. In a speech to his men, he told them of the three unfortunate soldiers who had dared to look for a pistol, informing them that one of the men had dropped it during the battle. Although their bodies were found, all hanging upside down from a tree, one of them had suffered a horrible death, for his hands and head had been cut off.[14] Having witnessed the violence of Indian warfare, the soldiers were willing to heed their commander's mandate. Anxiously, they awaited orders to commence the attack.

In preparation for the invasion of Monte del Tenuage, Elizondo encouraged some of his soldiers to buy horses from the neighboring haciendas. A strong cavalry charge, Elizondo reasoned, would force the rebels to run from their hiding places. First, foot soldiers would move against the Indian positions; then after a lively round of fire, his horsemen would attack and chase the fleeing warriors. Once the men were ready, the commander ordered them to stand in battle formation. Steadying their mounts, the dust-covered Catalonian Volunteers waited for the signal to begin the second battle against their foe.

On September 10, Elizondo's drummers and fifers sounded the signal to begin the attack. Dutifully, the sergeants checked to make certain that their men were moving along in the formation. Sporadic popping from their muskets could be heard, and the puff of burnt powder was visible, as the men increased their fire against the warriors. After fighting bitterly for the next two days, the rebel Indians broke and ran from the woods; but they did not surrender. By September 12, the Spanish horsemen had pursued the Indians to Pilar de Ibarburu in Cerro Prieto.[15] A week later, fighting small bands along the way, the same troops clashed with the rebels at Aribaipaia several leagues from Monte del Tenuage. After an additional sixteen days of march, the pursuit was called off, and the troops, dirty and sweaty, returned to Pitic in an exhausted condition.[16] In the second battle, the Spaniards had redeemed their pride, but not before they had learned invaluable lessons in Indian warfare.

Still, there was no rest with Elizondo in command, for he soon ordered a repetition of the tactics already employed. His plan, to drive the enemy into Cerro Prieto and attack them there, seemed to be working. For the next few months, the commander sent detachment after detachment against the rebels, widening the arc of sweeping movements from Guaymas to Pitic. Elizondo sent Captain Miguel Gallo and his dragoons to invade the neighboring province of Ostimuri, as the area between the Yaqui and Mayo rivers had been named.[17] His objective was to force escaping renegades back to Cerro Prieto. At Sierra de los Pilares, in the Sierra Madres, Gallo and his men, in pursuit of a band of warriors, were pulled into an ambush. Fighting their way out of the trap, the force suffered only two wounded men. Gallo's foray apparently pushed some of the rebels back to the sanctuary of the

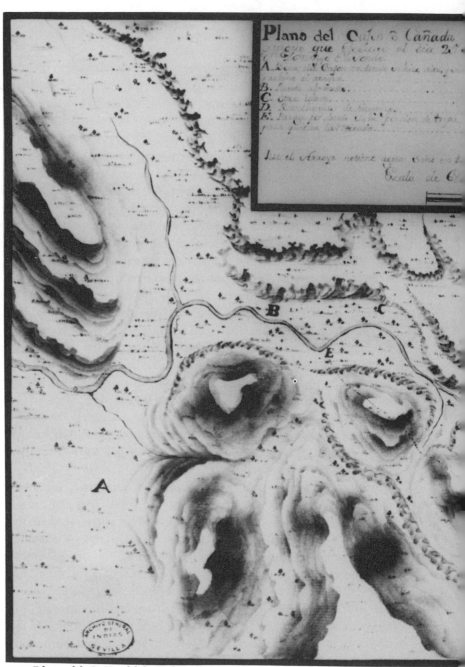

Plano del Cajón del la Palma (Campaign Map, 1767–72).
(Archivo General de Indias, Sevilla)

Sonoran mountains. Confident of his plan, Elizondo concentrated his efforts on Cerro Prieto.

Throughout the early autumn of 1768, Elizondo continued to send several scouting parties from Pitic and Guaymas into Cerro Prieto. By October, scouts reported seeing numerous Indian camps in the various canyons. One scout leader, Pedro de Alberni, sublieutenant of the Catalonian Volunteers, reported on several rebel strongholds there. Don Pedro had acquired a reputation as a scout, and before the campaign was over, the twenty-three-year-old bachelor from Tortosa, Catalonia, had led twenty-six missions into that mountain range.[18] Similarly, his report, along with those of others, confirmed to Elizondo the locations of the enemy hideouts. After a few more encounters, his scouts reported that the majority of Piatos, Seris, and Sibubapas were hiding in Cajón de la Palma.[19]

Surrounded by many escape passages, Cajón de la Palma, in "the heart of Cerro Prieto," was a formidable enemy stronghold. Diligently, Elizondo commanded that all entrances leading to it be taken. By October 20, after two days of skirmishing, the Spaniards controlled all passages leading to the canyon. The Seri and Sibubapa warriors were trapped, along with their families. In addition to those successes, captured Indians informed the commander that a few of the rebels desired peace. Reasoning that a general attack would convince them all to surrender, the colonel and his staff met and formed a plan of attack. To ensure that the encirclement was complete, Elizondo ordered that all canyons adjacent to Cajón de la Palma be occupied. Within a few weeks, reinforcements from Guaymas and Pitic crossed over the rugged wastelands and occupied Cajón de Arroyo, Cajón de Loreto, and Cajón de Cosari.[20]

Development of troops had been taking place throughout the operation. Of the 320 troops at Cajón de Loreto, 55 were Catalonian Volunteers. They had been there since October 18 and had engaged in a midmorning skirmish two days later.[21] Crouching in the warm autumn sun, the Volunteers held their position, occasionally conversing with one another, and perhaps complaining, as soldiers often did, about their rations of parched corn, jerky, and water. Probably, they also discussed Elizondo's delay in ordering the attack on the canyon. After all, they had been told that the attack would be made from Cajón de Loreto because of its accessibility to Cajón de la Palma.[22]

November came and the weather began to cool, especially at night.

The wait continued. Finally on the morning of November 23, troops from Guaymas and Pitic were sent to the mouth of Cajón de la Palma in preparation for the assault on the rebels. Unexpectedly, however, Elizondo called off the attack.[23] The experienced colonel was concerned about the dark clouds forming overhead and the gust of wind suddenly beginning to blow. Within a short time it started to rain. Just as Don Domingo had feared, the winter rains had arrived.

By afternoon of the next day, the sky had cleared. About 3:00 P.M., the troops began to move into their assigned battle positions along the floor and walls of Cajón de la Palma. Moving cautiously on the canyon floor, dismounted cavalrymen pulled their horses behind them as they followed captured Indian guides, who had been promised freedom for their services. For six hours the guides led troops through the maze of canyons to their positions.[24] Upon approaching the rebel camp in the dark, the soldiers crawled along the rocky ground. So close had they come to the rebel camp, they could hear the Indians chanting and could even see their faces in the light of their campfires.[25] Fearful of being detected, the soldiers dared move no closer.

In the meantime, along the canyon walls, other troops had been climbing to their positions. It was almost midnight when forty Catalonian Volunteers were ordered to camp near a group of friendly Pima auxiliary troops, who were bedding down for the night on one of the flat elevations. As the Catalan soldiers began their ascent, the light of a full moon broke through the winter clouds, casting an eerie pall over the boulders in the canyon. Upon reaching the flat, the Volunteers began to settle down near their Pima neighbors. The climb had been exhausting and their rest would be short; for at daybreak they would climb still higher so that they could spy on the rebel camp and take count of the warriors and their women and children.[26] Nearby, a nervous Elizondo watched his soldiers move about to take up their positions. He could hardly wait until morning to launch a perfect surprise attack on the enemy.

Shortly after midnight, twelve Fusileros de Montaña, who had been trailing some thirty paces behind the Catalonian Volunteers, approached the camp of the Pima auxiliaries, who were innocently sitting and talking among themselves. One of the fusiliers, peering at the shadowy figures of the Pimas in the dark, thought they were the enemy about to slaughter the Catalonians. Without a second thought, he raised his musket and opened fire. Reacting to the shot, nine of his comrades began shooting, too. Six Indian friends were wounded that night, and two of them died the next day.[27] For the moment, however, the element of surprise was lost. What appeared to be a certain victory turned into a night skirmish.

As the Volunteers scrambled for their weapons, the besieged rebels, accidently alarmed by the musket shots, instinctively ran for safety. At the same time, Spanish soldiers positioned high in the canyon opened fire after they were surprised by a number of Indians dashing through their positions.[28] In the confusion, the soldiers were unable to distinguish the auxiliaries from the enemy. Worse still, three times during the fighting, heavy rain showers fell. And right before Elizondo's eyes, a Fusilero de Montaña was killed when his wet musket failed to fire as his knife-wielding adversary charged him, slitting his abdomen so effectively that he died instantly.[29]

Nearby, Catalonian Volunteers Estévan Stá, Mauricio Faulia, and Francisco García set up a lively fire. All three were familiar with the canyon, for they had scouted it previously. They were joined by Estévan Solá[30] and Luis Rojas,[31] two Mountain Fusiliers who later transferred to the Volunteer company. Faulia, at thirty-five, was the oldest of the five men.[32] And Stá, from Santa María Sellen, Catalonia, was twenty-nine years old at the time.[33] Solá was the most experienced with New World warfare. Before he went to New Spain, he served with the Havana Coast Guard, and in action against the Dutch he had been wounded several times. Earlier, Solá had been a presidial guard at San Agustín, Florida. None of them, however, had ever been in a fight like the one at Cajón de la Palma. Callis was there, and so was Alberni. Both of them led their men in a charge on the canyon floor. After the fight, Colonel Elizondo praised the Catalonian Volunteers for having delivered "a lively and steady fire."[34]

After the outbreak, Elizondo ordered that the canyon be searched as soon as a cloud lifted which had settled at ground level. In the meantime, his officers gave him a casualty report. Unofficially, aside from the single fusilier killed, only two men had been wounded.[35] Of 319 troops at Cajón de la Palma, Elizondo noted that 39 Catalonian Volunteers had been with Callis and Alberni when they led their charge.[36] Miraculously, none of them had been wounded.

Once the cloud had lifted, a scouting party entered the canyon. There, they found six women, ten children, forty-one horses, and many deer hides—signs that the enemy had left in a hurry. The scouts estimated the enemy force on the canyon floor to have been about one hundred men.[37] Judging from the amount of blood found on the ground, they concluded that an undetermined but appreciable number of the enemy had been wounded.[38] In the early sunlight, the soldiers followed the blood trail a certain distance and noted its direction. Soon after, they returned to camp and reported to their commander.

At daybreak, Elizondo's camp was buzzing with excitement caused by the night action of a few hours before. While the men tended to their bruises and wounds, Callis went about interviewing the fusiliers who had been involved in the accidental shooting that had triggered the fight. After talking to the ones who had fired the shots, Callis made his report to a brusk Elizondo, who was angry because the mistake had cost him a victory. Still, Elizondo was not satisfied, and he ordered the Guaymas troops and the Catalonian Volunteers to march out and find the enemy. They were gone two days before Elizondo recalled them.[39]

In the meantime, a party of soldiers returning to Cajón de la Palma spotted some warriors who had reoccupied their former campsites, apparently confident that the Spaniards had left the area. Upon seeing the soldiers, the warriors retreated into the landscape without returning fire with their arrows. A short time later, Spanish scouts found a trail of blood leading into the mountains of Cerro Prieto, which they followed but lost.[40] Five days after the fateful night fight, Elizondo decided to regroup his command. To that end, he ordered the soldiers back to their respective bases at Pitic and Guaymas.[41]

On December 2, the Catalonian Volunteers and the other Guaymas troops en route to their base found fresh tracks of the enemy and followed them back to Cerro Prieto. Pursuing the warriors through the Cajón de Avispa, the soldiers found water. There, they watered their horses and filled their water bags before pushing ahead. The next day, they followed the tracks of Indian war ponies. A short distance away, the soldiers skirmished with the enemy, some of whom were fugitives from the battle of Cajón de la Palma. In the fight, the soldiers captured twenty horses.[42] The rebels broke and ran. The chase continued.

Near a place called Pozos de Fastiola, scouts found fresh blood on the ground. Cautiously, they followed the blood trail. By and by, they came upon a Yaqui woman, who told them that three braves, upon seeing that they were being followed, had fled to the nearby foothills. Pointing to a mountain, the woman told them the warriors would be at Cara Pintada—Painted Face. Quickly, the soldiers sent word to the main body of troops, and together they continued the pursuit.

Meanwhile, Elizondo, aware of the activities near Cara Pintada, ordered another forced march. This time, over four hundred men marched twenty-five leagues (nearly sixty-three miles) in fifty-two hours, most of it without water because the trail was extremely dry.[43] Pursued through the canyons of Cerro Prieto, the Indians made their stand in their mountain stronghold. The one-day battle of Cara Pintada took place on February 25, 1769. The same tactic as that used in the second battle of Monte del Tenuage was employed. Foot soldiers, like the forty-six Catalonian Volunteers under Callis, began the attack. Then a cavalry charge was unleashed against the enemy. Unable to resist, the Indians retreated. To the Indians, armed mostly with bows and arrows, the fire power of the five hundred troops led by Elizondo was awesome. Skillfully, the warriors escaped to the rocky ground where their trail could not be followed. Having punished the enemy once again, Elizondo ordered his men back to Guaymas.[44]

Again and again, small patrols scouted the Indian strongholds at Cerro Prieto. Before long, the expeditionary force had amassed a long record of skirmishes, scouting missions and battles. By 1770, Elizondo had ordered four major attacks on Cerro Prieto, including a second battle of Cajón de la Palma in October 1769. The soldiers had even chased the Seri to Tiburon Island and fought them off the coast of Sonora. Elizondo's troops had not only fought Piatos, Sibubapas, Yaqui, Pima, and other similar groups; they were also forced to contend with Apache raiders, who entered the war as spoilers. The Apaches became especially frustrating to Elizondo, when suddenly, in 1770, they shifted their attacks to the haciendas and towns of Nueva Vizcaya in the direction of Chihuahua. When that happened, the settlers from across the Sierra Madres began to clamor for protection, and Spanish officials began to evaluate the utility of the Sonora expedition in relation to the Bourbon plan of defense.

By the end of 1770, Elizondo, under orders from Viceroy Antonio María de Bucareli, began to withdraw his command from Sonora. After three years and two months of warfare, Agustín Callis and his Catalonian Volunteers marched southward over the mountain of Nayarit and then west to Mexico City. In mid-April 1771, the bedraggled Compañía de Voluntarios entered the viceregal capital to await orders for a new assignment.[45] Most of the other troops of the Sonora expedition had been withdrawn by that time, and only a remnant force was stationed there to protect the province's frontiersmen.

Sitting at his desk, Callis dipped his plume into the brown sepia inkwell and began writing the report of his unit. Although his company had been commended by Elizondo, the Catalonian Volunteers had not survived the war unscathed. About half of the original company was with him. Less than one-third of his men had deserted, taking fourteen fusils and thirty bayonets as they fled;[46] and another twenty-five men had been detached to Alta California, where they had been since 1769. Aside from the desertions, Callis had to contend with the retirement of one of his sublieutenants, Estévan de Vilaseca, and with the re-cruitment of new troops to fill the depleted ranks of this command. In particular, Vilaseca, who had been praised for his "honor, valor, and zeal" during the campaign, had served the unit well.[47] Aside from being a good officer, he was the *comisario de campaña*.[48] As such, he inventoried the supplies and made certain that they were distributed among his men. He was the company accountant as well as its bookkeeper. In the midst of reforming his company, Callis did not immediately replace Vilaseca.

3 / The Establishment of California

For a long time California was all but totally ignored by Spanish officials. From 1602 to 1768, the California coast was visited by mariners either exploring New Spain's northwestern littoral or stopping there to recuperate from the ravages of scurvy suffered during the trans-Pacific voyage from the Philippines. While it does seem that little was accomplished in occupying California as an area of settlement during this period, these years represent a silent unfolding of Spanish planning. Much of the data reported by seagoing Spaniards regarding the land, coupled with intelligence concerning the danger of Russian encroachment on Spanish claims in the northwest, generated a sort of historical force pointing toward the eventual settlement of California.

Although Spanish fears regarding the possible loss of territory to Russia prompted a newfound vigilance concerning California, other factors presented themselves in 1768 for Spain's consideration of a California colony. The fear that Englishmen would eventually discover the Strait of Anian, or a Northwest Passage, also stimulated Spanish interest in the north. Heretofore ignored missionary petitions to evangelize the Indians of the northwest Pacific coast received renewed importance. Certainly, the Sonora expedition of 1767 was another factor leading to the colonization of strategic points in California. The Sonora expedition introduced a group of bureaucratically minded men into New Spain's northern frontier; men who envisioned military expansion into Alta California as part of the Bourbon defense plan. One of these men was Visitador General José de Gálvez, who not only planned part of the campaign against marauding Indians in Sonora, but also made a personal investigation of the state of affairs of Spain's Baja California possessions.

With the arrival of Gálvez, old schemes to create harbors for the Manila galleons and to missionize the natives of the north were reactivated to fit the designs of the overall plan for defense of empire. Furthermore, with the Sonora expedition came new military personnel, namely, the Catalonian Volunteers, who would be associated with the defense of California for the next three and a half decades. Simultaneous to such a military buildup was the 1768 establishment of an important seaport at San Blas. Spanish ships from California, and eventually from the Pacific Northwest and Alaska as well, anchored at San Blas. It was probably at San Blas that Gálvez conceptualized further his plan to colonize California.[1] Gálvez activated part of his scheme earlier, when, in September 1768, he ordered Lieutenant Pedro Fages and twenty-five Catalonians to San Blas from Guaymas where they were stationed.[2] Fages and his men had been with the Elizondo-led Sonora expedition. For a short time, this detachment of Volunteers guarded the *San Carlos,* alias *Toisón de Oro,* anchored in the port of San Blas as it was being readied for the trip northward.[3]

From San Blas the Catalans sailed to La Paz, in Baja California. Another ship, the *San Antonio,* alias *El Príncipe,* formed the second part of the sea expedition. These ships were under the command of Captains Vicente Vila and Juan Pérez, respectively. In addition to the sea expeditions, Gálvez prepared two land expeditionary forces, one led by the governor of Baja California, Gaspar de Portolá, and the other by Fernando Javier de Rivera y Moncada. Thus, a two-pronged attempt at settling California was planned. Supplies for the land expeditionary force were forwarded by sea, on board the *San Carlos* and *San Antonio.*

In early December 1768, the *San Carlos* arrived at La Paz from San Blas, with the Catalonian Volunteers aboard.[4] However, the leaky *San Carlos* had to be unloaded, careened, and reloaded. Working hard at this task were Gálvez, who personally lent a hand, and the Catalonian Volunteers, who assisted crew members.

While at La Paz, Fages received his instructions from the California assignment from Visitador Gálvez.[5] The significance of the orders is twofold. First, these orders spelled out the role that Catalonian Volunteer troopers were to play in establishing California; and second, the authority given Fages, the Catalan officer, as *Jefe de las armas* (commander of the military at sea), is explained. Principally, Fages was to maintain command of his soldiers on land until the arrival of Governor Portolá at Monterey.[6] Moreover, Gálvez entrusted Fages with the daily distribution of rations in the most economical way possible.[7] This particular order would later cause Fages trouble because he was criticized by his men for the way in which he distributed their daily rations.

Aware of the perils to men in confinement on a ship for a span of time, Gálvez warned Fages that strict discipline had to be observed. Gálvez recommended that the Catalonian troops keep harmony with crew members by helping with some of the labor on board ship,[8] just as they had helped unload, careen, and reload the *San Carlos* earlier at La Paz. Wisely, Gálvez instructed Fages that it would be best if his men ate their meals with the crew.[9] In this way, Gálvez hoped to create an atmosphere of harmony and comradeship among the men and thereby avoid dissension.

The first objective of the expedition was to reach San Diego. On January 9, 1769, the *San Carlos* was ready.[10] Members of the expedition went to confession, attended Mass, and received Holy Communion. Then they heard a speech presented by Gálvez. The message Gálvez imparted to the men was punctuated with words to the effect that they had been chosen to plant gloriously the flag and cross of Catholic Spain in the wilderness in the name of God, king, and viceroy. Gálvez reminded them that they were to maintain peace and harmony among themselves.[11] After Gálvez's presentation, Father Junípero Serra, who had sung the Mass, completed the devotional exercises by blessing Vila; Costansó; Fages; Father Fernando Parrón, chaplain of the expedition; the Catalonian Volunteers; the crew; the ship; and the standards.[12] In all, sixty-two men comprised this expeditionary force.[13] Aside from the crew members, the notables (mentioned above) who comprised the expedition included Pedro Prat, surgeon; Costansó, royal engineer; and Vila, captain of the ship.

Fages's command of Catalonian Volunteers (1769–1774) included seventeen men from the original one hundred men who sailed from Cádiz in May 1767. The rest were probably recruited from Antonio Pol's Compañía de Fusileros or from the various other companies which formed the Sonora expedition. Fages was reinforced from time to time during the five-year period, but reviews of his command for this period have not been located.

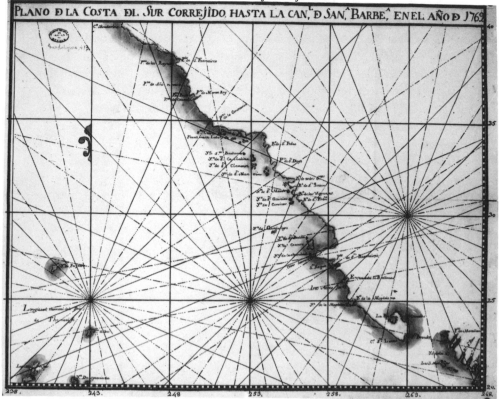

PLANO Ð LA COSTA ÐL. SUR CORREJÍDO, HASTA LA CAN, Ð SAN, BARBE, EN EL AÑO Ð 1769.

Map of Alta California, 1769. (Archivo General de Indias, Sevilla)

Among those who belonged to the original band of Catalonian Volunteers were Gerónimo Bulferic, Francisco Gombari, Pablo Ferrer, Domingo Malaret, José Molas, Antonio Montaña, Luis Moumarus, Miguel Pericas, Gerónimo Planes, Valentín Planello, Francisco Portella, Juan Puig, Domingo Clua, Domingo Arús or Ariús, Andrés Auguet of Huguet, Manuel Butrón, and Antonio Yorba (Torva). Others who joined the California expedition as Catalonian Volunteers included Ramón Bonnél, Francisco Cayuelas, Miguel Lineza, Miguel Manzana, Miguel Soberia Pengues, and José Sorde.[14] It is difficult to ascertain how many of the men listed above were with Fages on board the *San Carlos,* for no actual list of Fages's 1769 command has ever been found. Furthermore, Fages was later reinforced with twelve Catalonian Volunteers to make up for his losses of the first few months in San Diego.

Chapter 3

Within a day of Father Serra's ceremony, the *San Carlos* left La Paz. On board ship, Pedro Fages studied his instructions again. He reviewed Gálvez's plan regarding union with the land expedition led by Fernando de Rivera y Moncada. Upon arrival at San Diego, he must find a certain hill, located northwest of the port, for three fires marking Rivera's camp.[15] Hopefully, Rivera would precede the sea expeditionary forces by land and establish a base on that hill. In case Rivera had not arrived, Fages was instructed to land his troops with care and reconnoiter the land. From the Indians, wrote Gálvez, he was to "learn if Captain Rivera had been seen and if so, where would his camp be located."[16]

In the event that Rivera had not arrived, Fages, the Volunteers, and the crews of the two ships would establish a base and wait. The contact between the Catalan Volunteers and the natives was to be friendly. Gálvez felt that the first encounter would be important for the success of the missionization process. The *visitador* declared that "the commander of the troops ought to make the utmost effort possible to establish a good relationship with the Indians so that they will be disposed to receive, without repugnance, the establishment of a mission."[17] Once relations with the natives were stabilized, Engineer Miguel Costansó would select a site for buildings, and Fages and his men would begin construction of provisional shelters. Once a foothold was secured in San Diego, Fages and his Catalan soldiers were to maintain their position until Rivera and his troops arrived to establish themselves as presidial soldiers and mission guards.[18] Notwithstanding the order, the instructions directed Fages and his men to board the *San Antonio* and sail for Monterey if Rivera and his men had not arrived.[19] This portion of Gálvez's instructions to Fages clarified that a beachhead would also be established at Monterey. If possible, the Catalan Volunteers were also encouraged to make peace with the Indians there. Once in Monterey Bay, the Catalonians, armed with muskets, were to board a small launch and proceed cautiously to the beach. Once on the beach, Miguel Costansó, royal engineer, was instructed to select a site for a provisional fort. The Catalonian troops were to set up a camp on the chosen site, and the camp was to be fortified with a ditch, stockade, and cannons.[20] Again, as in Fages's instructions for the establishment of San Diego, the Catalonian leader and engineer Costansó were directed to send soldiers and Indian guides from Monterey to make contact with Rivera.[21] Although it was anticipated by Gálvez that the Indians would be as friendly as they had been "always with all travelers of yore," Fages was advised not to be too trusting because "the common enemy" constantly encouraged their mischievousness.[22] The Catalonian Volunteers were to be always on guard, ready with side arms or fire arms and proper ammunition. Sentinels were to be posted at all times, whether on a scouting mission, tending camp, or other such duties. They were to be on guard against any surprise attack. In the event of surprise hostilities, the Catalonian Volunteers were expected to overcome the initial shock of an assault.[23]

Trade with friendly Indians would be permitted on a limited basis, but no knives or potential weapons were to be given in trade. The trade was to comprise foodstuffs and native manufactures for whatever gifts the Spaniards took along for commercial purposes.[24]

Designed to direct operations at San Diego and Monterey, Gálvez's instructions to Fages were written to cover possible problems the expeditionary force might encounter. Thus, with these instructions in hand, Fages was academically prepared to meet the situations described by Gálvez. Fages's military experience, however, would prove most useful.

On January 14, 1769, the *San Carlos* reached the Bahía de San Bernabé, where the crew and troops spent a day recuperating.[25] They had been sailing for two weeks and had made little headway. Cursed by nature's elements, the voyage of the *San Carlos* became a living nightmare for those aboard. The vessel experienced contrary winds which drove the vessel seaward away from land. The winds alternated with calms, leaving the ship in doldrums for periods of time.[26] Calamities on the ship became more frequent as drinking water became scarce. Furthermore, the water casks leaked, causing some loss of water supply.[27] After two months at sea, the struggling *San Carlos* reached the halfway point, Cedros Island. Approaching the island, Captain Vila found it difficult to settle his ship because the anchor could not be secured due to the loose ocean bottom.[28] On March 26, a Fages-led scouting party found enough potable water to continue the voyage, and the vessel left Cedros Island shortly thereafter. After battling the sea and the wind, the creaky *San Carlos* reached San Diego with its crew and passengers suffering from scurvy after 110 days at sea.[29]

Scurvy had ravaged the health of all on board, without exception. Two were dead, while half of the Catalonians and most of the crew members were sick in the bunks. Only four weak sailors, assisted by

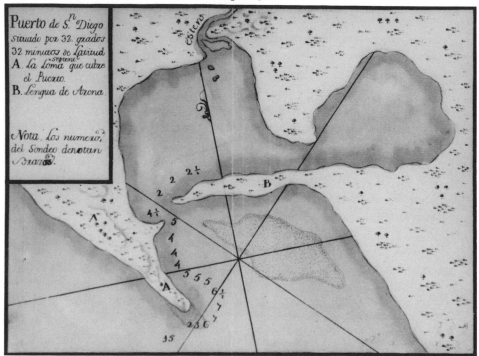

Plano del Puerto de San Diego Compiled by Fray Juan Crespi, 1772.
(Archivo General de Indias, Sevilla)

ailing Catalonian troopers, worked the ship.[30] Such was the condition of all personnel on the ship when they entered San Diego Bay.

On April 30, 1769, six cannon shots from the *San Antonio*[31] broke the quiet atmosphere of unspoiled California. The *San Antonio*, captained by Juan Pérez, had arrived in San Diego Bay after fifty-nine days at sea, but its crew was ridden with scurvy. The vessel had no soldiers on board. It was 7:00 A.M. when Captain Pérez saluted the arriving *San Carlos*.[32] To observers of the *San Antonio*, the *San Carlos* appeared quiet. However, Captain Vila wrote in his diary that Sunday Mass was said on his ship. Moreover, it was three hours before Juan Pérez and Fathers Juan Vizcaíno and Juan Gómes came on board.[33]

At midmorning, Fages, Costansó, Jorge Estorce, Vila's first mate, and his twenty-nine men who were still able to work boarded a long boat belonging to the *San Antonio*.[34] Their purpose was to scout the land near the bay and find potable water. Search for water by members

38

of the *San Antonio* had been undertaken unsuccessfully. These men had found some water by digging into the ground on the beach, but they soon realized it was brackish.

Thus, Fages and his men were compelled by necessity to find drinking water or perish in that lonely bay. The next day, Monday, May 1, 1769, the group found water. All day, they had been under observation by Indians. These Californians would thrust one end of their bows into the ground, and holding the other end they would dance rapidly around it. If the Spaniards came near them, however, they would quickly retreat a short distance. Finally, one of the Catalonian Volunteers stood out from the weary scouting party and thrust his musket into the ground, expressing an attitude of peace.[35]

Convinced of peaceful intentions on the part of these strangely dressed foreigners, the Indians approached them. Here, in a California wilderness, the Spaniards and Indians met as they had elsewhere many times since the days of Columbus and Cortés. On that spring day, members of the Fages party quickly brought out gifts of ribbons, beads, and baubles.[36] Next, the soldiers anxiously asked them for places where drinking water would be available to them. The Indians pointed to a wooded place within sight. The direction was northeast, and within the grove to which they pointed was a small river, which would soon be known as the San Diego River. Indian hospitality was even more impressive when they led the Spaniards to the river, three leagues distant. When they reached the river, the men seemed to forget momentarily their voyage, isolation, and plight, for the scenery was pleasant. Costansó described the landscape as arbored and filled with fragrant plants like sage, rosemary, and roses, among other wild plants in flower. Animal life, too, seemed plentiful to these Spanish scouts.[37] The land seemed to be a happy one, and the territory adjacent to the river appeared fertile. As for the river itself, Costansó recorded that it flowed southward into the bay from an inland mountain.[38] The company of men went forward to the Indian village, which was in the immediate vicinity of the river. There, they were received by men, women, and children, estimated by Costansó to be thirty or forty families. Making contact with friendly natives was a boon to the expeditionary forces. Fortunately, the problem of drinking water, important to the ailing men in San Diego Bay, had been solved. Fages and his men returned to the *San Carlos* at nine o'clock that evening.[39]

The following day, Vila determined it best to move the *San Carlos*

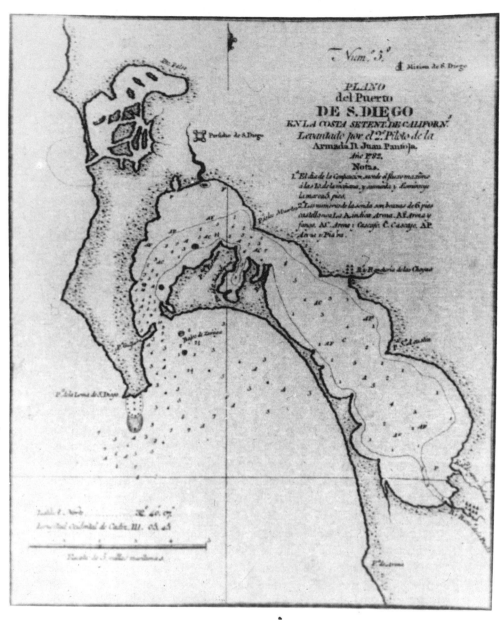

Plano del Puerto de San Diego, 1785.
(Archivo General de Indias, Sevilla)

as close to the river as possible. With the help of eight Catalonian Volunteers and two sailors, the sea captain directed that the *San Antonio* be tied to the *San Carlos* so that the two ships could be of service to each other. Those Catalan soldiers who were able to work, despite their weakened health, were expected to anchor and man the *San Carlos*.[40]

Movement on the stricken vessels was sparse. For the next few days between Tuesday, May 2, and Thursday, May 4, those who were not too sick tended the dying. Twelve Catalonian soldiers with their leader, Pedro Fages, were among the sick who were still strong enough to carry out necessary duties, which undoubtedly saved their lives. There was only one doctor on the *San Carlos* to direct care for the sick: Pedro Prat, a Frenchman and surgeon of the Spanish Royal Army.[41] Prat had been in the Sonora expedition with Fages and his Catalonians when they were pulled from the campaign to join the California adventure. José de Gálvez was disappointed that Prat had arrived in La Paz with few medicines. Gálvez asked Prat to leave a memorandum requesting medical necessities and told him they would be sent to him at Monterey on the packetboat *San Joseph,* which would leave La Paz for that distant port three months hence.[42] Thus, lacking drugs and medicines, Prat had to trust his ingenuity to save lives. Dr. Prat's knowledge of herbs provided relief to the suffering men. Costansó recorded that Prat's concoctions helped relieve and strengthen them. Prat himself, suffering the ravages of scurvy, was valiant in his efforts to collect herbs to make whatever remedies he could,[43] but those who died did so slowly. Burial details were composed of Catalonian Volunteers. One such burial took place on May 3.[44]

The stricken *San Carlos* had been in San Diego Bay less than a week when some of the ailing survivors were able to construct barracks and to move the seriously ill to the beach. Construction of shelters took place on the weekend of May 5–7, under the direction of Costansó. It was the ailing Fages and his reduced command who carried out the evacuation of the sick and dying from the *San Carlos* to the beach. The poor supply of medicine and insufficient diet were not the only sources of aggravation to this wretched group; for once on land, the cold sea breezes at night tended to increase the suffering.[45] Shortly, death began "its ravages in the canvas pest-house on the beach."[46] Costansó related that so great was the factor of exposure to the elements that the men began dying "two and three at a time." The expeditionary force was reduced to twelve soldiers and a few mariners who were able to assist in guarding the ships and camp, navigate the launches, and help the sick.[47] Such responsibility placed on so few men reveals the uncertainty of their situation. The erection of living quarters continued for a few more days. The Catalonian soldiers and mariners not only unloaded cannons, ammunition, and men from the *San Carlos:* they also performed the same services for the *San Antonio.* The death toll continued to climb as the sick showed no improvement. On May 9, the stricken groups were established on the beach. On that day, Fages sent his soldiers with a few mariners to bring water in barrels. The Catalonian troopers went as guards and helpers. Up to that date, twelve Catalonians were still able to work. By the end of the day, Fages's effective command was eight soldiers.[48] On this cold and windy day, more men died throughout the afternoon and night; and the water did not arrive until after midnight.[49] Details for more water were sent the next day, while the cold winds continued to aggravate the sick and dying.[50]

Throughout the ordeal, Fages, Vila, and Pérez had no alternative but to ignore their instructions from Gálvez. It was now four months since they had left La Paz, and still there was no sign of Rivera. Fages did explore the immediate vicinity of the bay for horse tracks and other signs of Rivera's men, but to no avail.[51] Costansó wrote that the men "did not know what to think of Rivera's tardiness." Then, on May 14, Indian runners brought electrifying news to the camp. Pointing southward, they told of soldiers, armed and mounted, who were coming toward the bay.[52] Joyously, the survivors prepared for their arrival. A volley of shots saluted Rivera's advance guard. Both groups were happy to see each other, for each hoped to find alleviation of its respective suffering.[53] Soon the rest of Rivera's land expedition appeared. Father Juan Crespi wrote that they found on the beach a general hospital comprising both crews and the Catalonian Volunteers. He reported twenty-three people dead.[54] Later, on July 3, 1769, Father Serra wrote that three Catalonian Volunteers had succumbed and, among those remaining, the "great number had little hope to live."[55]

Fortunately, Rivera could account for all of his personnel: few were ill and no one had been lost except by desertion.[56] Rivera's men had suffered much and were short on rations. They camped near the survivors of the sea expedition and divided their supplies to aid them. Then, Rivera had both camps moved closer to the river. Fages and Costansó had not moved there earlier because they could not divide the few healthy men into two groups to guard the camp and the ships at the same time. Instead, Fages and Costansó decided to remain on the beach within sight of their vessels, where they could guard all of their property at once.[57] The camp was transferred one league north to the bank of the river. The campsite was fortified, and huts and corrals were built. On May 17, the sick were transported to their new camp.[58] Five weeks later the Portolá forces arrived. On June 29, Governor Portolá's men made their appearance in the camp. During the five weeks between the arrival of Rivera and Portolá's men, Dr. Prat attended the sick with greater hope of their recovery. The arrival of Rivera and, later, Portolá brought relief to those who had preceded them to San Diego.

Meanwhile, Juan Pérez was elected to take whatever crew he could assemble to San Blas to inform Visitador Gálvez of the state of the forces in San Diego.[59] Vila remained behind for whatever service he could render under a new set of orders, should they be forthcoming from either Gálvez or Portolá. Vila had lost almost all of his officer staff, as well as his boatswain, quartermaster, and coxswain; and he had no replacements for these positions.[60] Thus, when Portolá suggested that Vila sail with an expeditionary force to Monterey, he refused despite the governor's offer of twenty-nine men. Vila felt that these men were useless to him, because of their lack of naval experience.[61] Portolá then modified his plans.

Taking stock of supplies and assuming that the San Joseph was on its way to Monterey[62] with supplies that Gálvez had promised, Portolá decided to send a force by land. The decision to leave as soon as possible was prompted by information that the weather varied. When the *San Carlos* arrived in April with its stricken crew, its members claimed to have seen snow on nearby mountain peaks. The possibility of an early winter had to be considered. It was now summer and Portolá pondered whether the expedition would reach Monterey if it left late and was caught by cold weather. The expeditionary forces to Monterey, reasoned Portolá, would have to march through mountain passes that could be closed in winter.[63] Therefore, Governor Portolá decided to assemble the expedition to Monterey as soon as possible. Among those chosen to go were Fernando de Rivera y Moncada, Miguel Costansó, Pedro Fages, six Catalonian Volunteers, twenty-seven leather-jacket soldiers, Friar Juan Crespi, and fifteen California natives. The leader of the group was the governor himself. The sick were left in San Diego to be attended by those who were well.

From a few letters and diary comments, it is possible to trace the condition of the Catalonian Volunteers up to that time. In his diary, Vila stated that by May 29[64] all of his crew members and Catalonian Volunteers were ill, with the exception of five crew members who were still capable of handling the ship. On June 9, 1769, Father Juan Crespi wrote that up to that point twenty-one crew members of both ships had died as well as one or two of the Catalonians.[65] Crespi also mentioned that "of those on the two vessels, the strongest are the lieutenant of the Volunteers (Fages), Señor Costansó, the captain of *El Príncipe,* and his pilot." Crespi's observations of the Catalonian Volunteers was that "only three are well, all the rest being sick, many dying, the majority with cramps in the legs or all over the body."[66] Less than a fortnight later, Crespi wrote again that twenty-three had died, "most of them sailors, but including two of the soldiers mentioned."[67] On July 3, 1769, Father Junípero Serra recorded that three Volunteers had succumbed and, of those remaining, the "great number had little hope to live."[68] By July 14, at least two more Catalonians had died of their sickness.[69] The casualty list of the dead members of the sea expeditions was reported in San Diego while the first expedition to Monterey was in progress. Certainly, on the eve of departure to Monterey, Fages's effective command was six Catalonian soldiers; fourteen seriously ill, who remained behind in San Diego with Father Junípero Serra;[70] and five dead.[71] Those Catalonian troopers who remained with Serra because they were seriously ill were expected, if they recovered, to help the priests begin construction of buildings on the mission site.[72]

It was late afternoon, Friday, July 14, 1769, when the exploration party left San Diego.[73] The men filed out of the camp. At the head of the line were Portolá, Fages, and Rivera, followed by the Catalonian Volunteers and a few friendly Indians carrying shovels, axes, crowbars, hoes, and other tools essential for military operations. This contingent was followed by muleteers, presidial soldiers, and another group of friendly Indians, followers of Rivera, who handled the remuda of horses and mules.[74] Father Crespi was also in the lineup as diarist, chaplain, and missionary priest, no less an explorer than the others.

After traveling northwest for two and a half leagues, they stopped to camp. They had marched for almost three hours when they encountered "heathens" who brought sardines to the Spanish camp. The Spaniards called the area "Pools of the Valley of San Diego."[75] The next week, from July 15 to 22, they continued their march north passing through the Soledad Valley; San Dieguito Canyon near Del Mar; Buena Vista Creek near Carlsbad, the future site of San Luis Rey Mission; Las Pulgas Canyon; and Cristianitos Canyon, north of San Onofre.[76] On this march, they noted the flora and fauna, the terrain, and the people.

On Sunday, July 23, they began their march at 7:00 A.M., after Mass was said. On this date, they entered a valley which they called Santa María Magdalena, the later site of San Juan Capistrano.[77] Skirting the foothills of the Santa Ana Valley near El Toro, they traded with friendly Indians to whom the priests introduced Christianity. Meanwhile, a scouting party of Spanish soldiers returned the next day to tell of six islands they had seen the day before. Of these islands, one was identified as San Clemente.[78] They reasoned that they were about five leagues from the bay of San Pedro. By July 27, they reached Santiago Creek and pitched camp in the hills northeast of Orange. The next day, Friday, they experienced a "horrifying earthquake." The first shock was violent. As the party tended their camp near a river just after noon, the rumble and swaying of the earth began. The major tremor was followed by three aftershocks which shook the land. The last tremor was felt at about 4:00 P.M.[79] Crespi called the river Jesús de los Temblores, but the soldiers called it the Santa Ana.

On Sunday, July 30, the explorers reached La Habra after passing Fullerton. They entered a valley which they called San Miguel Arcángel, today known as the San Gabriel River Valley, where they set up camp along that river near Bassett.[80] That afternoon they felt another tremor. By the last day of July they had marched from San Diego to a campsite near El Monte, south of present-day Mission San Gabriel.[81]

The expedition continued marching throughout the month of August. By the second day of that month they were camped along the Los Angeles River. The earth tremors persisted as these men marched near the Elsinore fault line into the San Fernando Valley, where they camped on August 7. The camp was located northwest of Mission San Gabriel.[82] In this general area of Greater Los Angeles, the soldiers hunted antelope and wild goat, and while exploring, noted the Brea Pits. One of the hunters was a Catalonian Volunteer who was responsible for the naming of a spot known to these explorers as the "Springs of El Berrendo." It seems that on August 4, this Catalan trooper, nameless in Crespi's diary, shot at a deer, breaking one of its legs. Unable to overtake the deer that afternoon, it was tracked and captured alive the next day by the soldiers near Santa Monica.[83]

The rest of August was spent on a march north from Sepulveda Canyon, past the Santa Inéz River. Along the way they camped near Encino, then passed through Newhall to the Santa Clara River. From the river they marched northward toward Fillmore, and in the next few days they reached the site of Ventura.[84] The march was slow and by Friday, August 18, they had marched as far as Santa Bárbara. At the end of August the travelers camped near present-day San Antonio Creek,[85] past the Santa Inéz River.

During the march, the soldiers scouted the trail in advance, guarded campsites, cut trails, made friendly contact with natives, and contributed to permanent place-names of sites along their route of travel. Some of these names, which Crespi credited to the soldiers, still persist today. Pitas (Whistle) Point, north of Ventura, received its name from sentinels who warily passed the night of August 15, 1769, suspiciously watching natives dance to the music of pipes or whistles. The Spaniards complained that they were kept awake all night by the noise of these flutelike instruments.[86]

Near Rincón Point, on Rincón Creek, Crespi named an Indian town Santa Clara de Monte Falco. However, the soldiers called it the Town of El Bailarín because the chieftain, who was an exceptional dancer, performed for them on August 16.[87] La Carpintería, near Santa Bárbara, was also named by these soldiers on August 18. The inspiration for such a name was the sight of Chumash Indians building a canoe. The Spaniards noted that these natives had many well-built canoes.[88] The death of a seagull on Thursday, August 25, inspired the name of present-day Gaviota near Santa Bárbara. Soldiers exploring along the coast shot and killed the gull in the area, which otherwise might have been known as San Luis, for the king of France, a name recommended by Father Crespi.[89]

North of La Gaviota is Cañada del Cojo, a campsite used by these explorers on August 26. Nearby was a village of twenty-four Indian houses. Their chief was lame in one leg; hence, the soldiers called the village Ranchería del Cojo. The name Cañada del Cojo derives from a soldier's observation.[90]

A soldier's carelessness is the clue for the name of Espada Creek. On August 27, an absent-minded soldier, absorbed in watching a group of natives fishing in their canoe, was robbed of his sword by a stealthy brave. The soldier, failing to notice that he had been relieved of his weapon, marched off. However, an honest Californian saw the theft and chased the thief into the water, took the sword, and returned it to the soldier. The hero was rewarded with beads. The soldier was admonished, and the place was named Ranchería de la Espada as a reminder. Espada Creek takes its name from this incident.[91]

The explorers continued their march northward throughout the month of September, reaching Monterey on October 1, 1769. On October 4, they held a meeting in their camp near the mouth of the Salinas River. The order of business was the failure to specifically locate Monterey Bay. Two days earlier, scouting parties had been sent out and their reports were discouraging.[92] Portolá was using 1734 maps and descriptions of an old Manila galleon pilot, Joseph Gonzáles Cabrera Bueno. Accordingly, Portolá expressed his disappointment in having missed Monterey Bay, and advised his officers that the best alternative was to continue northward.[93] Portolá's thinking was that they had not reached the proper latitude. Pedro Fages concurred, writing:

> We knew not if the place where we were was that of our destination; still after having carefully examined it and compared it with the relations of the ancient voyagers, we resolved to continue our march; for after having taken the latitude, we found that we were in 36°44' while, according to the reports of the pilot, Cabrera Bueno, Monterey should be in 37°, and so serious an error was not supposable on the part of a man of well known skill. The configuration of the coast did not agree either with the relations which served us as a guide.[94]

The explorers continued their trek northward to San Francisco Bay, which they discovered at this time and there they realized their mistake. In the process, however, they had discovered an even greater bay, that of San Francisco. On November 28, 1769, they began their return trip south to San Diego, which they reached on January 24, 1770.

Once in San Diego, review was taken of the sad state of the men and an inventory made of the remaining provisions. Meanwhile, Fages was informed that eight more Catalonian Volunteers had died, bringing the dealth toll to thirteen. Of the twenty-five Catalonians who had left Sonora with Fages, only twelve had survived the ordeal in San Diego Bay.[95] At the same time, Rivera y Moncada was sent to the new Baja California Mission of Velicatá on the peninsula for supplies and reinforcements. Fages himself petitioned for twelve more soldiers to complete his command. Next, Portolá decided to make one more attempt

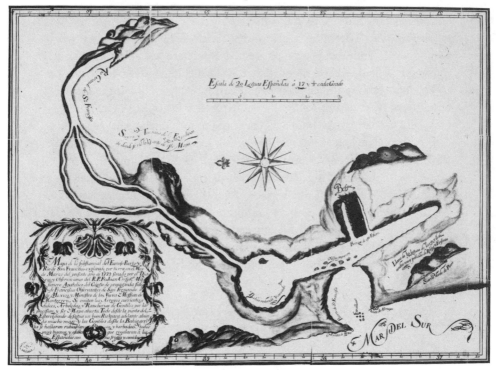

Plano del Puerto de San Francisco Compiled by Fray Juan Crespi, 1772.
(Archivo General de Indias, Sevilla)

to find Monterey. Fortunately, the *San Antonio* returned from San Blas with food and medicines, thus raising the morale of all concerned. By late May 1770, the explorers were back in the vicinity of Monterey Bay. This time, they made a careful survey of the bay and realized that their original mistake was due to their lack of faith in their own calculations. They had been more willing to believe the printed work of an ancient mariner despite its disparity with the reality they had witnessed. On May 31, the *San Antonio,* with Father Serra on board, arrived in the bay less than a week after the discovery of the port had been confirmed.[96] On this second land expedition to Monterey, Fages had with him twelve Catalonian Volunteers and seven *soldados de cuera,* or leather-jacket soldiers.[97] These men witnessed the act-of-possession ceremony of Monterey Bay on June 3, 1770. First, the Spanish standards were planted in the ground; then Father Serra sang a Mass. Next came the formal act of sovereignty, after which everyone sang the *Te Deum Laudamus*. Salvos from artillery and the soldiers' muskets terminated the ceremony.[98]

Fages later signed a statement of testimony confirming that formal possession had been taken; to wit:

> As Lieutenant of the Free Company of Volunteers of Catalonia, assigned by Your Majesty to this New Kingdom of Spain, I certify that the commandant of this expedition, Don Gaspar de Portolá, has taken possession of the Port of Monterey and its environs, the day cited in the name of Your Catholic Majesty, and with attention given the history of Californias of the voyage of Sebastián Vizcaíno, and by collection of sea charts of Cabrero Bueno, he [Portolá] found signs, similarly by sea as by land without any [signs] missing, and so that it be certified wherever necessary, I sign it today, June 11, 1770.
>
> Pedro Fages [Rubric][99]

Following the ceremony, the laborious task of constructing the mission and presidio at Monterey ensued. Supervision of the work was the responsibility of Pedro Fages, who became commander of California when Portolá departed from Monterey on the *San Antonio* on July 9, 1769. The choice of Fages, a known taskmaster and strict disciplinarian, was lamented by certain individuals, who filed complaints to their superiors in Mexico. Fages was not discriminatory in assigning duties to his men, for Catalonian Volunteers were treated similarly to *soldados de cuera,* as attested by the service record of Corporal Miguel Pericas, a Catalan Volunteer.

Corporal Pericas was a career soldier who enlisted in the lower ranks in 1757, and retired to Catalonia in 1789, after having been promoted to sublieutenant.[100] As a professional soldier, Pericas had seen hardship and death many times. He was one of the original Catalonian Volunteers who sailed from Cádiz in 1767, and he served briefly in the Sonora campaign until called to the California expedition with Fages in 1768. Having survived the near-disaster at San Diego, Pericas was present at the ceremony of possession at Monterey in June 1770, and he served in California from 1769 to 1774. During that time, Corporal Pericas personally helped in the construction of the presidio and mission of Monterey. He cut wood for lumber and helped make adobes for the buildings. Pericas was involved in the actual construction of homes for the priests as well as the building of warehouses and fortifications. Usually after a hard day's work, Pericas pulled guard duty at night, watching for marauders. At that time Pericas was thirty-seven years old. Other Catalonians who were at Monterey with Pericas suffered considerably because of the general situation, which included recovery and relapse of scurvy, deprivation, lack of food, hard work, and sleepless nights, as well as death for some. Those Catalan troops included Sergeant Juan Puig, Manuel Butrón, Antonio Montaña, Domingo Arúz, Antonio Yorba, Francisco Cayuelas, Francisco Portella, Andrés Auguet, and Domingo Malaret. Francisco Portella died in Monterey on April 24, 1774, two months before these troops were pulled out of Monterey and sent to Tepic. Andrés Auguet died in Tepic on September 29, 1774, and Domingo Malaret passed away there on October 2, 1774.[101] Undoubtedly, their hardship at Monterey contributed to their deaths.

Such was the contribution of the Catalonian Volunteers in establishing California in accordance with the plan of defense of the Spanish empire. Of particular importance to Spanish claims to that area was the Catalonian Volunteers' participation in the first land exploration of California.

4 / The Exploration of California's Interior

P edro Fages and his Catalonians were among the first Europeans to explore California by land. In the sixteenth century, members of the Coronado expedition were on the eastern edge of present-day California; but they were looking for Hernando de Alarcón's ship, with which they had failed to rendezvous. Blazing a trail northward from Velicatá in Baja California in 1766, Father Wenceslao Linck reached Cieneguilla in Baja California.[1] This trail was used three years later by Fernando de Rivera y Moncada, who opened a trail from Cieneguilla to San Diego. Effective exploration of the California interior took place after 1769. Penetration into the interior was accomplished by others after that date, but the Catalonian Volunteers were among the first to do so.

Exploration of the Golden State began when Fages and his scurvy-ridden comrades conducted a search for potable water in the San Diego Bay area on May 5, 1769. Having been led by Indians to the San Diego River, Fages explored the river's mouth to determine if it could be entered by launch to obtain water. Fages concluded that a small boat could make the entry at high tide. During this period, Fages and his men traded with the natives, an experience which proved valuable for Fages in his later explorations of California. For the moment, however, Fages was involved in a struggle for survival in San Diego Bay. With the arrival of Fernando de Rivera y Moncada, Fages began a more extensive investigation of the San Diego River and vicinity. On June

21, Fages and six Catalan troopers left their camp to determine the length of the river valley inland.[2] After three leagues of travel, the party reached the place where the river enters Mission Valley from Mission Gorge in today's San Diego. Although the Spaniards noted the fertility of the upper valley, they were equally impressed with the abundance of flora in the land through which they traveled.[3] Such were the origins of the eighteenth-century explorations of the California interior.

The first major exploration of California was the planned expedition to Monterey Bay undertaken by Portolá, in which Catalonian Volunteers were present. The failure of this expedition to find Monterey Bay has been discussed in the previous chapter. After the first attempt to find the bay failed, a second trip resulted in the establishment of a settlement at Monterey Bay. Moreover, Pedro Fages and his men participated in both explorations and were present for the formal act of possession performed by Portolá. The first attempt to find Monterey Bay had reached the vicinity of San Francisco. Such an adventure tantalized the imagination of Lieutenant Fages, for he planned a return trip to that region in the following year.

On November 21, 1770, Fages left Monterey with six soldiers and a muleteer.[4] His objective was to find a way to Point Reyes by traveling inland in an effort to find a more direct route to the northern end of San Francisco Bay.[5] The route taken by Fages followed a northeast direction across the wide Salinas Valley, past the sites of present-day Hollister, Gilroy, Coyote, and San José and to the mouth of the Guadalupe River.[6] Five days later, the explorers reached the Berkeley area. On November 28, Fages wrote,

> Four soldiers went out to explore the country, and at night they came back, saying that they had gone about seven leagues toward the north. They said that the land was very good, and level; that they had climbed to the top of a hill, but had not been able to discern the end of an inlet which lay before them and communicated with the one which was at our right hand.[8]

These four soldiers had ascended a point from which they saw the mouth of the estuary and two arms of San Francisco Bay. In all likelihood, they were looking at the opening to the sea where the Golden Gate Bridge would later stand. Thus, it can be ascertained that when

Spanish plans for occupying the San Francisco area were resumed in 1775, the present-day site of the Golden Gate Bridge had been seen by land at least twice, once by Sergeant José Ortega in 1769, and the second time in 1770, by Fages's men, probably led by Sergeant Juan Puig of the Catalonian Volunteers.[9]

The Fages group had been pathfinding to an extent, for they had traversed Ortega's old trail and modified it to suit their circumstance.[10] Although Ortega had actually stood on one of the arms forming the estuary, Fages's men viewed the Golden Gate from across the bay and remarked on their discovery. In fact, Fages's scouts reported that they had seen the estuary and believed it had its "entrance through the bay of the port of San Francisco." Fages doublechecked the discovery and remarked, "I made certain by having viewed it."[11] But the land route to Point Reyes was impassable; for running across the land into the bay was a river that blocked the path to the cape. In his entry for November 29, a discouraged Fages wrote:

> On this day we determined to return to our starting-point, on seeing that it was impossible for us to pass over to the other side of the Punta de los Reyes without wasting many days' time, also because of the anxiety that I felt about the camp, the farmwork, and the care of the cattle.[12]

And so it happened that Pedro Fages and his men returned to Monterey, without incident, after fourteen days of travel. However, the thought of scouting the San Francisco area persisted in Don Pedro's mind, and in 1772 he planned another expedition to the north.

Although the entrance to the bay had been sighted, the search for a route to Point Reyes challenged Fages. In his 1772 expedition, Fages's objective was still the same, to circumvent the huge estuary or somehow cross the "arm of the sea" which lay between Monterey and Point Reyes.

It was half-past ten on the morning of March 20, when Fages, Fray Juan Crespi, six Catalonian Volunteers, six leather-jacket soldiers, Crespi's Indian servant named Paje, and a muleteer waved farewell to their friends in the Monterey presidio.[13] Fages followed generally the routes taken by the 1769 and 1770 expeditions. By March 24, the explorers were in the Santa Clara Valley,[14] a great plain which the Spaniards called Robles del Puerto de San Francisco.

Fages reported that natives had been seen along the way, and Crespi

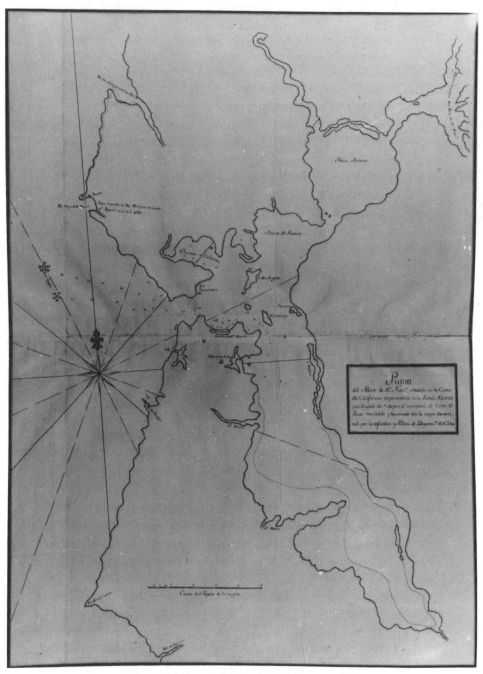

Plano del Puerto de San Francisco, c. 1785.
(Archivo General de Indias, Sevilla)

54

concurred in adding that they were timid. The next day, Wednesday, March 25, Fages recorded that after Mass they broke camp at seven o'clock in the morning; and after traveling through a flat area, they sighted more Indians who appeared to shout to them in welcome. However, the highlight of the day for Fages was the mistaken realization that he was three or four leagues from the estuary.[15] Here, tired from their day's march, they stopped at a place they called San Salvador de Horta (San Lorenzo Creek).[16] Fages was apparently mistaken about the distance to the estuary, for the next day they walked six more leagues. On March 27, their direction was northwest.[17] At this point, they were in Oakland skirting the estuary, where Fages mentioned he sighted "five islands" and "three form a triangle."[18] Obviously, these islands were Alcatraz Island, Yerba Buena Island, and Angel Island. Fages was making his observation opposite the present-day site of the Golden Gate Bridge. The next day was one with little to report with reference to the progress made toward reaching Point Reyes. They camped near Richmond.

March 29 was a Sunday. It was seven o'clock in the morning and after Mass was heard when the expeditionary force continued its march. Climbing hills and crossing arroyos, they came to where the hills formed a round estuary like a large bay. There, they saw two or three young whales.[19] Fages and his men were at San Pablo Bay.[20] That day, Fages noted that they had marched eight leagues. The Catalonian officer and his men believed that their objective of reaching Point Reyes could now be easily accomplished. They concluded that San Pablo Bay was the end of the estuary they had been trying to circumvent. All that they had to do was to go around it and continue to Point Reyes.[21] Had that been accomplished, Fages and his men would have been the first Europeans to find a direct land route connecting together all points of San Francisco Bay. Unfortunately, when they tried to go around the bay they discovered that the water continued inland in the form of a channel, Carquinez Strait.[22] It proved to be an impassable obstacle to the Fages expeditionary party.

Early the next day, the expedition continued in a northeastern direction, still following the channel. Events of the day included encounters with friendly Indians and the entrance of the explorers into a large plain.[23] Fages described the plain as teeming with animal life. Ascending a pass to its highest point, the Spaniards made their observation of the panoramic view. Crespi wrote:

we saw that the land opened into a great plain as level as the palm of the hand, the valley opening about half the quadrant, sixteen quarters from northwest to southeast, all level land as far as the eye could reach. Below the pass we beheld the estuary that we were following and saw that it was formed by two large rivers.[24]

The two rivers they saw were the Sacramento and the San Joaquín.[25] Thus the Spaniards had made their most significant discovery. Fages and his men were the first Europeans to gaze upon the great Central Valley.

For Fages, there could be only one conclusion regarding his objective: it would be impossible to cross on foot or horseback the Strait of Carquinez or the two rivers, neither of which could be circumvented at this time. Fages then divided his command to explore the land. Three men investigated the direction of the channel to the north, and the other three were sent south to find a better way to return to Monterey.[26] After a few days, the explorers rendezvoused in the California wilderness. On March 31, 1772, the disappointed explorers began their return to Monterey from a camp that Fages called the "Camp of the Return," near present-day Pittsburg, California.[27] The party arrived in Monterey on Sunday, April 5.

From the point of view of finding a land route to Point Reyes, the expedition was unsuccessful. However, the explorers were successful in discovering San Pablo Bay and the Central Valley. Moreover, they gathered valuable information for future settlers of San Francisco Bay. Significantly, Fages and his men were the first to enter California's Central Valley from the north in 1772. Late that year, Fages and a small detachment of soldiers, searching for deserters, left San Diego en route to San Luis Obispo.[28] Following an established route which would have passed through Mission San Gabriel, Fages changed the line of march toward the west through El Cajon Pass; thus, Fages avoided visiting Father Paterna at the mission because he was angry at the priest. Traveling northwest along the San Gabriel mountain range, the Catalonian officer followed the Mojave Desert, via the Palmdale area, to Antelope Valley. The explorers proceeded through Grapevine Valley to Buena Vista Hills and village.[29] Fages was impressed by the immensity of the valley, which runs diagonally from northwest to southeast. Of the terrain, the observant Catalonian wrote:

From the village of Buena Vista, the plain continues toward the south for seven leagues more, over good lands with some water. And at the end of these seven leagues one goes toward the south through a pass, partly of valleys and arroyos, very thickly grown with groves of live oaks, as are also all the hills and sierras which form these valleys. Going now three leagues more in the same direction, one comes to a very large plain, which keeps getting wider and wider, both toward the east and toward the south, leaving to the north and northwest many sierras.[30]

It was Fages who named the village Buena Vista, resulting in the present-day names for Buena Vista Lake and Buena Vista Hills.[31]

And so it was that Pedro Fages and his detachment of troops were among the first Europeans to enter the South San Joaquín Valley, four years before Father Francisco Garcés. The Catalan officer and his soldiers entered the South San Joaquín Valley in 1772.[32]

Fages was the first to realize the continuity and extent of the San Joaquín end of the Central Valley, for he was the first to enter it not only from the north but also from the south.[33]

Interestingly, Fages's discovery of the South San Joaquín Valley was accidental, for if his desire to avoid Father Paterna's mission had not detoured his itinerary in the search for deserters the Catalonian might very well have taken the established route north.

Pedro Fages and his detachment of Catalonian Volunteers had played leading roles in pushing Spain's defenses and claims north to Alta California. Less than two decades later, another group of Volunteers led by Pedro de Alberni were assigned to Nootka, on the west coast of Vancouver Island, to bolster defenses and claims of Spain in the Pacific Northwest.

5 / Pedro Fages, El Oso

On the afternoon of December 2, 1781,[1] Spanish troops watched, with apprehension, dust clouds in the distance. These soldiers were part of a rescue detachment that had left Pitic near present-day Hermosillo, Sonora, on September 16. They had traversed the desert lands northward toward the Colorado River, their destination. Their mission was to evaluate the extent of destruction and magnitude of a Yuma uprising which had taken place months before; also, they hoped to ransom any survivors.

As these soldiers stood watching the dust kick up from the hooves of Indian war ponies, they must have recalled a meeting their commander had arranged the day before with a group of Yumas. The object of that meeting was to acquire information concerning captives held by the rebels. Unarmed, to avoid mistrust of their intentions, the officer, accompanied by his second in command, approached about thirty Yumas, who told him of the captives, but remarked with disdain that they had invited two or three nations to unite against the Spanish force. Undaunted, the tough-minded officer replied, "Let them come; we are enough for them all."[2] The place was Concepción near Yuma, Arizona, and the commander was Lieutenant Colonel Pedro Fages, captain of the Catalonian Volunteers.

As the Yumas approached the waiting soldiers, their intentions became clear: they wanted another meeting. Most of the Yumas had remained about a league away when their leaders came to talk to Fages.

The result was the rescue of a ten-year-old girl in exchange for a blind Yuma youth. Moreover, the Yumas promised the release of "the rest of the women" captives.[3]

The next day Fages prepared an ambush for the Yumas in the hope of capturing their leaders for ransom of the remaining prisoners. Thirty presidial soldiers and ten Pima auxiliaries were hidden in the foothills around the camp, and fifteen Pimas were hidden along the river bank, near where they hoped the Yumas would come. The plan did not succeed because the wily Yumas kept their distance, and Fages feared scaring them into killing their captives. Another ransom was made, and Fages traded one Indian captive for seven Spanish women. However, the shrewd Catalonian kept two Yuma prisoners until one "Christian woman, still in their power, was released."[4]

The rest of December was spent challenging the Yuma for more prisoners and searching for the remains of victims mutilated in the tragic Yuma uprising. Skirmishes with the Yumas were recurrent throughout the expedition, which ended with some success in late December. Fages spent Christmas Day on the return march to Pitic, arriving there on the thirtieth day of the month.

The Pedro Fages of 1781 was a mature frontier army officer with fourteen years experience in New Spain. His style of dealing with Indians, though belligerent, showed confidence and courage. By that time Fages was an expert pathfinder, a talent he had displayed many years before. In 1781, Fages was a well-seasoned professional soldier. He had always been a rugged individual, but his campaign of 1781 proved him to be a wise and shrewd negotiator, and one apparently respected by enemy Indians. Whereas a younger Fages may have been inclined to antagonize his enemy into a fight—as he had been accused of doing in the Santa Bárbara Channel of Alta California nine years before—an older Fages dealt firmly and fairly with the Yumas and saved the lives of their captives. Certainly, in 1781, Fages was capable of an efficient and intelligent leadership. Moreover, it was a leadership which he had developed over many years of military discipline.

Pedro Fages, a native of Guisona, Catalonia, was born some time in 1734.[5] His career as an officer began in 1762, as sublieutenant in the campaign against Portugal. Fages spent the next four years, ten and a half months in the Second Regiment of Light Infantry of Catalonia. In 1767, when calls were sounded for volunteers to form a new company destined for service in the Americas, Fages was one of the officers who responded. The thirty-three-year-old Catalonian was promoted to lieutenant on May 12, 1767,[6] placing him second in command of the newly formed Free Company of Catalonian Volunteers. Lieutenant Fages left Cádiz on May 27, 1767, under orders to proceed with his company to Mexico to join the Sonora expedition led by Domingo Elizondo. Although Fages served less than one year in the Sonora campaign, his service record indicates that he made several sallies[7] into the Sonoran wasteland against enemy Indians.

One of the first glimpses of Fages was seen when he left Cádiz as second in command of the Volunteers. However, Clio's magnifying glass sharpened the focus on Fages in one of his first letters written from New Spain on June 28, 1768. Like most soldiers far from home, Fages had a certain someone, unnamed in his correspondence, whom he wanted to help. Fages arranged that a certain kinswoman in Barcelona should receive 120 *reales vellón* per month beginning in January 1769.[8] He wrote, from the barracks in Guaymas, that the money should be given to Doña Rosa Callis, wife of Captain Agustín Callis, so that she could give the money to "my expressed kinswoman."[9] The money was to be taken from Fages's pay. No further details of the arrangement were made, although Fages did say that it was his desire "in the service of God to help her in whatever possible." Whatever the situation was in Barcelona, Fages felt sufficient kindness and responsibility toward that person to guarantee that she would not be abandoned by her benefactor across the ocean. Speculation on the matter would seem to indicate that Fages had taken care of an obligation, for in subsequent years he seemed to have buried himself in his work.

There is little in Fages's service record that yet hinted of his leadership qualities, his abilities as expert trail blazer and explorer, or his temperament. These traits would be dramatically revealed in his first assignment to California. Subsequent Fages-led expeditions would demonstrate his talents as Indian fighter and rugged frontiersman in northern New Spain.

Fages first experienced Indian fighting in the Sonoran campaign under Elizondo. However, he had been in Sonora hardly one year when he was chosen to lead twenty-five Catalonian Volunteers on the sea wing of the California expedition of 1769, on board the packetboat *San Carlos*. Fages and his men arrived in La Paz, Baja California, in December 1768, and in January set sail for San Diego Bay. After a harrowing experience at sea, the *San Carlos* arrived in San Diego with scurvy-ridden personnel who had suffered 110 days of deprivation. Although Fages was lieutenant of Catalonian Volunteers, his position in the expedition was *Jefe de las Armas,* commander of the military at sea. Thus Fages was the highest ranking officer in California until the arrival of Governor Gaspar de Portolá. Even though Fages and his men were deathly ill from the effects of scurvy, they managed to establish a foothold in Spanish California at San Diego Bay.

With the arrival by late June 1769 of Portolá, Father Serra, Fernando de Rivera y Moncada and their respective troops from the two land expeditionary forces, a new phase of the California founding expedition began. Fages was prepared to participate in the second objective of establishing California, the founding of Monterey. This journey took Fages as far north as San Francisco Bay. After establishing Monterey in the second attempt from San Diego in 1770, Fages undertook another exploring venture to the San Francisco area in 1772.

Fages was in California from 1769 to 1774, during his first tour of duty there. He was later commended for his accomplishments in a difficult assignment. Aside from exploring the California wilderness, Fages was praised for his part in

> the discovery and pacification of upper California and the port of Monterey, establishment of the missions, cultivation of the land, and so on, thus throwing up, with certainty, the first lines [of defense] which today guarantee the continuation, subsistence, and probable growth of such an important work in the service of God and king and propagation of the faith in those remote lands.[10]

Although Fages won recognition for his accomplishments, he also gained a reputation among the people with whom he worked as a difficult personality. It was during this period of his life that Fages came under increased criticism from priests and soldiers. Whatever the charges made against Fages, the undeniable historical perspective is that he behaved as an officer in an authoritarian age. This is the context within which this officer's relationship with his subordinates must be weighed. Such was the case of Fages, who seemed, in his general philosophy of command, to hold the extreme view of authority.[11] However, it should be noted that Fages's command in California was his first assignment of real responsibility in his eight years of military service. Nevertheless, despite the criticism voiced against him by his contemporaries, Fages proved himself a doer.

Donald A. Nuttall, Fages's biographer, analyzed the Catalonian as a loyal and conscientious officer who left no detail of his work unattended. Moreover, Fages was an intelligent and courageous individual who never shirked his duty.[12] These qualities of Fages are especially evident in his explorations of California.

Fages was a highly ambitious career soldier who aimed to please his superiors, for such an attitude was sure to win him recognition and promotion. Nonetheless, Fages did possess certain traits which tended to undermine his potential for leadership.

For eight years Fages had been a good follower. He had learned to serve well and therefore expected no less from those who served under him. Consequently, such expectation was sure to cause friction, as eventually occurred. Another source of criticism directed at Fages was the result of his temperament.[13] The brash Catalonian was given to violent outbursts, and on one occasion he did threaten physical abuse to one of his soldiers, which of course did not come to pass. Fages's seemingly arrogant attitude toward those who served under him was sure to breed discontent.

The charges made by missionary priests in California against Fages were well known among his contemporaries. Apparently, the object of such charges was to secure the removal of the uncooperative Fages. Seemingly, the testimony of soldiers under Fages tended to reinforce and disguise the removal of Fages at Serra's urgings.

The complaints leveled at Fages by Father Serra included bad treatment and arrogant remarks made by Fages to his soldiers, creating antipathy among them toward their leader. Discrimination against the leather-jacket soldiers by Fages and his inability to lead them was another complaint. This last charge tended to exhibit Fages as incompetent. Moreover, Fages was said to favor his Catalan Volunteers, an assertion which proved to be an exaggeration. Father Serra's list accused Fages of refusal to transfer soldiers for bad conduct at the request of the priests. Yet the Catalonian officer was charged with punishing neophytes over which he had no jurisdiction except in grave offenses as well as interfering with mission management. Serra said that Fages had refused to assign a certain soldier as assistant to a certain priest on grounds that the soldier had become personally attached to said priest, with such attachment deemed to be subversive to military authority. Fages was further accused of tampering with mission mail, specifically with opening letters of priests, delaying their delivery, and neglecting to tell the priests the schedule of outgoing mail. Serra stated that Fages had retarded the construction of missions by assigning the only blacksmith available to presidial duty, taking mission mules for use by soldiers, and expropriating mission cattle for presidial use. Such were the charges made by Serra against Fages.[14] Serra's complaints were supported by soldiers who served under the Catalan commander.

It was said, with some degree of truth, that Pedro Fages, captain of Catalonian Volunteers, was discriminatory against the *soldados de cuera*. However, this charge must be weighed with testimony from contemporary accounts of Catalan troopers who served with Fages in California. Most had been with him in Sonora. Among them were Juan Puig, Miguel Pericas, Manuel Butrón, Antonio Montaña, Domingo Aruz, Antonio Yorba, Francisco Cayuelas, Francisco Portella, Andrés Auguet, Domingo Malaret, Domingo Clua, Pablo Ferrer, Gerónimo Bulferic, Gerónimo Planes, Francisco Gombari, and Valentín Planello.

Grievances against Fages by his fellow Catalonians dated to the landing in San Diego Bay. Corporal Pericas related that "it was common saying of all the men that more died by famine than from sickness."[15] Pericas then proceeded to explain the phrase by recalling the incident when Dr. Prat was in need of food for the sick and requested of Fages some chickens which belonged to him "because there was no use in asking for any which were royal property." The surgeon walked away in tears at Fages's refusal, for he could not help his patients without nourishing food. Pericas narrated that "Don Pedro always maintained that the chickens were his, and so he ate them all himself one by one. Never was it known that a chicken was killed for the sick."[16] Pericas himself had suffered abuse from Fages for his remark about one of the commandant's orders. The corporal was put in chains.[17] Perhaps it was this act by Fages which prompted Pericas to become one of his most outspoken critics years later.

So great had the rift between officer and men become that throughout 1773 Catalonian troopers in California petitioned for transfers from their assignment. Juan Puig, Domingo Clua, Pedro Ferrer, Gerónimo Planes, Francisco Gombari, Valentín Planello, Domingo Malaret, and Miguel Pericas asked Father Junípero Serra to intercede for them in their case against Fages. These soldiers also wrote to Captain Agustín Callis, commander of the Catalonian Volunteers and stationed in Mexico

City. Serra and Callis corresponded on the matter.[18] Callis appreciated the confidence the men had placed in him, but he was not in a position to help them.

Because of royal ordinances, soldiers were expected to act through proper channels of command, especially when requests for changes in duty were made from lower to higher authority.[19] Callis reminded Serra that these men should have made their request first to Fages as their commander at Monterey. Their next step, in case of failure, was to contact the inspector general, and finally the viceroy. Thus, Callis declined to act in the case for reasons of propriety.[20] That Fages was bypassed as the proper authority for petitions of reassignment by these men indicates that they felt he would not be inclined to look favorably upon their requests or that he would take reprisals against them. Father Serra certified that their work should be taken as truth.[21] Ultimately, the Catalonians took their case to the viceroy, as seen in their complaints concerning rations dispensed by Fages.

In a letter to Viceroy Antonio María Bucareli y Ursúa dated March 11, 1775, after the Catalonian Volunteers had left California, Sergeant Juan Puig and Corporal Miguel Pericas described the hardships they suffered while serving with Fages in California.[22] Although these soldiers requested monetary compensation for themselves or for surviving families of deceased Catalan Volunteers, the testimony they presented against Fages aimed at justifying their application for compensation. Spanish soldiers would be compensated for rations not received if they could prove their case.

Juan Puig stated that when Fages went to Monterey in 1770, he stayed in San Diego with eighteen soldiers. Puig wrote that he and his men were left virtually without food. Apparently, Puig alluded to Fages having divided the rations so that Puig and his men almost starved, and were saved only by natives who took their clothes in trade for food.[23]

Corporal Pericas was on a march with Fages from June 14, 1769, to January 24, 1770. Pericas stated that Fages issued rations up to the end of September, but between October 1 and December 29 the soldiers were given five tortillas daily, and from December 30, 1769 to January 24, 1770, the troopers were given one pound of mule meat.[24] Strict rationing of food by Fages continued over a period of time. As cited by Puig, Fages rationed food from May 8 to June 15, 1775, in which time they were given eight ounces of bear meat per day; and until

November 8, they received five pounds of flour. When Fages went on a search for deserters, he left Puig in Monterey with instructions detailing rations of one small sweet cake daily, along with twelve pounds, eight ounces of bull meat; seven cups of wheat; and two pounds of flour, which was to last them twenty-four days. Unfortunately, these troops went forty-two days without rations. In desperation Sergeant Puig and three soldiers went to San Diego where they waited twenty days for rations, during which time they were given no more than six pounds of meat.[25]

Corporal Pericas complained that when he was at Mission San Antonio de Padua with eight soldiers between May 25 and July 31, 1772, they were given a small ration of corn every eight days and six ounces of bear meat daily between July 3 and July 31. During the month of July they were allowed one pound of flour. Pericas detailed the month of August as follows: from August 1 to 4, six ounces only of bear meat per day; from August 4 to 28, no rations; and from August 28 to 31, one-half pound of wheat and one ounce of lard per day, with this latter ration continued until September 24. Rations were reduced to one ounce of lard and "nothing else" in the last week of September. Pericas continued detailing the daily menu of rations for the period lasting until May 1773.[26]

Such were the rations described by these Catalonian Volunteers who complained of suffering hunger pangs caused by poor distribution of food. Complicating the food shortages was the work schedule imposed upon the men for two years, these Catalonian Volunteers helped in cultivating the first lands in California for farm produce, and built the mission churches, rectories, barracks, warehouses, and fortifications.[27] They also pulled guard duty, hunted for deserters, and explored California. For their suffering they asked monetary compensation based on the food they did not receive. Moreover, the point they made was that Fages determined the amount of rations to be distributed to the troops. Obviously his own Catalonian soldiers were not favored, contrary to charges made by members of the *soldados de cuera*. Nevertheless, that criticism came from other troops serving under Fages's direction.

It was Corporal Mariano Carrillo, a *soldado de cuera*, who wrote a complaint against Fages in 1772 detailing his attitude toward those troops.[28] Carrillo's account begins soon after formal possession of Monterey had been taken. At that point in time, soldiers were converted into workmen who built large warehouses in twelve days and filled them by unloading the supplies from the *San Antonio*. Next, they labored in constructing the presidio from sunrise to sunset, stopping only for meals. At night, certain soldiers had guard duty to perform. Carrillo complained that there was no letup in the work, for the soldiers "knew that if they sat down to rest awhile or to roll a cigarette and the *comandante* caught them, he would rebuke them harshly. Thus, the men became so disgruntled that there was not one among them who did anything cheerfully."[29] Carrillo stated that Fages personally tormented his men and was constantly "on the heels of the soldiers." It was said that Fages was never satisfied with work done by the soldiers and trusted no one.

The commandant set a quota of logs to be cut per day as follows:

> Fifty logs of from three to four *varas* in length, if a good width; if they were thinner, then sixty must be cut daily. The work of those who transported the logs depended on the distance they had to carry them. In everything else, however, a day's task was rigidly set, so that no one had any spare time during the day . . . In short, he had us do whatever occurred to him, whether we wanted or not.[30]

Although these accusations against Fages appear sound at first glance, a careful study of rations given to the Catalonian Volunteers certainly does not indicate that they were favored over the *soldados de cuera*. As regards the work schedule, the service record of Miguel Pericas offers an example of the work performed by Catalonians. Pericas, who was in California from 1768 to 1774, participated in construction of presidio and mission of Monterey. He not only cut wood for lumber and made adobes, but he was also among those who stood guard duty at night after a hard day's work.[31]

Apparently, Fages lacked respect for the *soldados de cuera* because they were recruited from the lower ranks of society. Through the colonial bias held by Fages, these soldiers were considered undisciplined and given to laziness. Their leader Fernando de Rivera y Moncada was popular with them, in Fages's view, because of his lax leadership.[32] Actually, Rivera y Moncada, a mestizo, was as good as any colonial frontier officer in the Spanish empire.

Apparently, Fages had evaluated the precariousness of the situation and had instituted a plan akin to a declaration of martial law. Without strict discipline, the founding expedition of California was doomed to failure. Notwithstanding his contribution in establishing California, Fages was removed in 1774.

It was during this period of his life that Fages was nicknamed "El Oso," "the Bear," because of the many bear hunts he had undertaken. In fact, his reputation as a hunter of the predators was well known among the Indians near Monterey, who were grateful to him for "ridding their country of troublesome bears."[33] A few months earlier, Fages with fourteen men had spent some three months hunting bears in the Cañada de los Osos near San Luis Obispo. Fages was said to have boasted that he "would pull bears right out of the ground."[34] Fages's nickname may just as well have derived from his personality, for he was a strong, aggressive person. Significantly, Fages's bear hunts were said to bring relief of hunger until a supply ship arrived in Monterey.[35] Like his English colonial counterpart, Daniel Boone, Fages would earn his share of frontier accolades.

Although Fages and his men were instrumental in establishing several missions in California, they were the subject of a set of regulations that would set the pace for soldiering in that northern province. Undoubtedly, the list of complaints presented in Mexico City to the viceroy by Father Serra had made this point. However, the chief incident in Serra's mind may have been Fages's refusal to assign a guard for the founding of San Buenaventura Mission because the Catalan officer said that he did not have enough troops. There was truth in Fages's explanation; however, Father Serra saw only the retardation of the growth of his mission field.

The Fages–Serra disputes were of long duration. One of the first incidents between the two concerned two cases of lanterns found on board the *San Antonio* in 1770. Serra felt that the lanterns were suitable for land use, and he was eager to use them at the mission. However, Don Pedro said that they were intended for the ships. Serra wrote:

> Whatever be their origin, they were very welcome. And if they were intended as Don Pedro said, for the boats, or for any other destination, one word from Your Most Illustrious Lordship—but not from anyone else less exalted—will settle the matter, and dispose of them wherever it please Your Most Illustrious Lordship.[36]

The results of the first encounter between Fages and Serra triggered a rivalry which culminated, in part, in 1774. The groundwork for the removal of Fages had been laid, for in 1773 it was believed that such discord could ruin the California project.[37] Resolution for the disposition of affairs in California resulted in a set of regulations governing military conduct and duties. Such rules were established by a *junta de guerra* on May 6, 1773. Point six of the regulations provided for the removal of Fages from California.[38]

Despite arguments between Fages and his associates, which dominated a great deal of time and correspondence, much work had taken place. Fages and his men had witnessed the erection of several missions and presidios while undertaking exploration of California's interior wilderness. Notwithstanding his removal from California in 1774, Fages was awarded fifteen hundred pesos as a bonus in 1776 for his meritorious contributions.[39]

Fages's career between 1773 and 1776 appeared to hang in balance. Although Viceroy Bucareli executed the removal of Fages from California, years later he wrote that he had regretted withdrawal of the Catalonian "after I had come to know him."[40] Evidently, Bucareli's reevaluation of Fages was tempered with the thought that the Catalonian enjoyed the special favor of the powerful José de Gálvez, now Minister of the Indies.[41] Gálvez had not agreed with Bucareli's removal of Fages, and suggested that the Catalonian, whose valor and merit were known, be given a command at a presidio so that his reputation might not suffer as a result of the California affair.[42]

When Fages left California, he proceeded to Mexico City via Tepic, Guadalajara, Irapuato, and Querétaro. The trip was marked by a stay in Irapuato, during which time Fages convalesced from a sudden illness.[43] By the end of 1774, an ailing Fages arrived in Mexico City. He spent the year 1775 writing several reports concerning the California project. Among these reports was a historical and political as well as natural account of California.[44] In this particular report Fages wrote about Monterey, San Diego, and San Francisco Solano. The report is of particular ethnological interest because of Fages's references to native Californians. Fages included a brief dictionary of Indian words and their Spanish equivalents. Insights into California's natural history merit attention in Fages's explication of birds and animals. Fages also included a brief discussion of fruits and seeds in California.

Probably, Fages's stay in Mexico City redeemed him from obscurity, for he seems to have impressed his superiors with his intellectual ability.

By early 1776,[45] Fages was in command of the Second Company of Catalonian Volunteers in Guadalajara. However, before Fages could settle into the routine style of sedentary garrison life, requests for troops came from California in the wake of destruction caused by hostile Indians near Mission San Diego.[46] Pedro Fages served as recruiter for twenty-five men in Guadalajara and Tepic. There is, however, no evidence that Fages accompanied these men to California. Fages remained in Guadalajara until 1778. In the meantime, he requested and received the hand in marriage of Eulalia Callis, daughter of Agustín Callis.[47] Although Fages's service record of 1776[48] indicates that he was forty-two years old at that time, Eulalia apparently was much younger than he, for she was probably born in 1751.[49] In 1777 Fages was captain of Catalonian Volunteers,[50] and his father-in-law Agustín Callis was captain of the First Free Company of Catalonian Volunteers and lieutenant colonel in the regular army. Thus, Fages had taken a wife, but his primary devotion seemed to be to his career; for by mid-December 1777, Fages and his Catalonian Volunteers left Guadalajara bound for Sonora.[51] Their actual destination was El Pitic, present-day Hermosillo, which they reached on April 22.[52]

However, in preparation for a campaign against Apaches, Teodoro de Croix ordered Fages and his men to the presidio of Santa Cruz near Terrenate, an assignment which proved to be extremely dangerous and difficult. Croix wrote of the difficulty of Fages's assignment:

> The company of Santa Cruz of regular dotation was unable to defend the post. Reenforced with volunteers composed of eighty men, it was suffering daily attacks of the enemies. It was never able to prevent the ingress of these into the interior of the province and already the troops were becoming possessed with terror of panic.[53]

The year was 1778, and while Fages's career seemed inauspicious he was rewarded with promotion to lieutenant colonel while he was still at Santa Cruz.[54] However, by 1780 Fages was back in Mexico City recruiting troops, for his own command had been depleted by deaths, desertions, and retirements.[55]

Although Fages had been away from California for several years, from time to time the priests kept track of his career. One such example is a letter written by Fray Pablo Mugártegui, who remarked in passing:

69

The news around here is that the Apaches have finished off
Don Pedro Fages and two companies of volunteers, I take that
as a fable, although it may have some truth in it.[56]

The statement was false, for Don Pedro Fages would soon return to
govern California in 1782. Meanwhile, in 1781, Fages had recruited
his men and prepared to return to Sonora.[57] This time, Fages was
accompanied by his wife Eulalia Callis de Fages.[58]

By May 1781, Fages's party was in Arizpe, capital of Sonora. The
arrival of the group came none too soon, for on the night of May 30,
Eulalia gave birth to Pedro José Fernando Fages. "Pedrito" was baptized
on June 4, 1781.[59]

Fages's stay in Arizpe was short-lived, for he and his Catalan troopers
were moved out to Pitic to put down a rebellion against an enemy
Fages had fought before, the Seri.[60] The year was 1781, and it appeared
that Fages would be finally stationed in a permanent position. However,
such was not to be the case, for in September 1781, Fages was called
upon to lead an expedition against the Yumas, far to the north along
the Colorado River. The chief cause of the Yuma revolt was the establishment of the Spanish settlement of San Pedro y San Pablo de Bicúñer
and Misión Purísima Concepción near tribal lands. Many Yumans felt
that their way of life had been threatened by the encroaching settlement
and mission. The immediate cause occurred when Captain Fernando
de Rivera y Moncada and a detachment of soldiers camped near a Yuman
corn field and permitted their horses to forage in it. Rivera and his
men were among the first casualties of the rebellion.

Following the Colorado River campaign, Fages's career as a Catalonian Volunteer gave way to a position in California. Fages served as
gobernador of California from 1782 to 1791, after which he retired to
Mexico. Don Pedro Fages died in Mexico City in late 1794, where he
resided as an officer, *sin destino* (without assignment).[61] Notwithstanding
twenty-four years of hazardous military life in New Spain, the fifty-
seven-year-old Fages had lived out his adventures in New Spain.

6 / Spaniards, Russians, and Englishmen: The Catalonian Volunteers in the Pacific Northwest

During the decade of the 1770s, Spanish authorities were alarmed by many reports of increased foreign activity in New Spain's northernmost area of claim extending from California to the Aleutian Islands. Notwithstanding the pressure of possible foreign encroachments on Spanish possessions in the north Pacific, Viceroy Antonio María de Bucareli y Ursúa decided to increase Spanish exploration northward by using California and San Blas as supply bases for ships.[1] Among those mariners ordered north was Juan Pérez, commander of the *Santiago,* who sailed in 1774 reaching Queen Charlotte Island.[2] In 1775 Bruno de Hezeta, who commanded the *Santiago,* and Juan de la Bodega y Quadra of the *Sonora* set sail for Trinidad Bay to take possession of that area. Bodega y Quadra separated from the expedition, reaching a latitude of 58° north latitude,[3] probably near Sitka. The Hezeta–Bodega expedition enabled Spain to make paper claims to lands in the far northwest of New Spain. These claims were considered an extension of Alta California.

During that same period, Captain James Cook, sailing for England, made three voyages to the Pacific Ocean. It was his third voyage, made from 1776 to 1779, which concerned the Spaniards.[4] Cook made a landing at Nootka Sound,[5] on the west side of Vancouver Island. Although Cook did not perform an act of possession there, his voyage stimulated interest in Nootka because of possible fur trade with the natives on the island. Realizing a threat to Spanish claims and fearing

71

penetration of New Spain's defenses by foreigners, another Spanish expeditionary force was sent north in 1779 under Ignacio Arteaga and Juan de la Bodega y Quadra, who commanded the *Favorita* and the *Princesa,* respectively.[6] Arteaga and Bodega y Quadra found no sign of Englishmen, Russians, or Americans. Their report was reassuring and caused a temporary halt to Spanish voyages in support of the threatened northwestern claims. By 1780, northward-bound Spanish expeditions ceased.

In 1788, new reports of foreign trespassers began to upset Spanish authorities. The result was another expedition north under the command of Estevan José Martínez.[7] Martínez took two ships, the *Princesa* and the *San Carlos,* to investigate reports of Russians, who were said to be on islands named Kodiak and Unalaska. Actually the Russians had been there in 1779, and Arteaga had failed to find them. Nonetheless, Martínez made contact with the Russians, who informed him of Russian plans to colonize Nootka Sound.[8] Suddenly, Nootka became an area of intensive interest to the Spaniards. That same year, 1789, Martínez was sent to colonize Nootka, and a rudimentary establishment was begun. However, Martínez had other problems. When he arrived in Nootka, he was dismayed to find foreign ships under the commands of the Americans John Kendrick of the *Columbia* and Robert Gray of the *Lady Washington* as well as an Englishman, James Colnett, who was directing English ships in those waters.[9] Undaunted by Colnett's failure to identify himself properly, Martínez had him arrested and taken with his ships to Mexico.[10] The result was a sharp response by the English government, demanding indemnity. The situation placed England and Spain on the brink of war over an incident which came to be called the Nootka Sound Controversy. In October 1790, Spain and England, who had taken the path to negotiation instead of war, signed the first of the Nootka Sound conventions. Under the provisions of this Nootka Sound Convention, Spain agreed to recognize the right of another power to trade freely on the Pacific coast. Spain, moreover, was compelled to make restitution for English ships taken by Martínez. England, on the other hand, was free to trade north of California, and English ships gained the right to enter any California port for provisioning but not for trade,[11] unless specified. Obviously, Spanish concessions there foretold the decline of Spanish claims in the Pacific northwest,[12] as well as the dissolution of the Family Compact, for France failed to support Spain in this crisis.

Meanwhile, during the first hectic months of the Nootka Sound Controversy, the Catalonian Volunteers were mobilized for a military mission in the northern Pacific. In August 1789, the First Company of Catalonian Volunteers under Pedro de Alberni was alerted to mobilize and march from Guadalajara to the Port of San Blas and embark from there for Nootka.[13] By September 4, the Catalonian Volunteer mobilization was impeded because the company needed fifteen men to complete the effective force.[14] Captain Alberni applied for recruits, hoping to enlist the men from the Regimiento de Puebla.[15] These fifteen men, said to be Catalonians recently sent from Spain in transit to the Philippines, were temporarily attached to the Puebla regiment.[16] In addition to the lack of troopers to complete the company roll, Alberni had other problems affecting his manpower shortage. Twenty-three men were on the sick list of the Catalonian company.[17] Another man, Miguel Pericas, a sublieutenant, had applied for retirement.[18] Thus, Alberni asked for twenty-three more men to make up for the old and infirm soldiers.[19] It was not until January 1790, then, that Alberni and his men were prepared to march to San Blas. During that time, Alberni, still in Guadalajara, reviewed the state of armaments of his troops and found them to be unsatisfactory.[20] A request for new weapons was made by the Catalan captain, delaying further the mobilization of his troops. Next, after Alberni realized that the new assignment was in a cold climate, he requested warm clothing for his men.[21] Aside from equipping his men, Alberni had other administrative duties to perform. For example, he had to leave the Guadalajara post in reasonable order for incoming troops assigned to replace the outgoing Catalonians.

Alberni had also taken Volunteers from Mesa del Tonati in Nayarit, which was part of his command. Their replacements were troops from the Regimiento de Milicias de Guadalajara and Dragones Provinciales de Puebla.[22] Also, members of the Second Company of Catalonian Volunteers stationed in Sonora were being assigned to Guadalajara. Leading them was Captain Estévan Solá, whose wounds from Apache arrows tended to bother him, causing him to ask for an assignment in Guadalajara. He had with him soldiers who were soon to retire, but the rest of his command remained in Sonora with Solá's successor, Pedro Nata Viñolas.[23]

During that time, Alberni was very much concerned about a young sublieutenant who had suffered a serious head injury. Alberni's preoccupation with the young officer, whom he had favored, was another reason

for the delay in mobilization of his command. The injured sublieutenant, Francisco María Bucareli, seemed temporarily unable to join
his comrades. His subsequent efforts to join the company, despite advice
not to do so, convinced his superiors that he was permanently disabled.
On January 22, three days after Bucareli's effort, Juan de Dios Morelos,
a surgeon in Guadalajara, strongly advised that the sublieutenant was
not healthy enough to join the Volunteers on their new assignment.[24]
Moreover, wrote Morelos, Bucareli, who was gravely injured and "hys-
terical," attempted to join the troops at San Blas, where he was detained.
Alberni ordered that Bucareli should be left behind,[25] and Juan Francisco de la Bodega y Quadra conceded to honor Alberni's and Morelos's
request.[26] Meanwhile, Bucareli would remain in Tepic until he recovered.[27] Unfortunately, he became progressively worse and each day
he appeared to become "more demented." Finally, a hospital was recommended.[28] In March 1790, Bucareli entered the Hospital de San
Hipolito in Guadalajara.[29] His injuries, however, were beyond medical
help, for he died on August 23, 1790.[30]

Meanwhile, as the Bucareli episode came to pass, mobilization of
the Catalonian Volunteers continued its slow progress. Alberni had
requested new firearms because the Catalonians had not been rearmed
in thirteen years. In fact, the last time the Catalonian Volunteers had
been issued new weapons was on May 20, 1776. Alberni noted that
extensive use of the weapons on marches and the lack of gunsmiths for
the company over the years had resulted in the deplorable state of the
firearms.[31] Alberni said that the guns were in bad condition despite
efforts made to keep them serviceable.[32] Although the Catalonians
received some weapons at Tepic, the rest were ordered from El Perote,
which arrived while the Catalonian Volunteers were in Nootka. In
February 1790, seventy-eight muskets and bayonets were sent to San
Blas.[33] These new, clean, and well-boxed weapons were later forwarded
aboard the frigates *Princesa* and *Aranzazu* to Alberni in Nootka. Alberni
received them in March as well as orders to send back the old weapons
so that they could be repaired.[34]

Although Alberni had been ordered to bring his command to full
strength and to rearm them for a new assignment, official orders regarding the Catalonian mission to Nootka were not released until
December 7, 1789.[35] Included in these orders to Juan Francisco de la
Bodega y Quadra were instructions regarding the second Spanish occupation, following the 1789 effort by Martínez, of the port at Nootka.

Bodega y Quadra was specifically instructed to assign a detachment of the Catalonian Volunteers,[36] under Captain Alberni and his lieutenant Maricio Faulia, to occupy and guard that port. Although the main function of the Volunteers was to defend Nootka from foreign aggression, the Catalan troopers were also used as an amphibious force. The Spanish used soldiers on their vessels[37] as guards and as troops for landings.

The orders of December 7, 1789, to Bodega y Quadra from the viceroy, explained the reason for Spanish maneuvers in the Pacific Northwest. Specifically cited in the orders was the Russian plan to settle Nootka. Nonetheless, the Spaniards hoped to get there first and to be firmly established.[38] The Spaniards planned to win the race to Nootka.

Despite the slow mobilization of the Catalonian Volunteers, Alberni was ordered to proceed immediately to San Blas and board ship for that northern port.[39] Three weeks later, the Catalonian company was still in Guadalajara. It was not until January 1, 1790, that Alberni sent soldiers ahead of his command to prepare lodging facilities for his men en route to San Blas.[40]

Reasons for Alberni's delay in Guadalajara included the wait for new recruits; armament which did not arrive; warm clothing which had to be given to his men; and the hope that Sublieutenant Bucareli and three sick soldiers would recuperate. The ailing troopers, José Rubin, Francisco Herrera, and Gerónimo Bulferic, were ultimately left behind with Bucareli.[41] Although the Catalonian Volunteers departed Guadalajara for San Blas on January 2, Alberni did not do so until January 4.[42] The Catalonian captain had remained to care for his men.

It was February 3, 1790, when the anchors of three Spanish vessels were raised in preparation to leave San Blas for Nootka. Sailing from San Blas were the frigate *Concepción,* commanded by Francisco Eliza; the packetboat *San Carlos,* captained by Salvador Fidalgo, and the *Princesa Real,* under Manuel Quimper.[43] Francisco Eliza was appointed commandant of the fortifications to be built at Nootka. With Eliza were Alberni and his Catalonian Volunteers, who would militarily strengthen the occupation of that place. Eliza had been given secret instructions by Bodega y Quadra in San Blas on January 28.[44]

Francisco Eliza, a very capable officer of many years experience at sea, began his naval career in 1773 and successfully ascended through the ranks, achieving the status of lieutenant in 1784. In 1809, years

Map of the Spanish Claim to Alaska, 1790.
(Biblioteca Nacional, Madrid)

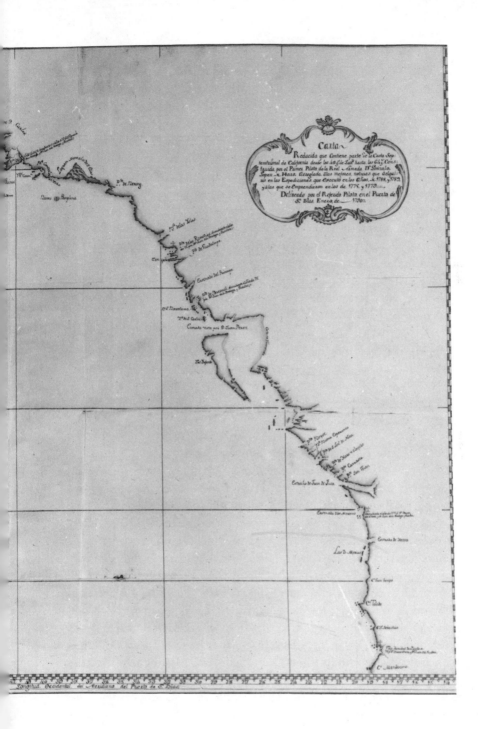

after the Nootka expedition, Eliza was promoted to captain in the Spanish navy.[45] His assignment in 1790 was to seize and fortify Santa Cruz de Nuca before any foreign power, namely Russia, could do so.[46]

Establishment and fortification of Nootka was to be made in co-operation with the Catalonian Volunteers under Captain Alberni, who was placed in charge of the outpost there.[47] Further exploration for purposes of gathering intelligence about the terrain, mineral wealth, and the position of foreigners and natives was a major objective of the expedition.[48] To that end, detachments of Catalan Volunteers from Alberni's company of seventy-six men would be assigned to various expeditions made from Nootka to the Strait of Juan de Fuca, the islands of the Aleutian chain, and other points of Spanish interest in the Pacific Northwest. Furthermore, Eliza was instructed to use the Volunteers in military engagements if necessary. Bodega y Quadra's instructions to Eliza pointed out that if

> during the brief interval of the absence of our arms someone has taken advantage, you will make known the right and preference we have, and the orders you carry to evict anyone intending to oppose you, and only in this case or insult to our flag should you use force to contain and punish the offense.[49]

Nonetheless, Eliza was reminded to carry out a peaceful mission. The erection of a fort with twenty cannons, garrisoned by the Catalonian Volunteers, was intended to be a show of force deterring foreign opposition to Eliza's commands.[50] Spanish officials calculated that the show of military force would gain respect for Commander Eliza's peaceful overtures. Moreover, the impressive fortifications constructed at Nootka by the Volunteers and sailors resulted, aside from military purposes, from convictions held by Alberni and Eliza that daily exercise in fresh air forestalled illness and discontent. Therefore, soldiers and sailors alike were put to work clearing the land of undergrowth and trees and rebuilding their fort at the entrance of Friendly Cove. Construction of barracks, sheds, storehouses, and the administration building was done by the industrious Catalonians and crew masters. Because of the distance to fresh drinking-water sources, the men were also put to work digging wells near the construction site.[51] Undoubtedly, their efforts were impressive to foreigners who could appreciate the smugness of the Spaniards in their military installation at Nootka. Furthermore,

TABLE 1. Monthly Statistical Report of Catalonian Volunteers at Nootka, 1790–93.

	Jan.	Feb.	Mar.	Apr.	May	June	July	Aug.	Sept.	Oct.	Nov.	Dec.
1790	79	80	80	78	78	78	78	78	78	78	78	77
1791	76	76	76	76	76	76	76	76	75	75	75	73
1792	73	72	72	64	64	64	64	65	66	67	67	66
1793	62	61	59									

Alberni was duly credited for planting a garden at Nootka, which ultimately proved to be useful in provisioning other mariners for years to come. So impressive had Alberni's personal contribution been at Nootka that one of his contemporaries, the illustrious Alexander Von Humboldt, included in his famous *Ensayo Político sobre el Reino de la Nueva España* (1811) a tributary comment on Alberni's work at Friendly Cove.[52]

In Nootka, the Catalonian Volunteers were used in various assignments. Pedro de Alberni, their captain, kept careful statistics regarding his men. Alberni's records indicate which men were sick, deserted, dead, or reassigned to the port of San Blas for disciplinary action. Moreover, Captain Alberni's review of troops gives the names of the men and their assignments. Alberni kept careful account of his command, which was full strength at eighty men but dropped to a low of fifty-nine troopers because of deaths and desertions. Table 1 illustrates the statistical report of the First Company of Catalonian Volunteers under Alberni assigned to Nootka; the dates cover January 1790 through March 1793.[53] The officer staff included Captain Alberni, Lieutenant Mauricio Faulia, and Sublieutenant Francisco María Bucareli. However, Bucareli, as noted above, died on August 23, 1790, and Lieutenant Faulia died at sea on March 10, 1791.[54] In his report, Juan Pantoja y Arriaga, pilot of the packetboat *San Carlos,* which left San Blas on February 4, 1791, wrote of the circumstances of Faulia's death and the sufferings of the Catalonian Volunteers:

> As soon as we dropped anchor First Lieutenant Don Francisco Eliza, the commandant of the establishment, came on board and stated that the crew of the two frigates under his command, the

Concepción and *Princesa,* and the Company of Volunteers of Catalonia had suffered many hardships in this first winter on account of its severity. Five sailors had died and the *Princesa* had left March 10, for one of the Ports of New California with 32 sick, among them, the lieutenant of the company and five soldiers, mostly gravely ill with scurvy and blood diarrhea, to see if their health could be restored as the climate there was milder and better remedies existed.[55]

Another source explaining the death of Mauricio Faulia at sea is a letter from Bodega y Quadra to Viceroy Revillagigedo in January 1792. Bodega wrote that the sick were taken from Nootka to Monterey to the frigate *Princesa* by Jacinto Caamaño, and that Faulia died a few days after the ship had left Nootka.[56]

The sicknesses suffered by the Volunteers from Catalonia were colds, colic, rheumatism, scurvy, and diarrhea or "bloody dysentery." Pantoja believed that scurvy and dysentery were common and incurable in Nootka.[57]

With the deaths of his two subordinate officers, Alberni continued to delegate authority through Sergeant Joaquín Tico. Tico was not promoted, nor were Bucareli and Faulia replaced with subordinate officers in Nootka. Although replacements for the two deceased officers were nominated, they did not go to Nootka. Instead, they remained in Mexico. Replacements for Bucareli and Faulia were Simón Suárez, first sergeant from the Regimiento de Infantería de México,[58] and José Font, brevet captain of the Milicias de Toluca.[59] Font and Suárez were paid and ordered to go to Tepic.[60] Earlier, Suárez, as sublieutenant, had been ordered to California to join a detachment of the First Company of Volunteers from Catalonia. However, it is doubtful that Font and Suárez went beyond Tepic because Alberni's records do not show them listed either under his Nootka command or in detachments sent to California. Instead, Captain Alberni included them in the review of his command in Tepic on December 31, 1792.[61]

The uses of the Catalonian Volunteers in Nootka were incidental to the occupation of Friendly Cove and the various important Spanish explorations of the Pacific Northwest. Alberni kept a basic number of men with him to garrison the fort at Friendly Cove. The rest were assigned to Spanish vessels operating in the area. At Nootka, Alberni maintained thirty-seven volunteers as guards under his direct command, as follows: seven corporals and four men were in the fort; another eleven men were on board the *Concepción,* a large warship anchored in waters near the entrance of Friendly Cove as part of the show of strength; and fifteen men were kept on land guarding the ship and the fort in their view.[62] At a glance, it appears that Alberni had set up three practical lines of defense. Since attack was to be expected from the sea, the *Concepción* was the primary defense. In the event of attack from the forests, however, the troops on land would become the first line of defense. The third line of defense was always the fort, which symbolized possession. Immediately upon arriving at San Blas in January 1790, the Catalonian Volunteers assumed their duties as guards of ships on the particular mission. Alberni had assigned twenty-two Volunteers to watch the packetboat *San Carlos* and three troopers to guard the *Princesa Real.* The rest of the men were with Alberni on the *Concepción* sailing to Nootka.[63]

The Catalonian Volunteers, during the course of their stay in the Pacific Northwest, participated in several important explorations in those waters as guards on Spanish vessels well known in their day. These expeditions, which were exploratory in character, added much to the knowledge of the cartography of the North Pacific.

Although Nootka was occupied, the Spaniards soon realized that effective establishment of fortifications at Nootka would not adequately preserve Spain's hold in that area. Despite the failure of Russian plans to settle Nootka, the Spaniards felt that additional intelligence was needed to determine the strength and position of the Russians. And so, on May 4, 1790,[64] Salvador Fidalgo left Nootka destined for Alaskan waters. Among Fidalgo's crew were English and Russian interpreters, as well as fifteen Catalonian Volunteers who completed the roster. First Corporal Juan Yñiguez, Juan Sánchez, Antonio Baldes, José Tórres, José Antonio Ferre, Antonio Cañizares, Juan Manzanilla, Juan Ortel, Francisco Pérez, another Francisco Pérez, Cayettano Valls, Rafael Romero, Estévan Cabre, and Antonio Bonilla[65] were assigned to guard the *San Carlos.*

Once inside Prince William Sound, Fidalgo performed an act of possession claiming and naming present-day Cordova Bay.[66] Fidalgo also named Valdez in honor of Spain's minister of Marine and Indies. Sailing northward, they encountered glaciers blocking their passage. Acts of possession were performed at Mendez Bay and Port Gravina. Presently they entered Cook Inlet, and found there a guarded Russian fort on July 4.[67] In an effort to avoid an encounter, Fidalgo bypassed the fort after quickly gathering whatever intelligence he could;[68] then, he turned south to a place he named Revillagigedo, where he performed an act of sovereignty. Fidalgo avoided any encounters with foreigners as he maneuvered his warship to Kodiak Island, which he reached on August 15. After finding the Russian post there, Fidalgo attempted to return to Nootka, but contrary winds forced him to set his course for Monterey.[69]

A second expedition was sent south from Nootka to the Strait of Juan de Fuca on May 31, 1790. The commander of that expedition was Manuel Quimper of the *Princesa Real*. These waters had not been adequately explored, and penetration of the strait was the first ever made of that waterway.[70] On this voyage, Quimper, whose pilot was Gonzalo López de Haro, one of the most experienced navigators of his day, directed his ship south, stopping at Opitsat, an Indian village in Clayoquot Sound, to visit and trade for several days. Thereafter, the explorers continued their voyage southeast, investigating strategic bays and naming, as well as sounding, all likely landings. Their investigation was thorough, for they gathered intelligence regarding Indian behavior, climate, prevailing winds, fresh-water sources, and firewood as well as knowledge of the fertility of the soil in that area. Some place-names credited to this expedition are Port of San Juan, Haro Strait, Puerto de Revillagigedo (Sooke Inlet), Rada de Valdes y Bazan (Royal Roads), Puerto de Córdova (Esquimalt Harbor, near Victoria), and Port Bodega y Quadra (Port Discovery).[71] They did not find Puget Sound, although they had mapped the waterway leading directly to it. Quimper and his men then continued to a place he named Núñez Gaona (today's Neah Bay) after a high-ranking Spanish naval officer, Commodore Manuel Núñez Gaona.[72] The importance of the Bay of Núñez Gaona was its location at the entrance of the Strait of Juan de Fuca. After taking formal possession of the bay, Quimper sailed for Nootka, but adverse sailing conditions likewise forced him to go to Monterey.[73] Nine Catalonians were with Quimper on the expedition to the Strait of Juan de Fuca in 1790. Acting as Quimper's guards and troops were Francisco Fabregatt, Antonio Marín, Damian Seguera, Sebastián Escribano, Francisco Murguía, Domingo Albarez, Francisco Martí, Francisco Rodríguez, and Simón Gonzáles.[74] These men participated in an act of sovereignty performed at Núñez Gaona by Quimper by firing the customary three volleys at the conclusion of the ceremony.[75]

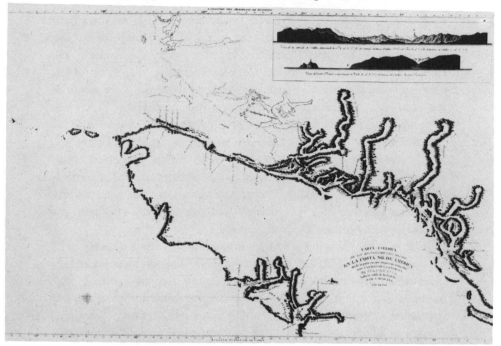

The Canals at the Entrance of the Strait of Juan de Fuca, 1793.
(Archivo del Servicio Histórico Militar, Madrid)

These Catalonian Volunteers who had been with Fidalgo and Quimper were afterward temporarily detached to Monterey because the vessels they were on had been unable to return to Nootka as planned. Although Alberni kept a record of them, for they were still part of his command, he was without twenty-three men for the rest of the time he spent at Nootka. Later, the detachment of Volunteers in Monterey was used in various other assignments to Nootka. First, these men were taken to San Blas and housed with the Compañía Fija de San Blas in early 1792.[76] Four months later, fifteen of them were assigned to the 1792 voyage to the Strait of Juan de Fuca on the *Princesa*,[77] under the command of Salvador Fidalgo. Most of these men had been with Fidalgo in 1790. The Catalonian Volunteers were to see extensive duty on various ships from 1790 to 1793, acting as guards on important explorations.

Quimper's exploration of the Strait of Fuca in 1790 was important because of the information acquired. Spanish authorities felt that knowledge of the Pacific Northwest would help them in securing their claim more effectively. With this in mind, another expedition was prepared for the purpose of gathering more accurate information of the coastline and waterways, which might lead into the interior of the continent. At any rate, the Spaniards desired to verify if, in fact, the mythical Strait of Anian or the Northwest Passage did exist. The place to start was the Strait of Juan de Fuca. It had always been supposed that the mariner Juan de Fuca, after whom the strait had been named, had sailed north almost two hundred years before Quimper's 1790 voyage, discovering a passage leading into the interior of the continent.[78] If such a passage did exist, the Spaniards in 1791 were willing to expend effort to find it. Quimper had reopened the trail with his discovery of the Strait of López de Haro.

In 1791, Francisco Eliza was commanded by Juan Francisco de la Bodega y Quadra to explore those points which had not been examined. Eliza was instructed to investigate thoroughly the coast from Mount St. Elias to the Port of Trinidad in the Pacific Northwest.[79] Eliza was instructed to leave no detail unattended in the report of his exploration. Bodega y Quadra requested information regarding the coastline, soundings of harbors, and distances as well as factual comments describing animals, birds, fish, insects, plants, and mineral wealth.[80]

Eliza sailed on May 4, 1791, on the *San Carlos,* which was accompanied by the *Santa Saturnina* under José María Narvaez.[81] The destination of these explorers was Alaska's Mount St. Elias, but Eliza encountered unfavorable weather after a few days out to sea and turned south to investigate the Strait of Juan de Fuca.[82] Eliza also prepared for any possible encounters, although his was to be a peaceful mission. Nevertheless, the *San Carlos* was armed with sixteen four-pound cannons, and the *Santa Saturnina* carried four three-pound guns.[83] Eliza also took with him ten Catalonian Volunteers. Pedro Alberni assigned to Eliza's expeditionary force Second Sergeant Miguel Serera, First Corporal Francisco Gutiérrez, Francisco Terricabres, Rafael Coca, Felipe Gutiérrez, Vicente Montenegro, Pablo Ferrer, Saturnino Budet, Miguel Ramos, and Francisco Corbella.[84] Eliza did not neglect his defense of Friendly Cove, for in his absence he left Pedro Alberni and his troops to guard the Spanish establishment, and placed ensign Ramón Saavedra in command of the *Concepción.*[85] Eliza's voyage proved to be of importance to the knowledge and cartography of the area he explored.

On the afternoon of May 7, Eliza's ships anchored in Clayoquot

Sound. The ships were met by many natives who had rowed out in their canoes to greet them. Two days later, Eliza dispatched the *Santa Saturnina* to explore Barkley Sound. Their rendezvous was to be at Esquimalt Harbor.[86] Ten days later, however, the *Santa Saturnina* returned from its assignment with the desired information.

On June 14, Second Pilot Juan Pantoja was sent on a heavily guarded longboat to explore an interior part of the Strait of López de Haro for the second time. From May 11 to 19, Pantoja had taken an armed longboat to the interior of an inlet to the northwest, but he was forced to retreat in the face of hostile-looking natives.[87] Actually, this was the third time armed longboats had been sent into the Strait of López de Haro. On May 31, Ensign José Verdía had encountered Indian resistance. Undoubtedly, Verdía was accompanied by Catalonian Volunteers because he reported that the Indians paid no attention to the firearms shown them in a Spanish display of force. Verdía retreated to the cannon-carrying *Santa Saturnina*.[88] Thus, Pantoja's mid-June attempt to explore the strait was also punitive in purpose. To explore the strait, Eliza ordered Pantoja's fully armed longboat to be supported by the *Santa Saturnina*, supplied with twenty-five shots for the six cannons and swivel guns on board. Accompanying Pantoja were eight able-bodied Catalonian Volunteers. The Second Pilot was instructed to examine carefully the Strait of López de Haro and punish the Indians if they threatened to attack as they had assaulted the longboat of José Verdía.[89] Ultimately, no Indian hostility was encountered.

It was on Eliza's 1791 voyage that a detailed mapping was made of the Strait of Georgia, known to the Spaniards as Canal de Nuestra Señora del Rosario. Another significant event during the expedition was the discovery of the mouth of the Fraser River, which was named in 1808 by Simon Fraser after running the course of the river to its mouth.[90] One other important find made by Eliza's explorers was Puget Sound (Admiralty Inlet). Unfortunately, the Spaniards neglected to explore it thoroughly or to publicize it. Spanish failure to realize the extent of Puget Sound explains in part the absence of credit given Eliza's expeditionary forces.[91] The credit went instead to the British captain George Vancouver.

On July 25, Eliza determined to leave the Strait of Juan de Fuca and return to Nootka.[92] On the way back to Friendly Cove, Eliza discovered and named the port of Nuestra Señora de Los Angeles,[93] present-day Port Angeles. Such were the accomplishments of Eliza's

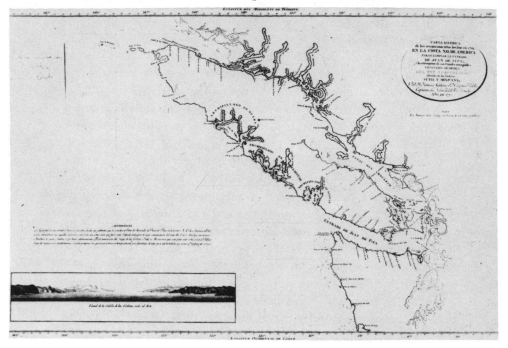

*Vancouver Island, the Strait of Juan de Fuca and the Canal de Rosario.
(Archivo del Servicio Histórico Militar, Madrid)*

voyage to the Strait of Juan de Fuca. At last, the Spaniards had learned
the answer to the age-old riddle: Fuca's passage through the continent
did not exist. Eliza's voyage had stamped an indelible mark of doubt
on the word of the legendary ancient mariner.

The expedition was a success from another point of view—only one
life was lost during the voyage, that of Miguel Serera, sergeant of
Catalonian Volunteers, who succumbed to inflammation of the abdomen. Alberni recorded Serera's death as having occurred on August 27,
1791.[94] Eliza himself had taken sick during the voyage, but he recovered on the way back to Nootka.

His return to Nootka signaled a new phase in the Spanish occupation
of Nootka Sound. Early in 1791, Bodega y Quadra had issued orders
to Eliza regarding defenses at Nootka. Eliza was not to molest Englishmen who came to the port. Furthermore, if the English established
a base near Friendly Cove, he was not to prevent them by force from
doing so. All that was expected of Don Francisco was a written protest.[95]

Moreover, his orders were designed to withdraw the Catalonian Volunteers from Nootka. Bodega y Quadra instructed Eliza that

> although His Excellency thinks that . . . one frigate and the Company of Catalonia will be sufficient to guard the port and that one should return, believing that by that time a friendly arrangement will be concluded between our court and that of London, yet as he is desirous of not making a mistake, he leaves it to your judgment to determine the matter as you are on the ground to appreciate the greater or less urgency of it.[96]

Don Francisco complied with his orders.

By July 1, 1792, Alberni and part of his command had left Nootka on the frigate *Concepción*. Their destination was Monterey.[97] The rest of his men were scattered in various assignments. Fifteen Catalan troopers were assigned to Fidalgo's 1792 voyage to the Strait of Fuca on the *Princesa*. Thirteen others were on the Aranzazu in Alaskan waters under Jacinto Caamaño; three were with Dionisio Alcalá Galiano on the schooner *Mexicana* in the Strait of Juan de Fuca; and ten Volunteers were on the brigantine *Activa* commanded by Salvador Menéndez,[98] all in the Pacific Northwest.

Ironically, as Alberni and his detachment were being pulled out of Nootka, Spanish activities in the Pacific Northwest were increasing in 1792. During that time, Bodega y Quadra arrived in Nootka on the *Expedición de los Límites* to negotiate with the British commissioner there. Fidalgo attempted a settlement in Neah Bay; Galiano explored the Strait of Fuca once again; and Caamaño was in Alaska exploring.

In order to strengthen Spain's hold on the Strait of Juan de Fuca, Viceroy Revillagigedo planned a settlement at Neah Bay, Quimper's Bay of Nuñéz Gaona. In charge of the project was Salvador Fidalgo, accompanied by the aforementioned Catalonian Volunteers.[99]

The fort at Neah Bay, established in 1792 by Fidalgo, became the first attempted white settlement west of the Rockies and north of San Francisco in future United States territory.[100] During the period spent at Neah Bay, Fidalgo's men constructed houses and corrals. Unfortunately, Fidalgo did not encourage friendship with the Indians there, and he almost started a general Indian war by avenging the death of one of his officers, who had been killed by Neah Bay natives. Nonetheless, the project of settlement was short-lived. In 1796, when William Broughton commanded the *Providence* there, he found it deserted.[101] Interestingly, Alberni last listed fifteen Catalonian Volunteers on board the *Princesa* in his review of troops in August 1792.[102] Thereafter, Alberni listed sixteen men, eleven of whom had been with Fidalgo, who were assigned to guarding the establishment at Nootka,[103] although Alberni may have been referring to Neah Bay. At any rate, these men were still there in March 1793,[104] when Alberni reviewed his command in Guadalajara.

Alberni's return trip from Nootka to Guadalajara was without incident, however long in duration. As mentioned previously, Alberni left Nootka by July 1, 1792.[105] Within a month, the Catalonian officer, with sixteen of his men, were in Monterey.[106] Three months later, on November 1, Alberni was in San Diego,[107] awaiting transport to San Blas. By November 22, Alberni and his sixteen men arrived in San Blas on board the *Concepción*.[108] Three others who had been with Galiano on the *Mexicana* also arrived on the same day. Alberni noted at that time that he had left behind two corporals and twenty soldiers at Nootka.[109] Continuing the march, Alberni proceeded to Tepic and arrived there in the first week of January 1793, with himself as well as his soldiers ill and exhausted.[110] By the end of February, Alberni ordered his men to continue their march to Guadalajara so that they could relieve the militia there. Slowly, the Catalonian captain and his men traveled to Guadalajara, for they were recovering from their illnesses.[111] On March 12, 1793, Alberni and one officer, probably Font, and a weakened force of forty-two men arrived in Guadalajara. Thirty-six men were needed to complete Alberni's effective force in Guadalajara.[112] A review of the Catalonian Volunteers in March 1793 showed forty-eight men in Guadalajara and sixteen at Nootka, totaling sixty-four men.[113] By March 22, Alberni was strong enough to report to the viceroy that he and his men had arrived in Guadalajara.[114]

The Catalonian Volunteers had once again performed their duty. Their presence at Nootka and the fort they rebuilt there was evidence of the need for the anticipated force required to resist foreign encroachments on Spanish claims to the Pacific Northwest. However, the enemy did not turn out to be foreign troopers, but rather diplomats, who would eventually settle the Nootka Sound claims, depriving Spain of her possession in the Pacific Northwest. By 1819 Spanish claims to any part of the Northwest would be part of the past.

7 / *Pedro de Alberni, Stalwart Soldier*

One of the more interesting Catalonian Volunteers was Pedro de Alberni. Little of Alberni's personality can be detected from a cursory reading of his correspondence. However, upon careful examination of Alberni's letters and official reports, a picture of a quiet, forceful, and loyal man emerges. Alberni wrote little of himself in a self-embellishing manner. His applications for promotion are tempered by an official style of writing. Alberni's vocabulary was often direct and simple, for Don Pedro had a knack for presenting his arguments logically and clearly. He seems to have possessed a capacity for order, and he always seemed to execute his assignments as directed. With the exception of one major incident, Alberni's behavior seems to have been consistently exemplary.

The major incident, which led to charges of insubordination against Alberni, occurred at San Blas on September 23, 1789.[1] The circumstances for such an accusation grew out of an application made by Alberni for the payment of his Catalonian troops, who had been ordered to Nootka. Alberni presented his case with the following argument. On the morning of the incident,[2] Alberni and his sublieutenant Francisco María Bucareli entered the office of *Intendente de Comisario* Antonio Villa Urrútia for the purpose of inquiring about the delay in the payment of the troops. Soldiers under Alberni's command had not been paid for July and August. Don Pedro's patience had run thin because, as he explained, he had approached Villa Urrútia and his scribe, José

Mateos, on "eighteen occasions."[3] Earlier, José Mateos had been instructed to review and make adjustments of the payment application. Alberni noted that the minister of Real Hacienda had remitted the forms to Villa Urrútia with their approval.[4] Nevertheless, five days prior to the incident, Alberni had stopped at the office to check if the *intendente* had approved payment of the troops. On the morning in question, Alberni was greeted by José Mateos, who supposedly told Alberni that there were other matters of greater priority than payment of his troops.[5] At that point, Alberni, incensed by the scribe's attitude, raised his voice in objecting to what he perceived as sarcasm. Just as quickly, the scribe rudely told Alberni to "shut up and leave."[6] Alberni noted in his report that he was treated like a servant deprived of the "honor . . . which the king has conceded to me." As tempers escalated between Alberni and Mateos, Villa Urrútia heard the commotion outside his office and entered the reception room. The royal official was met by an angry Alberni, who quickly accused him of delaying the quick payment of his troops.[7] Then Alberni did the unpardonable, verbally attacking Villa Urrútia and waving his hands menacingly at the *intendente*'s face while raising his voice to a shout.[8] Villa Urrútia's report of Alberni's behavior noted that the Catalan had accused him of not liking Catalonian troopers, a charge he quickly denied, saying, "I am far from looking at these troops with disaffection."[9] Before the incident, Villa Urrútia had visited Alberni in his quarters, indicating that he and the Catalonian had gotten along well. *Intendente* Villa Urrútia refuted Alberni's allegations concerning discrimination against Catalonians by stating that on several previous occasions he had given Alberni good review comments in official records.[10] In addition to his negative display of temperament, Alberni refused to obey Villa Urrútia's order that he place himself under house arrest. Alberni's response to his arrest was disobedience on grounds that Villa Urrútia was not his superior.[11] Official response to the unfortunate incident tended to favor the *intendente* in the long run.

It was resolved that officials of the Real Hacienda would appoint someone else to make adjustments on the payment of the Catalonian Volunteers and that Alberni was to recognize officials with more respect.[12] Alberni had succeeded in getting some action directed toward payment of his troops. However, he was left vulnerable to Villa Urrútia's vindictiveness. In the next few months Alberni was the subject of the *intendent*'s correspondence to Viceroy Revillagigedo. Villa Urrútia charged that Alberni continued to be insolent toward him. Coincidentally, the Catalonian troops under Alberni had been ordered to make preparations for an expedition to Nootka, in today's British Columbia. Villa Urrútia wrote Revillagigedo regarding troop preparations for San Blas.[13] Shortly thereafter, Juan Francisco de la Bodega y Quadra, commandant of the Department of San Blas, was ordered to place Alberni under arrest until the expedition anchored in Nootka. Bodega y Quadra was informed that Alberni had shown repeated insubordination and disrespect to *Intendente* Villa Urrútia.[14] The seventy days arrest of Alberni was imposed by the viceroy. On July 5, 1790, a repentant Alberni, now in Nootka, wrote to the viceroy wishing him good health. Alberni told the viceroy that he respected his superiors, despite his arrest,[15] during the long sea voyage from San Blas to Nootka. In another letter to Revillagigedo, written on the same day as the first, Alberni said that he would defend Nootka "to his death."[16] Such repentance was sure to make a good impression on the viceroy. Although these letters were written in a serious tone, they seem to impart a humorous effect. Certainly, the viceroy must have smiled at Alberni's good nature. In 1792, an impressed Bodega y Quadra wrote to Viceroy Revillagigedo in praise of Alberni's accomplishments at Nootka and recommending him to the viceroy's good graces.[17]

Born in 1745, Alberni was forty-five years old when he led Catalonian troops to Nootka in 1790.[18] He was the son of Jaime de Alberni and Josefa Texedor. A native of Tortosa, Catalonia, Alberni married Juana Vélez of Tepic, and she bore him one daughter.[19]

Between the years 1771 and 1788 Alberni served in the garrisons at Guadalajara in Jalisco and Mesa del Tonati in Nayarit. In 1782, Alberni assumed command of the Volunteers when Agustín Callis died in Real del Monte.[20] At that time Alberni was a lieutenant of the Catalan Volunteers, a rank he had held since March 1776.[21] Until 1782, Alberni's career had been without luster. He had carried out his tours of duty as a subordinate to others. After 1782, Alberni's career took a sharp turn and he became a notable figure in Spain's northward advance.

Although Alberni's service record indicates that he began his military career in the Second Regiment of Light Infantry of Catalonia as a cadet in 1762, the records of Inspector Pasqual de Cisneros show that in 1782 Alberni had been in military service for twenty-five years, eight months, and fourteen days.[22] Thus, it appears that Alberni began his military life in 1757 at the age of twelve and as a soldier. Military service at such a young age was not unusual in that period.[23] Nevertheless, in 1762, seventeen-year-old Alberni was listed as cadet in the Second Regiment. Between 1762 and 1767 Alberni rose through the ranks from cadet to first and second sergeant. During this time Alberni participated in the 1762 campaign against Portugal.[24]

In 1767 Alberni's career took its first major change. Volunteering for service in the Americas, Alberni was promoted to sublieutenant under the command of Agustín Callis, captain of the newly organized Company of Catalonian Volunteers. With the new company, Alberni saw action for the second time in the Sonora expedition, from 1767 to 1771. His record during the Sonora Indian wars was exemplary. Still, little in Alberni's record indicated any signs of the brilliance he was to exhibit after his rise to captain in 1782. When the Sonora campaigns ended in 1771, Alberni was among those soldiers who were shifted back to Mexico City for reassignment. Alberni's career is marked by a peculiar characteristic which was noticed a century later by Hubert Howe Bancroft. Writing of Alberni's rise to importance in California, Bancroft wrote that Alberni's "high positions in the province [were] purely accidental."[25]

Apparently such had been the case throughout Alberni's career. When Alberni came to Mexico in 1767, he was listed fourth in command of the Catalan Volunteers. By 1771 he was second in command, although he was still a sublieutenant. The events paving the way for Alberni's quick advancement were, first, the reassignment and eventual promotion of Lieutenant Pedro Fages to the California expedition as commander of a detachment of Catalonian Volunteers in 1768; and, second, the resignation of Sublieutenant Estévan de Vilaseca in 1771. Thus, when Agustín Callis died in 1782, leaving vacant the rank of captain of the First Company of Catalonian Volunteers, Alberni, then a lieutenant, quickly applied for the vacancy of the deceased officer. By September 1782, Alberni was named interim commander of the Catalonian Volunteers until royal approval was granted for his promotion.[26]

Although Alberni undoubtedly deserved the promotion, it was recognized that he earned it through seniority, for it was written that the preferment was given Alberni *"por no tener otra salida para premio de su mérito."*[27] Nevertheless, the "accidental" rise of Alberni meant the discovery of an unusually talented man, as the subsequent years of his career would reveal.

Alberni left San Blas for Nootka on February 3, 1790,[28] with a command of eighty Catalonian Volunteers. Their mission was to guard Spanish vessels and reestablish fortifications in what is now known as British Columbia. Alberni's particular assignment was that of commandant of arms and governor of the fort of Nootka, a position he held from 1790 to 1792. It was in tasks incidental to his official duties that Alberni began to show true worth. Alberni distinguished himself through his own inventiveness. An imaginative person, the Catalan officer developed good relations with the Indians of Vancouver Island, who had heretofore despised and lacked confidence in Spanish diplomacy; and he carried on meteorological surveys which added useful information regarding Spanish activities in that area. Similarly, agricultural experiments by Alberni in the region provided not only dietary supplementation for all mariners who frequented the area, but added information concerning food plants which would grow in that northern climate. Alberni kept records of the quantity yielded by plants, and he studied the best planting periods for the various seeds. Captain Alberni's contributions also included a study of the language of Nootkans.[29]

With reference to the role that Alberni played in developing good relations with the natives in the port of Nootka, where he was stationed, it should be noted that before he came, the Nootkans had suffered threats to one of their principal chiefs, Maquinna, by Ensign Estévan José Martínez. Martínez accused Maquinna of robbery and threated to shoot him.[30]

The Nootkan chieftain had been wronged, and Alberni set his talents toward befriending him. Pedro de Alberni and Francisco Eliza of the *Concepción* are credited with devising and implementing a plan to restore native confidence. The plan was that Maquinna would be praised and flattered through the native "grape-vine." Eliza and Alberni would release the flattery to a Nootka commoner, who unwittingly would pass the good word along. All that the two Spaniards needed to do was sit and wait for Maquinna to hear from his own people the laudatory remarks the Spaniards had uttered about him. It was calculated that Maquinna would forgive all.[31]

Comprehending that something more was needed to attract Maquinna, Alberni energized the plan by composing a jingle in Nootkan dialect. Employing the few Nootkan words that he knew at the time, Alberni praised Maquinna's greatness and friendship. The jingle also claimed Spain's loyalty to this Nootkan chief and to his people:

Chapter 7

> Macuina, Macuina, Macuina
> Asco-Tais, hua-cas
> España, España, España
> Hua-cas, Macuina, Nutka
>
> Macuina, Macuina, Macuina
> Es un gran Princípe, amigo nuestro
> España, España, España
> Es amigo de Macuina y Nutka.[32]

The two verses, one Nootkan and the other Spanish, translate as follows:

> Maquinna, Maquinna, Maquinna
> Is a great prince and our friend
> Spain, Spain, Spain
> Is a friend of Maquinna and Nootka.

Alberni, the lyricist now turned maestro, had taught his soldiers to sing it to the tune of "El Mambrú" a popular Andalusian song.[33] Just as Alberni had hoped, the natives took notice of the song and passed the tidings to Maquinna. Soon the self-styled Catalonian choir was singing their new hit song to their number one fan, Maquinna. The Spanish naturalist Mariano Moziño wrote that "Maquinna arrived on the spot and asked that they, the Catalonians, sing his eulogy several times consecutively to him so that he could memorize it and repeat it."[34]

So impressed was Maquinna with the ditty that he repeated it to Moziño, who interviewed him two years later. Thus, Alberni ignited a friendship which otherwise would never have been formed. Shortly thereafter, Alberni and Eliza began to notice the importance of native support to the Spanish position at Nootka. Affirmation of their diplomatic success was manifested in the frequent donations of fish and deer meat by Nootkans to the tables of Eliza and Alberni's troops. Tlupananul, a Nootkan prince, personally delivered these foods to Alberni.[35] The affection professed by the Nootkans for Alberni was profound. Even after Alberni left Nootka in 1792, the Indians continued to remember him although they had lost hope of ever seeing him again.[36] Moziño wrote that Prince Nanquis, whom he met long after the Catalonian captain had departed, asked him to hug Alberni for him the next time he saw him. Moziño was impressed with the fond memories Alberni had shared with the natives. Juan Francisco Bodega y Quadra, in his visit to Nootka in 1792, was pleased to inform Viceroy Revillagigedo of the affection the natives continued to feel for Alberni.[37]

Alberni's interest in the natives went beyond mere friendship. During his tour of duty at Nootka, Alberni helped compile an eleven-page word list consisting of 633 Nootkan words and their Spanish definitions. The final draft of the brief dictionary was completed and submitted to officials by Moziño, who credited Alberni with much of the field work.[38] The Nootka experience seemed to be a catalyst for Alberni's talents. Moziño was inspired by other Alberni accomplishments, of which he wrote:

> To this industrious genius, which in no way contradicts the general character of his province [of Catalonia] is owed the houses, offices and gardens which have furnised help and comfort to many seafarers.[39]

Alberni had trained his soldiers to cultivate his gardens. He personally helped dig trenches for irrigation and raised a number of fowl for supplementation of dietary needs. It was Alberni who had set the standard and example for such works. Francisco Eliza paid tribute to Alberni's resourcefulness by planting gardens based on the Catalonian's findings. For example, it was noted that cabbage, garlic, and onions grew best in summer. Lettuce and radishes grew into late fall. Potatoes, beans, and peas grew in abundance as did carrots and artichokes. Garbanzos, corn, wheat, tomatoes, and squash did not seem to do as well in Nootka as elsewhere. Squash, for instance, was possible in various species but grew small; tomatoes did not ripen well, and garbanzo plants grew large but did not granulate.[40]

The establishment at Nootka was complete with livestock. Two cows, one bull, and one calf comprised the large animals. Small farm animals, such as one goat, one lamb, twenty pigs, and seventy chickens with four hundred chicks,[41] were, barring a catastrophe, raised with a good chance of reproduction.

Alberni collected seeds and took care to plant each plot of grain at weekly intervals in order to determine the best possible time for planting.[42] The Catalonian officer was aware of the short planting season and peculiarities of the climate. Although Alberni was not the first

Spaniard to break ground at Nootka, his agricultural experiments were given much notice and recognition, perhaps because he had produced crops on a significantly larger scale and perhaps because more and important Spanish and foreign visitors frequented Nootka at this late date in Spain's effort there.

Pertinent to Alberni's search for the best planting period was his meteorological studies. Alejandro Malaspina in "Descripción Física de las Costas del Norte de la America,"[43] emphasized the importance of Alberni's inquiries:

> the fortunate pioneering discovery of Pedro Alberni and the notices which he has communicated has placed us in a situation enabling us to detail many circumstances which certainly can be seen as important toward the future measurement of the temperature of Nootka.[44]

Malaspina compiled a chart of weather conditions based on information obviously collected by Alberni.[45] The chart runs two columns, by month, for the years 1790 and 1791.

Thus did Alberni make another contribution not only to his contemporaries, but also to future researchers desiring to piece together a picture of the climate of another era. Alberni and his men returned to San Blas from Nootka in 1792. Obviously, Alberni's superiors were pleased with his successes at Nootka, for in that year he was promoted to lieutenant colonel in the Spanish army,[47] although he was still captain of the First Company of Volunteers from Catalonia.

For the next two years, Alberni was in Guadalajara attending to his family and soldierly duties. In 1795, Alberni and seventy-two Catalonian Volunteers were sent to California from San Blas. The reason for the transfer of these troops to California was war with France. The old plan of defense of the empire provided the motive. Lieutenant Colonel Alberni picked his men—well-armed, healthy, and disciplined. Another attractive feature was that most of these men were married.[48] Movement of the Catalonian troops was coincidental to official plans to establish the civilian Villa of Branciforte. Alberni was among those chosen to select a site for the proposed settlement. The approval of the Villa de Branciforte was precipitated by fears of foreign Anglo-American or English aggression. Precautionary orders urging diligence along the

ALBERNI'S REPORT OF METEOROLOGICAL CONDITIONS.

	1790	1791
January		Variable with cold. Thunder on the twenty-ninth. Freezing on the thirty-first.
February		Much rain, and moderate winds from the southeast.
March		Cold, with interrupted rainfall. Strong storm from the southeast, with hail on the twenty-first.
April	Pleasant and clear.	Pleasant and temperate. Some showers.
May	Clear and moderate.	Excessive rainfall.
July	Rain, with southeast winds.	Rain until the thirteenth, followed by clear and very warm weather.
August	Very rainy.	Beautiful and warm. Slow sea breezes.
September	Beautiful.	
October	Much rain.	
November	Rain and fog. Biting freeze on the twenty-third.	
December	Variable, much rain, little cold.[46]	

California coast were issued frequently, while rumors of enemy plans to attack California were heard from time to time.

Only two foreign ships appeared along the California coast in 1796. One of them, a British man-of-war, the *Providence,* was commanded by William Robert Broughton.[49] On June 10, 1796, the *Providence* entered San Francisco Bay. The Spaniards took precautions. Pedro de Alberni ordered Broughton not to land. Word flashed across the coast, transmitting Alberni's order.[50] Broughton, however, was able to prove his peaceful intentions when he anchored in Monterey Bay and delivered some instruments intended for Juan Francisco de Bodega y Quadra.[51] After buying supplies from Governor Diego Borica, Broughton weighed anchor and attempted to explore the area of the Río San Antonio, but departed after he was fired upon by Spaniards.[52]

The foreign threat was met, and the incident justified more petitions from Spanish officials in California for more men. In 1797, nearly one hundred men were sent to that northern coast of Mexico; among them four Catalonian Volunteers under Lieutenant Simón Suárez.[53] Lieutenant-Colonel Pedro Alberni was appointed commandant of the San Francisco Presidio in 1796 by virtue of his superior rank.[54] Although Alberni's rank as captain of Catalonian Volunteers made him responsible for that company, his rank of lieutenant colonel in the Spanish army made him the highest-ranking military figure in California at that time. Thus, Alberni's responsibilities as commander of San Francisco involved assignment of presidial troops at that fort only. As captain of the Catalan troops, however, Alberni was responsible for eight men under Simón Suárez at Monterey; twenty-five men led by José Font at San Diego; twenty-five men at San Francisco; and fourteen men scattered in various assignments.[55] In 1800, when Alberni was assigned to the defenses at Monterey, he again became commandant of that post by reason of his superior rank over commanders of presidial companies of the district, Hermenegildo Sal and Raimundo Carrillo.[56]

The nineteenth century opened quietly in California. The years 1801–1802 appeared uneventful. Although orders continued to come from Mexico to watch for hostile foreigners, Alberni seems to have experienced few problems. Yet Californians continued to wait for the eventual attack from British or Anglo-American ships. The calm before the storm was broken by the 1810 Mexican War for Independence. Thereafter, California's isolation as a far away province was lost forever. By that time Alberni had passed from the scene, for he died in Monterey of dropsy at the age of fifty-seven, on March 11, 1802.[57] He was buried in the mission cemetery at Carmel. Alberni's estate was willed solely to his wife, Juana Vélez, for his daughter had preceded him in death. Pedro de Alberni, a forty-five-year career officer, left his mark in Sonora, California, and British Columbia. He commanded troops in Sonora,

Nootka, Nayarit, Guadalajara, Veracruz, San Francisco, Monterey, and Branciforte.[58] Yet only one landmark survives today of Alberni's presence. On Vancouver Island, Alberni's contemporaries noted on their maps of British Columbia a certain long inlet called Canal de Alberni. Today a town at the head of the inlet is named Port Alberni.

8 / The Catalonian Volunteers and Their Assignments in New Spain

The military services performed by the Catalonian Volunteers between 1767 and 1803 were of great utility to the Spanish plan of defense of the empire. During that period, the Volunteers underwent several changes. Although their assignments varied, the unit suffered the same trials and tribulations as all other military units in New Spain.[1] Accoutrements were often in short supply, and commands were rarely up to strength. The Volunteers faced a particular problem in keeping the unit purely Catalonian, and by the mid-1770s fewer soldiers in the unit were actually from Cataluña. Moreover, before Alberni's death in 1802, officers for the Volunteers in California were recruited from different commands. Certainly, by the middle 1780s, Fages's old command in Sonora was led by American-born officers. In 1810, the Catalonian Volunteers had been in existence for over forty years. Finally, the Catalonian Volunteers were dissolved as a result of the Mexican War for Independence.

In addition to their stylish uniforms,[2] their accoutrements were subject to the availability of supplies. As regards their weaponry, the Catalonian Volunteers used belt knives which had, typically, ten-inch blades. Although officers wore sidearms, Volunteer troopers carried the *escopeta*, a type of light musket. The dimensions of the *escopeta*[3] were:

Length: 54.5 inches
Barrel: 39 inches, octagon taper to round decorated
            barrel turnings
Lock: $5^{1}/_{2}$ inches $\times$ $1^{1}/_{2}$
Caliber: 69 (bore .75)
Furniture: Brass
Weight: 7 pounds

Another common-type musket used by the volunteers was probably the Light Infantry Fusil. The dimensions of the fusil[4] consisted of:

Length: 60 inches
Barrel: $43^{7}/_{8}$ $\times$ $1^{5}/_{8}$ inches
Caliber: 69 (bore .73)
Furniture: Brass (with Catalan style stock).

The type of weapon varied among the Catalonians. For example, Antonio Pol reported that his Compañía de Fusileros used a .19 caliber fusil[5] in 1771. A few months after his report, Pol's company was ordered to merge with Callis's command. Evidently, Callis's troopers were rearmed in 1776, but not again for thirteen years. When Alberni, successor of Callis, was preparing his command for the expedition to Nootka, he noticed that his men's fusils were in bad repair because new weapons had not been issued his company since 1776,[6] and because his company was without a gunsmith. Alberni at that time ordered new guns, and seventy-eight fusils were sent to him in Nootka from the storehouses at El Perote[7] via San Blas. The guns, including bayonets, were shipped on the frigate *Princesa* and on the *Aránzazu,* with instructions that Alberni must return the old weapons so that they could be repaired.[8] Thus, the Volunteers were issued new guns and were expected to use them over long periods of time. Undoubtedly, the Catalonian Volunteers were familiar with other types of weaponry, such as the lances used by presidial soldiers in Sonora and California.

The food of the Catalonians varied. On extended campaigns, the typical foods consisted solely of bread, meat, and vegetables;[9] or parched corn and jerky,[10] which were rationed to the men on the Sonora expedition with Domingo Elizondo. Food was considered a part of a soldier's payment for his duty; remuneration, however, was often compensated in money if the food rations were not adequate.

TABLE 2. Catalonian Volunteer Pay Scale in Pesos.[11]

	Monthly	Yearly
Captain	70	840
Lieutenant	40	480
Sublieutenant	32	384
First Sergeant	16	192
Second Sergeant	15	180
Drummer	12	144
First Corporal	13	156
Second Corporal	12	144
Soldier	11	132

Much mention of money is found in documentry sources regarding the pay and bonuses of the Catalonian Volunteers. The basic salary schedule was as shown in Table 2 (salary and income provided in pesos). Although this schedule does not express bonuses paid or other extra benefits like food rations, it does cite the pay of the Catalonian Volunteers specifically; however, there does seem to be an inconsistency, for Estévan de Vilaseca claimed to have received a yearly income of fifteen hundred pesos as sublieutenant when he retired in 1771.[12] Furthermore, the Reglamento de 1772—a set of military regulations issued for the purpose of standardizing and organizing military procedures— prescribed that guards stationed at Mesa del Tonati receive two hundred pesos yearly, and specified that the officer of Catalonian Volunteers assigned there would receive fifteen hundred pesos "above his salary." Moreover, soldiers were to be provided with mules at the cost of the Real Hacienda. Thus, there were other factors to consider in calculating the total yearly income of regular army troopers in New Spain.

The original group of Catalonian Volunteers, recruited in Barcelona in 1767, strongly identified as Catalonians, probably because of Catalan provincialism. By 1790, however, the company had become diluted through recruitment of Spaniards from other provinces. One of the first non-Catalonians to enlist in the troop was Sergeant Luís Rojas, from Córdova in Spain. Rojas was recruited in México, probably from Antonio Pol's Fusileros de Montaña. His service record indicates that he enlisted on March 11, 1767. Rojas of Córdova was promoted to sublieutenant of Catalan Volunteers on August 4, 1776.[13] During the 1780s, others like Rojas had transferred to the volunteer unit; but by 1789 the Free Company of Catalonian Volunteers was anything but Catalonian. The two companies of Volunteers comprised the following:

First Company
  8 Catalans
  5 from Castilla la Vieja
  7 Andalusians
  2 Valencians
  4 from Extremadura, Galicia, Piamonte and Navarre
 42 from New Spain
 68 total company strength

Second Company
  9 Catalans
 13 Andalusians
  9 from Castilla, Valencia, and Extremadura
  2 Galicians
  2 from Murcia and Leon
 37 "Americans," i.e., Hispanics born in the Americas
 72 total company strength[14]

Following the Sonora expedition of 1767, the Catalonian Volunteers and Antonio Pol's Compañía de Fusileros merged. The merger was the result of reorganization of the company as specified in the Reglamento de 1772, in its instructions modifying assignments and standardizing the ranks.[15] Although numbers for the Catalonian Volunteers are not provided by Viceroy Bucareli when they entered Mexico City in 1771,[16] Pol's command was reported as 23 men, considerably reduced from the 150 men Pol recruited in February 1767. The reduction in Pol's command resulted not only from deaths and desertions, but also from retirements, for 72 men left Pol's company at the time.[17] Apparently, the Catalonian Volunteers under Agustín Callis found need of additional troops, for on November 12, 1772, Inspector Pasqual de Cisneros issued orders to Callis to prepare recruitment for his command.[18] The policy prescribed that new recruits hopefully would be Catalonians, but that "should this not be possible, Europeans of good standing, age, health and disposition"[19] ought to be considered. Moreover, Cisneros suggested that Pol's company be given preference; and Pol's ineffective company merged with Callis's Catalonian Volunteers.[20] Thereafter, Callis commanded the unit and submitted monthly reports on the state of his company. Consequently, Pedro Fages reported the state of his troops in California to Callis.[21]

As of May 26, 1772, moreover, Callis's command was reduced to eighty men and three officers.[22] The reduction of twenty men from the original company strength of one hundred troops was a general rule which was applied through the eve of Mexico's independence from Spain.[23] When Sublieutenant Estévan de Vilaseca resigned in 1771, he was not replaced. The chain of command in 1771 was Captain Callis, Lieutenant Fages, and Sublieutenant Pedro de Alberni.

Throughout the last decades of the nineteenth century, the Catalonian Volunteers served as troubleshooters in New Spain. The very name *Compañía Franca de Voluntarios de Cataluña* suggested that the company would be unattached with respect to regimental organization. As a result, the Volunteers were often referred to as *compañía suelta* or "free company." Viceroy Antonio María Bucareli y Ursúa put it very clearly when he wrote that "the useful service to be made by the Free Companies, as in time of peace, [is the] employment [of] them in those assignments in which they are needed, being the welfare of Royal interests."[24]

Between 1771 and 1803 the assignments of the Catalonian Volunteers varied considerably. Although the Volunteers were foot soldiers, they were just as often mounted.[25] Catalonian Volunteers were used as horse soldiers in the Sonora campaign of 1767–71 and in Sonora after 1778, especially in the Fages-led Colorado River campaign of 1781–82. The conversion of the Catalonian Volunteers to cavalry was suggested by Teodoro de Croix, who wrote that Fages's Volunteers would never be useful in Sonora unless they were mounted.[26] He remarked that given the rugged terrain and the type of enemy to be fought, the Catalonians would need horses. Croix suggested that Colonel Juan Bautista de Anza supply the horses. Comandante Croix ordered Anza to furnish eighty Catalonian Volunteers either with two mules each or one horse and one mule, whichever would be convenient. The horse would be bought by officials of the Royal Treasury at Real de los Alamos, and the Catalonians would return their mounts to these officials whenever they left Croix's command. Thereupon, the officials agreed to sell the animals and recuperate some of the money originally spent.[27] Thus, in certain instances, the Volunteers were used as horse soldiers. Yet one reason the Catalonian Volunteers were assigned to Guadalajara in 1772 was because the use of cavalry in that very mountainous region was limited.[28] Depending on the situation, then, the versatile Volunteers were adaptable to walking or riding.

Guadalajara was the military base of operation for the Catalonian Volunteers. There, in 1772, the Catalonians replaced the Compañía de Pardos Provinciales, who were reassigned eventually to Veracruz, although some were assigned temporarily to San Blas.[29] While the majority of the Catalan troops were placed in Guadalajara, three detachments would be dispersed in other assignments.[30] One, under Fages, had already served in California since 1769. Another detachment was serving in Nayarit, in the presidio of Mesa del Tonati;[31] it was ordered there in March 1773, with one officer and fourteen men.[32] The officer at Mesa del Tonati was probably Pedro de Alberni. Another detachment alternated with troops at San Blas, relieving them every one or two years depending upon the urgency.[33] Although the stage was set for the activities of the Catalonian Volunteers to be permanently assigned to New Spain, and their base to be fixed at Guadalajara, these troops were moved about where they were needed in Sonora, California, and far to the north in present-day British Columbia. Agustín Callis himself alternated commands at Guadalajara and Real del Monte, where he and a detachment of Volunteers were sent in 1772 to quell disturbances at the mines.[34]

The detachment of Catalonian Volunteers in California stayed there until 1774. The significance of their service lies in the successful establishment of San Diego and Monterey as forward outposts in the plan of defense of the empire. Moreover, the Catalonians constructed the presidio and mission buildings, which stand as monuments to their labor. The reason for their withdrawal reflected a split over jurisdiction of authority between their commander, Pedro Fages, and Father Junípero Serra, president of the missions. Fages planned to leave Monterey on July 7, 1774, but he did not do so until July 19.[35] However, on July 7, thirteen Volunteers departed California on board the packetboat *San Antonio,* and two remained to accompany Fages by land.[36] In the meantime, *soldados de cuera* stationed in Baja California under the command of Fernando de Rivera y Moncada, Fages's successor to the post, received orders to replace the Volunteer unit in Alta California. For that reason, ten Catalan troopers stayed behind to guard Monterey just in case something should happen, until the leather-jacket soldiers ar-

Uniform of Pardos Libres (*Free Blacks*), *replacements for the
Catalonian Volunteers at Guadalajara in* 1790.
(*Archivo General de Indias, Sevilla*)

rived.[37] Eventually these Catalonian Volunteers returned to (
jara. On their way there, Andrés Auguet and Domingo Ma
known to have died in Tepic, while Francisco Portella died in I
two months before the withdrawal.[38]

Throughout the rest of the decade the Catalonians were shifted back
and forth between Guadalajara, San Blas, Mesa del Tonati, and Real
del Monte. Some bases were far apart, and some soldiers served under
different commands. For example, Juan Puig and Miguel Pericas, who
had been in Monterey with Fages from 1769 to 1774, were with Captain
Agustín Callis at Real del Monte north of Mexico City in March 1775.[39]
Other Volunteers were similarly reassigned throughout their careers.

In 1777, the First Free Company of Catalonian Volunteers under
Callis included one captain, one lieutenant, one sublieutenant, two
sergeants, and sixty-four men.[40] Fourteen were needed to complete the
eighty-man requirement specified in Inspector Pasqual de Cisneros's
orders of November 12, 1772. The Second Free Company of Catalonian
Volunteers under Pedro Fages comprised one captain, one lieutenant,
one sublieutenant, three sergeants and seventy-seven men.[41] This company was complete. Review of troops for the Second Company of
Volunteers led by Fages was not reported for the months January
through May of 1778, or for later months, because that detachment
was in Sonora under orders of Commandant General Teodoro de Croix.[42]
However, the force under Callis fluctuated during these months, probably because of illnesses, retirements, and deaths. Callis's command
consisted of three officers, two sergeants, and eighty men, but in
January nine men were needed for completion, six in April, and seven
in May.[43]

In 1777, Viceroy Bucareli, after having read Croix's report on the
status of forces in the Provincias Internas,[44] suggested the possible use
of Catalonian Volunteers in Sonora. Bucareli felt that the utility of the
Volunteers in Guadalajara was rather routine, aside from the Catalan
detachment at San Blas, which was used to guard ships at that port
while they prepared for further exploration of the northern California
coast.[45] Although the object of Caballero Croix's account of troops had
been to show the need for many more men, Bucareli realized the
shortage of military personnel in New Spain and delayed fulfilling the
request; and it was not until Croix, in November 1777, practically
demanded that the Catalonian Volunteers be sent to Sonora that the
shortage was seriously considered. Croix wrote that these fusiliers should

be sent to Real de los Alamos, with the understanding that they would serve under his command for as long as he considered it necessary.[46]

In October, Croix justified the use of the Company of Volunteers by stating,

> It would be very satisfactory for the Company of Fusiliers, which is found in Guadalajara, to pass to Sonora, because this troop, as it was formed for the military expedition of the province, has knowledge of that country and warfare of the Indians there.[47]

Croix's petition proved to be significant for Pedro Fages, because soon afterward his career began to change markedly. After his tour of duty in Sonora, Don Pedro served as governor of California until 1794. Meanwhile, Fages and his Catalonian Volunteers proceeded to Real de los Alamos to join the forces of Teodoro de Croix, arriving there on February 7, 1778.[48]

Although the military reviews, mentioned above for January through May and succeeding months, do not include a count of the Second Company of Catalonian Volunteers under Fages, the *junta de guerra* held in the spring of 1778 ultimately produced details about the Volunteers. With reference to this meeting, Juan Bautista de Anza wrote his commanding officer, Teodoro de Croix, that eighty Catalonian Volunteers and three officers[49] should be assigned where needed in Sonora.

In April 1778, Fages and his men were assigned to Pitic. Two months later an enthusiastic Teodoro de Croix wrote to José de Gálvez as follows:

> On April 22 past, the Free Company of Volunteers entered El Pitic, and at that same time the rebellious Seri began to surrender. Such a happy beginning corroborates the utility which was promised me of that veteran troop, and the same time announces better progress in its operation which it will execute against the Apaches, while it is found in perfect state for good service.[50]

Croix utilized the Volunteers well, for Catalan troopers were seen as far north in Sonora as Terrenate. There, one small party of five Catalonian Volunteers and two dragoons were attacked by Apaches in 1779. They took refuge in a house, quickly converting it into a fort, and held off a large raiding party of three hundred warriors. Two Volunteers were wounded, but they killed three Apaches and wounded "many others." The fight lasted throughout the day, and each trooper used over seventy shots before the Apaches gave up and left.[51] In other action at that time one Catalonian sergeant and nine troopers in Cocóspera were attacked by more than one hundred fifty Apache warriors. Four of the enemy were killed and the rest retreated with many wounded. The Volunteer sergeant reported no casualties.[52] The scrappy Volunteers obviously merited the praise lavished on them by Croix.

Evidently, Croix made extensive use of the Catalonian Volunteers while they served with his command. Moreover, by 1781, the Company of Volunteers under Fages, commandant of the presidio of Santa Cruz in Sonora, was at half-strength because of desertions, deaths, retirements, and soldiers on leave.[53] In January 1780, Croix ordered Fages to Mexico City to arrange replenishment of his command. Croix's report of 1781 indicated the following:

> In order to put the company of volunteers in a state of service, it was necessary to complete it with good European recruits and provide it with arms and clothing. None of these resources could be provided in the province. I saw myself forced to dispatch to México in January, '80, Lieutenant Colonel Don Pedro de Fages, captain of the above company. Having completed the recruiting, he has just returned to the province, and the mule trains which are bringing arms and clothing have not yet arrived.[54]

Shortly after his return from Mexico City, Fages, under special orders from Croix, proceeded with his Catalonian Volunteers to the Colorado River to investigate the extent of the Yuma uprising, to rescue any survivors, and to wage war against the rebels. The Colorado River campaign of 1781–82 offers a good example of the tactical use of the Catalonian Volunteers as well as disciplined procedures for campaigning in northern New Spain that were practiced by their field officer.

Fages's command for the campaign comprised fifty Catalonian Volunteers and forty presidial troops from Pitic. Under Captain Pedro Tueros were twenty soldiers from the presidio at Altar and some Indian auxiliaries.[55] Juan Noriega was sergeant of the Volunteers, and Miguel Palacios was the noncommissioned officer of the Pitic troops. This expeditionary force left Pitic on Sunday, September 16, 1781. Traveling north past Batobabi, where they camped on September 20, they found signs of the enemy. The next day, a short distance beyond, they met enemy resistance at a place called Charco del Canelo. Fages described the action, as follows:

> We continued on our march, but had gone hardly half a league when we saw a small light about half a league distant from the trail. Here I commanded the men to halt and set up intrenchments. We made camp at the same place, which is called El Canelo. Immediately, I commanded Sergeant Juan Noriega, with twelve volunteers, and Sergeant Miguel Palacios of Pitic, with twelve presidial guards, to advance upon the light with all possible dispatch. Considering that the enemy might be numerous, as in fact they were, I immediately sent a reinforcement of twelve volunteers and twelve *soldados de cuera* under Sergeants Miguel Rivera and Gaspar Tovar. Hearing continuous firing, I twice sent them an abundance of cartridges and other necessary supplies.[56]

The encounter lasted about an hour. Under cover of darkness the enemy slipped away through an arroyo covered with undergrowth. Three Catalan Volunteers were wounded, one seriously; and two presidial soldiers were also hit. In this skirmish, two women captives and an infant were resuc\ed.[57]

During this campaign the Catalonian Volunteers were used as scouts, skirmishers, and escorts for wounded soldiers and rescued survivors, as well as members of burial details for those killed in the tragic Colorado River massacre. Among the dead were Fernando de Rivera y Moncada, Fages's old rival, and Father Francisco Garcés, a well-known missionary and explorer. By October 18, Fages had led his men to the site where the killings had taken place. There, the remains of the dead were identified. Fages wrote: "Their bodies had been consumed, but that of Moncada was unmistakably identified by a break in one of the shin bones." The next day, Fages ordered the bones of Captain Rivera y Moncada "gathered up and interred."[58]

In the last week of October, Fages returned on the Camino del Diablo to Sonoita, which he had passed on his way to the Colorado River, to await supplies and the remainder of his men. In late November, the men were ready and the second march against the Yuma began.

Heading north from Sonoita, the expedition veered northwest to El Carrizal near today's Arizona–Mexico border. By December 1781, Fages's troops had pursued the Yumas to Concepción, near present-day Yuma,

Arizona. There, they made another exchange for more prisoners. Fages's plan for the campaign emphasized a steady pursuit of the enemy, punishing them wherever possible and negotiating for whatever prisoners could be traded. In the process, Fages took Indian prisoners for exchange purposes. Apparently, the Yumas negotiated because Fages's strategy had become costly to them. One such example of losses incurred by the Yumas along the Colorado River was described by Don Pedro in his entry for October 20, which explains his plan of pursuit against the Yumas.

> At this time we perceived that the Yumas were crossing the river at some distance from us, and that in another place they had already raised arms against us. I commanded Ensign Don Manuel Antonio Arbizu to move against them with Sergeants Miguel Palacios and Juan Franco and twenty-five Presidial soldiers. They killed five of the Yumas and stopped the passage of the others. One *soldado de cuera* of the party was wounded by an arrow. We ourselves killed five Yumas from the bank of the river, and those killed in our sight numbered twenty-five in all, among them being the subchief, José Antonio, son of [Salvador] Palma. The brother of Palma was badly wounded, and Palma himself was also slightly wounded, according to report.[59]

In this second pursuit of the Yumas, the remains of these martyred priests were found. By early December, Fages's persistent and aggressive tactics had taken effect on Salvador Palma and his large Yuma band, who apparently had decided to force a showdown with the intrepid Fages. The confrontation began slowly near Yuma. The place was Mission San Pedro, adjacent to the ruined town of San Pablo Bicuñer. On December 7, Fages was proceeding with a detachment of troops from a campsite near Concepción to the said mission and town to recover the bones of the martyred priests. While scouting the town's general environs, Fages and his troops found more cadavers of soldiers and settlers who had died in the Yuma uprising while defending the town.[60] Suddenly, reports were received that a massive Yuma war party, said by Fages's scouts to number fifteen hundred warriors, was attacking the camp near Concepción. Gathering his men, Fages hastened to reinforce the defense of his camp. The battle had raged for almost two hours, but the enemy had broken off the engagement a half-hour before Fages and his troops arrived.[61] Nonetheless, the defenders of the camp

ly defeated the enemy, but they also had seriously wounded
ma chieftain named Captain Ignacio. In the fight, one soldier
opportunity to shoot Palma, but his pistol misfired. Palma
_,, ..ot only leaving his horse but also losing a hat that Fages
had given him earlier.[62]

Fages praised the defenders of the camp. The Yuma offensive had
been broken, and Fages proceeded to bury and cremate the remains of
the victims of San Pedro and San Pablo de Bicúñer. The middle of
December was spent hunting for a portable altar used by the martyred
priests for saying Mass, as well as searching for a baptismal font and
other sacred objects belonging to the deceased missionaries. These
objects were probably part of the booty taken by the rebel Indians.
The Catalonian Volunteers were specifically assigned to seek the baptismal font, but it could not be found.[63] Shortly thereafter, the expeditionary force broke camp and returned to Sonora, regrettably failing
to find the altar and sacred objects. It was Sunday, December 30, when
Fages and his men arrived in Pitic to await orders to proceed to Monterey
and San Gabriel with fifteen men.[64]

The land between Sonora and Alta California had been closed for
some time, but the Fages-led troops reopened the trails between the
two points by 1782. In that year, Fages demonstrated that the trail
was open by leading a small detachment of troops through the danger
zone from Pitic to California's Mission San Gabriel. Fages left Pitic on
February 27, arriving in San Gabriel on April 1, 1782.[65]

The year 1782 witnessed a series of changes in the chain of command
of the two companies of Catalonian Volunteers. Two events changed
the seemingly stable personnel of the Volunteers. One was the death
of Agustín Callis in March 1782; the other was the appointment of
Pedro Fages to the governorship of California in the same year. The
changes cast optimistic portents for the careers of Pedro de Alberni
and Estévan Solá, both lieutenants, who quickly applied for the vacancies left by their former captains.[66]

The order of command for Fages's vacant position in the Second Free
Company of Catalonian Volunteers was Captain Estévan Solá, Lieutenant Francisco García, and Sublieutenant Miguel Pericas.[67] Three years
later, the Second Company of Volunteers experienced another change
in its command. Captain Solá petitioned to be replaced because of his
failing health. Solá explained that wounds received in battles with the
Apache tended to bother him and that life on the rugged Sonora frontier

had become difficult because of his ailments.[68] At the same time, Lieutenant García petitioned for retirement. He was replaced by Captain Pedro Nata Viñolas. Recommended for the lieutenancy was Juan Sortorio, a cadet in the Regiment of Infantry of Naples, who had served at the Santa Cruz Presidio in Sonora.[69] In 1790, Pedro Nata Viñolas, who commanded the presidio at San Bernardino de Fronteras de la Provincia de Sonora, had been promoted to captain of the Second Free Company of Catalonian Volunteers.[70] However, the more important command of the two, with respect to assignments in the last two decades of the eighteenth century, was Pedro de Alberni's First Free Company of Catalonian Volunteers.

With the ascension of Alberni to captain on September 3, 1782,[71] Juan Puig was commissioned lieutenant and Mauricio Faulia was promoted to sublieutenant.[72] Further changes in Alberni's command were caused by retirements. In 1785, five Catalonian Volunteers retired from active duty. These retirees included Corporals Antonio Jusmet, José Sierra, Miguel Serera, and Jaime Joven. The first had served over twenty-six years, the next two served twenty-five years each, and the last was a thirty-eight-year veteran.[73] Miguel Serera later came out of retirement to serve in the Nootka expedition of 1790. These changes were welcomed because they allowed for younger recruits to take the places of the older soldiers. In a sense, Alberni's company was a self-renovating, natural process, for the replacement of old troopers with younger soldiers better prepared the company physically to meet emergency assignments.

During the period from 1782 to 1789, Alberni's troops were assigned to Guadalajara, Mesa del Tonati, Real del Monte, and San Blas. A review of troops in 1787 showed that the Volunteers still numbered eighty men per company.[74] Alberni, while in Guadalajara, gave account of his men for that period. His command comprised Sublieutenant Mauricio Faulia and fifty-four men in Guadalajara. Among the identifiable Catalonian Volunteers were Francisco Rubiol, Juan Mariné, Matheo Bello, Antonio Marín, Ramón Patiño, and Julian Robredo. At Mesa del Tonati in Nayarit was Lieutenant Juan Puig with nine men.[75] A month later, Alberni reported that his command consisted of Lieutenant Juan Puig, Sublieutenants Mauricio Faulia and Miguel Pericas, three sergeants, two drummers, four corporals, and fifty-five men. Thirteen troops under Sublieutenant Pericas were in Nayarit.[76] Juan

Puig applied for retirement in late 1787; his successor was Mauricio Faulia, whose place was taken by Sublieutenant Francisco María Bucareli.[77]

Interestingly, Alberni's command had suffered two desertions, one in January by a soldier named José Torres; the other was Ramón Patiño, who was arrested in México, held without justification, then apparently released and still at large in February 1788.[78] Absences in Alberni's command seem typical of the pattern in the company when it was under Agustín Callis. Like Alberni's troops, Callis's company was constantly undermanned. Although desertions were common in the Spanish Army during peacetime, runaways seemed to be under control. Nevertheless, during this period, Alberni needed at least twelve men to bring his command to the required eighty men.

Between 1789 and 1793, Alberni's command was involved in an assignment to Nootka, in the Pacific Northwest, Spain's northernmost area of claim. Alberni's unit at Nootka began with eighty men. Due to deaths, desertions, and retirements, however, his company had dwindled to a force of fifty-nine men by 1793.[79] When Alberni was ordered to bring his company to full strength, he was allowed to recruit the needed troops from the militia at Guadalajara.[80] Once again, the complexion of the Catalonian Volunteers had changed.

For a short while, from 1793 to 1796, Alberni's command was based in Guadalajara. In 1796 the company was reassigned to California, where it remained until 1803. By 1800 the First Free Company of Catalonian Volunteers stationed in California included the following officers: Lieutenant Colonel and Captain Pedro de Alberni, who had an application pending for promotion to colonel since 1798;[81] Captain José Font y Bermúdes, a nobleman from Coruña, who was second in command; and Simón Suárez, who was a sublieutenant.

Font had been with the Catalonian Volunteers for almost eight years in 1800. Prior to joining the Volunteers, Font had seen service in northern Africa at Oran, in Buenos Aires, and in 1782 at Veracruz. Apparently, Font had risen swiftly through the ranks, for he began his career as a soldier and was recognized as a *soldado distinguido*. From the rank of soldier, Font was commissioned as a lieutenant. Obviously, his social position of hidalgo was a factor in his promotion.

Third in authority of the Catalan Volunteers was Sublieutenant Simón Suárez, a forty-nine-year-old nobleman from Navarre. Suárez had risen steadily through the ranks over a thirty-year period. Like Font, Suárez joined the Catalonian Volunteers in 1792. Sublieutenant Suárez had served with the Regimiento de Granada. He had served with the Infantry of México before becoming a Catalonian Volunteer.[83]

The sergeant in Alberni's company was Joaquín Tico, a forty-four-year-old Catalonian, who had served with the company nineteen years, three months, and twenty-seven days. Tico had been to Nootka with Alberni, and it was noted that he almost died there.[84]

These men were with Alberni in California until his death in 1802. In fact, First Sergeant Tico was the executor of Alberni's will.[85] With Alberni's death, the chain of command changed once again. Font, who had been a brevet captain, was promoted to a full captain of the Catalan Volunteers.[86] Simón Suárez likewise received promotion to lieutenant.[87] However, Joaquín Tico, who expected to be promoted to sublieutenant, was not considered for advancement because he was married.[88] These men were present in one of the last episodes of the Catalonian Volunteers in California.

It was early afternoon on August 14, 1803, when an American vessel anchored out of cannon-shot range in Monterey Bay. Challenging the landing was Commandant of Arms José Font, his lieutenant Simón Suárez, and fifteen Catalonian Volunteers.[89] Boarding a launch in the bay, they proceeded to greet the American, Captain John Brown, and escort him to the Spanish commander of the frigate *Princesa,* Don Braulio Otalora, for routine interrogation.

Brown's ship was the corvette *Alexander,* armed with fourteen six-pound cannons and two eighteen-pound carronades. His crew consisted of nineteen men, some suffering from scurvy. The *Alexander* had left Boston on June 19, 1802, on an exploration mission to the Pacific, but lacking provisions and wanting repairs, it anchored in San Francisco Bay on August 11.[90]

At San Francisco, authorities turned away the needy *Alexander* because of suspicious circumstances. The *Alexander* had first appeared in San Francisco earlier in May and had remained seven days, during which time it was provisioned with food, water, and wood.[91] When the *Alexander* appeared the second time, it was refused a landing. Rejected in San Francisco on August 11, Brown proceeded to Monterey, arriving three days later. There, the *Alexander* was provisioned and repaired. Unfortunately, the *Alexander,* under cover of darkness and trickery, ran away without paying her debts.[92] Correspondence between Font in Monterey and José Argüello in San Francisco reveals plans to arrest Brown if he went to San Francisco again.[93] In fact, it was decided to detain any vessels entering California ports at that time.[94]

The Spaniards were constantly alarmed about possible foreign attack by sea, and they began to feel that the means could be a subversive tactic involving a false plea for help from a foreign ship seemingly in distress.[95] Despite such an attitude, California's defense program began to receive improper attention. Reduction of troops was the first sign of weakening California's coast guard, for the Catalonian Volunteers were withdrawn from California in 1803. Of the event Hubert Howe Bancroft surmised,

> Notwithstanding the precautionary measures ordered, it was deemed wise to reduce the military guard of California by with-drawing the company of Catalan Volunteers, now numbering seventy officers and men, under the command of Font. There is no correspondence extant to show the motive for this step at such a time, without any special attempt to replace the company.[96]

It was autumn in California when the first contingents of Volunteers and their families departed on the *Princesa* and the *Activa*. The last of the Catalonians probably left the following year. The Catalonian Volunteers had served their time in Spain's plan of defense of empire, and had carried out their assignments only to return to Mexico in the end. The Spanish empire was now at ebb tide, and Spain's title to the New World began to recede slowly from her grasp. As for the Catalonian Volunteers, they returned to México in a period of the history of New Spain which, in a sense, represented the lull before the storm. In 1808, the two companies of Catalonian Volunteers numbered 160 men, 80 men each; obviously, they were not the same Volunteers who had arrived in 1767.

Perhaps the strangest event in the history of the Catalonian Volunteers occurred during this period. It involved Antonio Pol, whom British spies claimed to be Benedict Arnold. Born at Lugar de Monfolla,[97] near Gerona in Cataluña, Pol had served as a cadete de Granaderos in the Regimiento de Infantería de Zamora. Like Callis, Fages, Alberni, and Vilaseca, he had served in the war against Portugal in 1762. In 1765, he answered Juan de Villalba's call for troops to form the Regimiento de America. For a short while, he served as lieutenant of a militia unit in Havana, Cuba, and from 1767 to 1773 he took

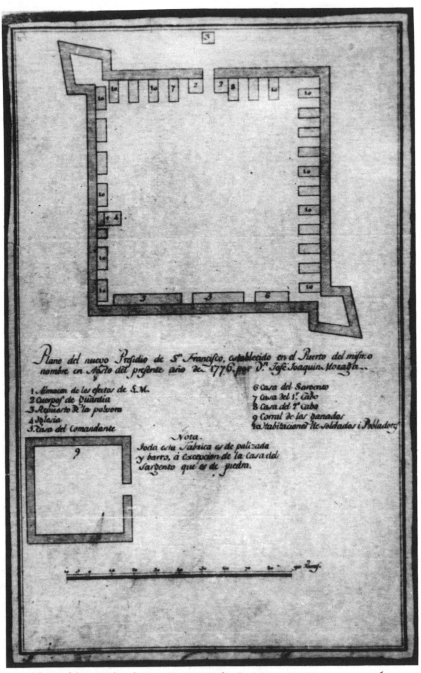

Plano del Presidio de San Francisco by José Joaquín Moraga, 1776.
(Servicio Geográfico del Ejército, Madrid)

part in the Sonora expedition, commanding a company of Mountain Fusiliers. After the Sonora campaign, Pol returned to Mexico City and applied to join the Catalonian Volunteers. Shortly before his transfer to the Second Company of Catalonian Volunteers, Pol had a confrontation with his superiors, and Pedro Fages, who favored a promotion for Pol, reported in 1774 that Pol was absent without leave.[98] Although he returned to his unit, the temporary disappearance of Pol spawned an incredible story about him.

In 1778 Francisco Rendón, a Spanish agent in Philadelphia who had been sent from Spain to evaluate the American Revolution, transmitted a copy of a letter to Madrid written by British spies. The letter sent from "G.D.D. to D.J."[99] explained that Pol had deserted the Spanish army and had changed his name to Benedict Arnold. G.D.D. claimed that Pol, after confronting his superiors, had left México by way of Veracruz, going to Cádiz, and from there to Paris. At Paris he received, with his new name, letters granting him permission to proceed to the Anglo-American colonies in revolt. Allegedly, the name Benedict Arnold was adopted by Pol so that he would not disgrace his family nor jeopardize the careers of his brothers who served in the Spanish army.

G.D.D. picked up the story that Pol, alis Benedict Arnold, had become a distinguished commander, and had been promoted to major because of his exceptional success on the battlefield against British regulars.[100] The physical similarity between Antonio Pol and Benedict Arnold may have been the spark to generate such an incredible tale. Nonetheless, Rendón was obligated to verify whether Pol was indeed Arnold. In the process, Rendón collected every bit of information about Arnold that he could find. Details of Arnold's betrayal of West Point; George Washington and Alexander Hamilton's attempt to arrest him; Arnold's escape on the British ship the *Vulture;* the hanging of Arnold in effigy in Philadelphia; and other sordid details were transmitted to Madrid.[101]

Although Pol never mentioned the episode in his correspondence, Rendón was satisfied that the Catalonian had served most of the rest of his career with the Catalonian Volunteers. Pol's career paralleled that of Pedro Fages, and both men died in 1794. Fages, a colonel, died in El Perote, *sin destino,* without assignment, after his term as governor of Alta California. Pol died soon after his retirement in México as a lieutenant colonel.[102] Benedict Arnold died in England in 1801.

9 / The Catalonian Volunteers as Colonizers

The Company of Catalan Volunteers was created to participate in the Spanish defensive advancement of New Spain. Although these Catalan troops were part of an organized Spanish military machine, it was hoped that they would serve a secondary function as settlers.

Almost from the very beginning, the hope was voiced that the Fusileros de Montaña assigned to Sonora would settle there.[1] In a lengthy letter to Viceroy Marqués de Croix, dated January 1768,[2] José de Gálvez spelled out the plan of defense for California and Sonora in which the Catalonian Volunteers would take part. Gálvez suggested the use of Fusileros de Montaña as farmer-soldiers. The first group of Catalonians to consider retirement in New Spain was from Antonio Pol's Compañía de Fusileros de Montaña. In 1772, Pol wrote that seventy-two of his men had applied for retirement, with the "sole aim of remaining in the province of Sonora to settle in it."[3] These settlers were promised land grants.

The Catalonians made their next major colonization efforts in 1778. The motive was not so much defense, even though the defense of property was critical in the precarious situation of New Spain's frontier; significantly, colonization provided a chance for wealth.

Plans for the project were the brain child of one Catalonian Volunteer, Sergeant Juan Puyol, who claimed to have found a mine in Sonora. Puyol made his application in 1778, and included a list of possible settlers.[4] The roster of colonists included Juan Puyol and his wife,

Isabel; Francisco Puyol, his brother from the Villa de Olot in Catalonia, who was a twenty-eight-year-old bachelor. Another was Joseph Basola, also twenty-eight, from the Villa de Olot, whose wife, Sabina Vivet, would remain in Barcelona. Juan Puig y Trillas, a twenty-two-year-old bachelor from Gerona, joined the group; and another Juan Puig Vidal from the Villa de Olot, a thirty-nine-year-old iron worker with a dark-complexion and a red beard, signed the roster. Apparently, neither of these Puigs was a relative of Juan Puig, a sergeant in the Catalonian Volunteers and stationed at that time at Real del Monte. The other colonists were Miguel Abdon Vives, a gunsmith, and Celedonio Veya, both from Catalonia.

These settlers left Cádiz in August 1778, on the frigate *Nuestra Señora de la Concepción* under the command of Captain Juan Marraach, destined first for Havana.[5] From Havana, which they left on November 17, 1778, the colonists proceeded to Veracruz, arriving there on December 18. Traveling through Mexico City, they stopped for an audience with the viceroy, who issued them their orders. Their next stop after Mexico City was the Port of San Blas.[6] From there the families were dispersed. Two went to Real del Monte, two to Arizpe, one to Fresnillo, one to Tepeaca, one to Limapan, and one to Acapulco. Puyol went to Real de Pachuca, and seven returned to Mexico City.[7] One other Catalonian Volunteer, Joseph Cardó, a soldier under Agustín Callis, is mentioned. His involvement in the colonizing venture is not clear; nonetheless, his name is on the list with no particular destination.[8]

The project had many drawbacks. For example, Puyol claimed that Pedro Fages was ruining the colonization effort. Fages had been appointed financial officer for the colonists, apparently by the viceroy. Puyol wrote to Viceroy Revillagigedo that Fages, who was responsible for dividing two thousand pesos among the colonists was acting too slowly.[9] By June 15, 1780, Fages was asked to return the money because the families had been so dispersed, making it difficult to hand out funds. After considerable discussion, the two thousand pesos were returned to the Real Hacienda[10] by Fages, who was told to do so by Teodoro de Croix, military commander to the Provincias Internas.

In his effort to colonize New Spain, Puyol failed. The significant factor, however, was that Catalonian people were brought from Spain by a Catalan Volunteer, and they evidently remained in their dispersed locations.

Colonization of Sonora was inevitable from the Spanish viewpoint.

However, while the northern frontier of New Spain did have such attractions as mining and land, it also had one main drawback—the ever-present possibility of Indian uprisings. These rebellions or constant raids were not only a deterrent to settlement, but also a great hindrance to European economic success. For example, in the period 1771–76, Indian raids along the Provincias Internas resulted in 1,674 dead, 154 captured, 116 abandoned haciendas, and 66,355 major livestock and 1,901 small animals stolen.[11] Such catastrophic losses meant that while the north, especially Sonora, was a basic area of expansion, it was truly a frontier area in need of the use of military personnel to create a Spanish sphere by influence of holding the enemy at bay while opening lands for settlement. Hopefully, Spanish soldiers would settle there. Opening the wild north for settlement was the role of the Catalonian Volunteers and other Spanish troopers who were assigned to Sonora in 1778.[12] Although organized colonization efforts did not meet great success with respect to establishing a group permanently at a given site, individual settlement efforts seemed more lasting.

The Catalonian experience in California represented still another facet in the process of Americanizing the Catalan troopers through the use of land, food rations, and money incentives. Father Serra reported on December 10, 1773, that three Catalonian Volunteers had married Indian women neophytes at Monterey.[13] These soldiers were later identified as Manuel Butrón, Antonio Yorba, and Domingo Arús.[14] At San Luis Obispo in 1774, three other Catalonians, Francisco Cayuelas, Antonio Montaña, and Gerónimo Bulferic, were contemplating marriage to "convert Christian women." These six Catalan soldiers were not only marrying into native families; they were asking for permission to leave military service so they could settle down in compliance with new regulations providing retired soldiers with two years of seaman's salary, a piece of land, and rations for five years. Butrón, Yorba, and Arús claimed that Fages had given them assurances to this effect, or else "they would not have married."[15]

Other soldiers, however, apparently had no plans for settlement. These soldiers requested a leave of absence because they were married in Spain. It is unclear if they were asking to return to Catalonia, because they do not seem to have ever left New Spain. Nevertheless, Sergeant Juan Puig, Pablo Ferrer, Francisco Bumbau, Gerónimo Planes, and Valentín Planello said they were married in Spain and wished a leave of absence.[16] It should be noted, however, that although Callis and Fages had married women born in Spain, Pedro de Alberni married Juana Vélez, a native of Tepic.

Settlement was always possible in the sparsely populated area of northern New Spain. Another major colonization effort involving the Catalonian Volunteers occurred late in the eighteenth century. From the point of view of the Spanish crown, establishment of a villa named Branciforte in Alta California was a rather urgent effort. The founding of the Villa de Branciforte in California was based on the premise of defense of empire. Just as the Catalan Volunteers had participated in the Sonora, California, and Nootka military expeditions, they would be chosen to lead a new colonizing effort to northern Alta California. In 1795, Spanish officials toyed with the idea of colonizing California with a civilian Spanish population for the purpose of civilizing the Indian rapidly and stemming foreign aggression on New Spain's far northern frontier.[17] Pedro de Alberni's Catalonians were to play out one of Spain's last efforts to protect her lands from encroaching foreigners.

Spain had already begun to lose her grasp of northern possession in the New World. In the last decades of the eighteenth century, Spanish diplomacy began to flounder. Diplomatic losses manifested themselves in the Nootka Sound Controversy, in the failure of the Jay–Gardoqui negotiations of 1784, and in Pinckney's Treaty of 1795. These diplomatic failures cast portents of more Spanish concessions in the north. Given Spain's inability to negotiate successfully with the United States and England between 1784 and 1795, Spanish fears of additional foreign encroachments were well founded.

On November 18, 1795, the report of the Royal Tribunal of Accounts was presented to the Viceroy Marqués de Branciforte, and it received an enthusiastic reception. The report, entitled *Branciforte, Informe del Real Tribunal sobre fundación de un pueblo que se llarmará Branciforte, 1795,* recommended that the governor of California, Diego de Borica, Engineer Alberto de Córdoba, and other military officers select a site and found a pueblo or villa to be named Branciforte in honor of the viceroy.[18] The purpose of establishing the Villa de Branciforte was to secure coastal defenses of Alta California with a militia-type population. Therefore, the solution was to settle the projected villa with farmer-soldiers and their families. The viceroy himself wanted to form a twofold plan of defense by which California would be armed and populated simultaneously. To that end, the Free Company of Volunteers from Catalonia received orders to settle in California. The plan was to grant lands in the projected Villa de Branciforte to these soldiers when they retired from military service.[19]

The presence of the Catalonian Volunteers as a military detachment offering potential settlers from its ranks posed the long-term advantage of an inexpensive defense program. The land-grant program included the added benefit of retaining the retired Catalonian soldiers as defenders against possible enemy invasion; in the meantime, these retired soldiers would farm their lands and become productive citizens. Hence, aside from being natural defenders of the region of the projected villa, the Catalonians would also promote prosperity. However, the main concern was that the use of married soldiers as settlers was not conducive to keeping a prepared military force in the long run.[20] Nevertheless, it was decided not to depend on these soldiers for reenlistment. As the time of the soldiers expired, they would not be permitted to reenlist; rather, new recruits from New Spain would be sent to take their places.[21]

Moreover, the project included the creation of a planned society. The precedence for such a plan was found in laws regulating existing pueblos in the Laws of the Indies. Such instructions, known as the Plan de Pitic which had led to the founding of the Villa of Pitic, were reviewed.[22] The instructions served as a model for Governor Borica to follow in the establishment of Branciforte. He pushed the founding of the new villa, recommending that one hundred families be recruited from the presidios at San Francisco, Santa Bárbara, San Diego, Los Angeles, and San Blas. The governor suggested, moreover, that the people be divided into certain classes. The first class was to comprise farmers accustomed to cold climates. The second class was to be composed of carpenters, blacksmiths, bricklayers, and stone cutters. The third category was made up of tailors, cobblers, millers, tanners, weavers, and various mechanics.[23] These civilians were to live side by side with the local Indians, thus encouraging native loyalty to the Spanish crown. The government was to be military in character, with Pedro de Alberni designated as commander and acting lieutenant-governor.[24]

Lieutenant Colonel Pedro de Alberni arrived in California with most of the Catalonian Volunteers in late March 1796. By early April, Alberni's force comprised one captain, two lieutenants, and seventy-two men. These troops were reunited and assigned in small detachments to San Diego, Monterey, and San Francisco.[25] Meanwhile, on March

3, 1796,[26] the king approved colonizing Villa Branciforte with retired soldiers, their families, and others who wished to move there.

Although the plan was recommended on paper, it still had to undergo implementation. Spanish officials seemed confident of the great success promised by the project. First, a good site for the villa had to be selected, for without that important detail, the project was certainly doomed to failure. Pedro de Alberni and Alberto de Córdoba were commissioned to select the site for the new villa.[27] Although Alberni and Córdoba each explored different areas of the same region, their reports seem to corroborate the findings of one another.

Alberni began his task by comparing the ideal description with the site to be selected. Writing to Governor Borica in early July 1796, Don Pedro spelled out his findings based upon what he believed the land should contain. The land to be chosen, he suggested, should have an abundance of water for drinking and irrigation, as well as trees for lumber and firewood. Knowing that houses, corrals, and storage bins would have to be constructed from materials on location, Alberni noted that soil texture for making adobes and limestone for building materials would be desirable, and pasturelands surrounding the site to be selected should be in abundance or at least available nearby.[28] Alberni's military experience at Nootka proved useful in identifying environmental factors necessary for a life-support system.

Governor Borica had assigned Alberni to reconnoiter the area between Santa Cruz Mission and Arroyo del Pajaro. Included in Alberni's search for a colonization site was the area adjoining Mission Santa Clara, the Parage de la Alameda (explored by Córdoba), and the surrounding terrain near the presidio, port, and mission at San Francisco.[29]

Alberni's report indicates acquiesence for Alberto de Córdoba's findings at the Alameda. Both agreed that the Alameda was not a good place because it had a small arroyo with little water potential; the arroyo was too deep for easy irrigation of the land. Furthermore, Alberni commented, there was too much land that needed irrigation, and firewood, lumber, and pastureland were not in substantial abundance.[29]

Alberni also scouted the San Francisco environs. The Catalan officer rejected San Francisco as a possible site because it was lacking in good soil and sufficient water to irrigate its lands. Alberni indicated that there was barely enough water for the few families already living in the presidio. Moreover, the water available was acquired with much difficulty. Alberni was not impressed with the area because of lack of wood for lumber or firewood. He estimated that lumber had to be brought from twelve to fourteen leagues away, and firewood was five or six leagues distant. In addition, Alberni noted that the pasturelands were hardly adequate for the few horses owned by soldiers in the garrison. Thus, of the various areas Alberni scouted, he felt that San Francisco and adjoining lands were the worst.[30]

However, the temper of Alberni's report is markedly enthusiastic concerning the lands between Mission Santa Cruz and the Arroyo del Pájaro. There, Alberni felt, was the best site for establishing a villa. Water for irrigation and drinking was plentiful. Pasturelands with much humidity and nearby woods made the area conducive to a successful settlement. Moreover, the woods varied in the types of lumber they produced. Another selling feature was the site's convenient proximity to the San Francisco presidio and Monterey.[31]

Even more favorable to the recommended site was Alberni's feeling that the Indians from the Santa Cruz mission would not suffer a loss of farming land because plenty of land was available.[32] Another concern Alberni harbored was the type of settler who ought to be considered for Branciforte. Alberni suggested that only bona fide laborers be sent to the new establishment. In Malthusian terms, he explained that laborers who came from cold climates were better workers and not prone to laziness. Alberni did recommend, however, that these people be given all advantages possible under the Laws of the Indies. The Catalonian officer strongly felt, moreover, that aid for building houses and enclosures for animals and storage of crops should be given to the settlers. And he suggested that buildings be constructed by the government for the colonists, so that they could tend to their crops without interruption.[33]

Alberni's letter to Borica included words of praise for those Catalonian Volunteers who wished to become settlers. The Catalonian leader lauded his soldiers of twenty-five to thirty years of service for their dedicated work. Don Pedro thought it would be difficult for soldiers, who had practiced for so many years the "glorious profession of arms," to take up "the ax, pickaxe, and plough."[34] Thus, with a recommendation of sorts, he hoped that his outgoing soldiers would be compensated for their many years of military life.

In a conclusion to his report, Alberni advertised the site he recommended on broader terms. Analyzing the advantages of such a villa as the proposed Branciforte, he wrote that production of flour, meat, and various seeds by the settlers would benefit the troops in the presidios and missions. Abundance of these products would also be beneficial for crews of ships that frequented the San Francisco harbor. In time of great surplus production, trade between California and the ports of San Blas and Acapulco could be increased.[35]

Three weeks later, Alberto de Córdoba reinforced Alberni's report, but added little more than his belief that the Catalonian Volunteers who chose to become colonizers should be compensated for their past service on equal or better terms than their civilian counterparts.[36] On the basis of both reports, Governor Borica submitted his recommendation that the site for Branciforte should be the area designated by Alberni to possess all the advantages for successful settlement.[37]

Once the site was selected, support for the venture began to solidify. Writing to the viceroy from his residence in the Colegio de San Fernando in Mexico City, Father Pedro Callejas, president of the missions, agreed to supply Governor Borica with materials available at Mission Santa Cruz. Such essentials, including seed, would be sold in accordance with prices set by law.[38] Thus, Governor Borica would be able to count on assistance for the settlers from such a nearby source as the Santa Cruz mission. However, this support from the mission would be short-lived. Another source for supplies, this time military in character, was the military installations at "Monterey, Yerba Buena, and San Francisco." Five eight-pound cannons were collected by Córdoba from such places. Alberni was charged with constructing breastworks for fortification at Branciforte. Evidently, the construction of the ramparts had been delayed for lack of suitable lumber. Erection of barracks for the troops outside a constructed palisade was also delayed. Alberni did receive orders to get the job accomplished,[39] signifying apprehension on the part of officials concerned over the first signs of obstacles impeding the establishment of the villa.

In addition to construction duties, Alberni was given custody of munitions and other instruments of war which were stored at Santa Cruz Mission.[40] Sweeping responsibilities were extended to Alberni, including the control of water for irrigation and the survey and inspection of rock quarries for building materials. Similarly, Alberni would oversee the use of lumber. Division of the land into contiguous strips for cultivation of wheat was another operation entrusted to the busy Catalan. And so it was that Branciforte was initiated through the efforts of a few men.

Planning the layout of the villa was accomplished by Alberto de Córdoba. Córdoba's scheme, a copy of the traditional Spanish town, featured the town square which dominated the blueprint-style plan. Represented on Córdoba's scale drawing of the Villa de Branciforte were locations for a church, hospital, *cabildo,* customs house, and homes for priests and settlers as well as corrals for their animals. All was designed around the typical Spanish town square.[41] On July 17, 1797,[42] a small band of seventeen settlers left the Monterey presidio, destined for the site of Branciforte. Three days later they arrived, provided with carts, oxen, tooks, and a leader, Gabriel Moraga, who was appointed their *comisionado,* or agent.[43]

Despite the preparations made by Alberni, Borica, and Córdoba, the Villa de Branciforte was a failure. Various reasons for its decline have included charges that the inhabitants were lazy and lawless; that the land was not fertile as reported by Alberni and Córdoba; and that the mission priests at Santa Cruz did not cooperate with the settlers. Whatever the reasons, the viceroy realized Branciforte's shortcomings and suspended operation of the villa on December 11, 1802.[44] Signs of the gasping Villa de Branciforte were manifested in its declining population. On November 28, 1801, Branciforte's eighty-three inhabitants included twenty retired soldiers, five of whom were single.[45] By the end of 1803 there were only five people residing there. Reasons for the sudden decline were not given.[46] Branciforte continued to survive its traumatic early years, so that by 1815 a new population numbered fifty-three people.[47]

Thus, the Villa de Branciforte, conceived late in the Spanish period, outlasted the patience and lives of those who planned it. It should be noted that Borica died in 1800 and Alberni in 1802. The Catalonian Volunteers, who would have retired there, withdrew in 1803 from California to México whence they had come. And so it was that a valuable and potential settler group was eliminated as future colonizers of Branciforte. Nevertheless, the Villa de Branciforte, eventually absorbed by Santa Cruz, was doomed to oblivion.

It is difficult to ascertain the significance of the Catalonian Volunteers as a settler group, other than for the period in which they lived, primarily because northern New Spain was an area in flux and the Volunteer troopers were transients there. Some Catalonians, like Miguel Pericas, retired and returned to Spain. Others, like Pedro de Alberni, died leaving little family. Families, like that of Agustín Callis, were small and nomadic in their life-styles. Pedro Fages and his wife, Eulalia Callis, were known to have had two children, who, with or without their father, moved about from assignment to assignment. Finally, Fages died in Mexico City without permanent residence or assignment. Yet there were others who left notable families behind, like Antonio Yorba in California, whose family today represents an important link to California's past, dating back to the 1769 founding expedition. Another Catalonian, Sergeant Joaquín Tico, who was with Alberni in the expedition to Nootka in 1789–92, was later assigned to California. Joaquín Tico's son Fernando was involved in California politics during the Mexican Period in the 1830s.[48]

The story of the Catalonian Volunteers as settlers is linked to the defensive character of the Bourbon Reforms. Moreover, an examination of the Volunteers and their assignments in New Spain gives perspective to their efforts as soldiers and frontiersmen.

10 / Estévan de Vilaseca, Soldier and Public Servant

In February 1788, an aging and ailing Estévan de Vilaseca applied for retirement from royal service in the treasury of San Blas.[1] For seventeen years Vilaseca had been retired from military life, and now he sought a military pension in addition to the retirement pay granted to public officials. The basis for his application for a military pension was his participation as a soldier from the Segundo Regimiento de Infantería Ligera de Cataluña and the Compañía Franca de Voluntarios de Cataluña.

Early in 1771, Vilaseca left the company of Catalan Volunteers that had been pulled out of the Sonora expedition. In April, Domingo Elizondo, colonel of the Regimiento de Dragones de España and commander of the Sonora expedition, wrote that Vilaseca had volunteered from the ranks of the Segundo Regimiento de Infantería Ligera de Cataluña to join the expedition against Seri, Piatos, and Sibubapas which had infested and raided Sonora since 1746.[2] Elizondo further commented that Vilaseca had participated in two of four general attacks on Cerro Prieto in his thirty-eight months in Sonora. During this time, wrote Elizondo, the "three barbarous nations" of Indians had been punished and the province pacified of the "hostilities, murders, and thefts" which had plagued the area for several decades.[3] Elizondo certified that Vilaseca had served with "honor, valor, and zeal" in the conduct of the campaign.

Three years later, Agustín Callis, captain of the Catalonian Volunteers, while writing his report of Vilaseca in 1774, annotated similar comments. Callis reasserted that Vilaseca had served under him since May 15, 1767, when he had officially received command of the Catalonian Volunteers.[4] In his report, Callis mentioned that Vilaseca had participated in the 1762 expedition against Portugal.[5] This statement was further corroborated in 1787 by Pedro de Alberni, who stated that Vilaseca was in the campaign against Portugal under the command of Lieutenant Colonel Juan de Vilara of the First Batallion of the Second Regiment of Light Infantry of Catalonia.[6]

In 1767, Alonso Cavallero, Comisario of Sevilla, listed Vilaseca as one of the *subtenientes* under the Catalonian Volunteer Captain Callis, who was preparing his troops to leave Sevilla for Cádiz.[7] The other sublieutenant was Pedro de Alberni. Vilaseca continued his journey with his fellow officers Callis, Fages, and Alberni, and all of them arrived in México on September 24, 1767.[8] These four officers received promotions upon volunteering in the company[9] ultimately destined for service in the Sonora campaign. Prior to his promotion, Sublieutenant Vilaseca was first sergeant in the Second Regiment of Light Infantry of Catalonia.[10] It was as a Catalonian Volunteer that Vilaseca gained experience as an Indian fighter. Callis's report on the state of his army shows Vilaseca's name listed third,[11] above Alberni's, indicating that Don Estevan was third in command of the Catalonian Volunteers.

During the three years and two months that the Catalonians were in Sonora, Vilaseca participated not only in the skirmishes at Cerro Prieto but also in the organization of supplies. Vilaseca served as *comisario de campaña*,[12] a job which entailed taking orders and inventory of goods as well as distributing them. As *comisario de campaña*, Vilaseca made sure that essential military supplies reached the men.

Exactly when Vilaseca began his work with the royal treasury at San Blas is not clear. However, it seems that his experience as *comisario de campaña*, which included bookkeeping, eventually led to his position of *pagador y tesorero interno*,[13] or paymaster and intern treasurer at San Blas, years after his retirement from the Catalonian Volunteers. Vilaseca officially served in the position of *tesorero interno* from 1783 to 1787.[14] Interestingly, when Vilaseca took a job at the Zapatillo saltworks in 1779, he had already worked with the treasury at San Blas, for it was noted that Martín de los Ríos replaced him in the treasury while Vilaseca was at Zapatillo.[15]

Don Estevan served as *administrador general* of the saltworks at Zapatillo from 1779 to 1782.[16] Precisely what duties were performed by Vilaseca in that position are unclear. Nevertheless, in 1781 when *administrador* Vilaseca turned in his books to the Real Hacienda of the Department of San Blas, he was complimented for having kept accurate ledgers of the accounts at Zapatillo.[17] Such a commendation suggests that Vilaseca was an honest man with a talent for bookkeeping and detail.

Following his term at Zapatillo, Vilaseca briefly served as *fiel de almacenes,*[18] a clerkship, in the naval dockyards at San Blas. Vilaseca's duties involved inspection of weights and measures. The year was 1783, and within that time Vilaseca resumed his duties with the Royal Treasury at San Blas, which was under the control of the Real Hacienda. Vilaseca worked as a treasurer until 1787. He must have been promoted to the rank of minister of the Royal Treasury of the Department of San Blas in 1788. In a decision made by the ministers of the Real Hacienda at San Blas involving a certain Pedro Carbajal, a surgeon, Vilaseca's signature appears among the ministers who signed the document.[19] Ten days prior to the Carbajal decision, Vilaseca petitioned for retirement pensions earned for his duties as a soldier. On August 9, 1788, members of the Real Tribunal de la Contaduría Mayor y Audiencia de Cuentas voted to give Vilaseca the 750 pesos income per year in retirement money which he had earned as a treasury man. The members of the tribunal, after reviewing Vilaseca's record as an official, felt that his retirement pension was a reward for his many years of good service.[20]

Vilaseca had been suffering from ill health over the years, and now that he was advancing in age he felt it was time to resign from his position. In his letter to Viceroy Flores on February 16, 1788, Vilaseca wrote that he was at the "end of my life" and that he was seeking a military pension, which he felt he had also earned as a soldier and officer, so that he could better support his wife and family.[21] Furthermore, Vilaseca sought to gain military retirement pay because it would be based on fifteen hundred pesos per year, which he claimed he had received as a sublieutenant.[22] Understandably, Vilaseca felt his retirement money should also be based on monies earned during his military service.

There is little doubt that Vilaseca's health was deteriorating. Three navy surgeons, including Pedro Carbajal, certified that Vilaseca, whom they had come to know affectionately, was old and suffered constantly from fevers. They felt that the "climate at San Blas" had been too "rigorous" for the aging treasurer.[23] Thus, Vilaseca was able to claim that his advancing age and declining health were responsible for his retirement. He had presented a good case for retirement from his official positions, but the tribunal was not inclined to grant a military pension in addition to retirement money he was already receiving. Instead, the tribunal members sidestepped his request praising Vilaseca for his good and loyal service, and felt that granting him his salary earned as a royal official was sufficient. Thus a disappointed Vilaseca, who had hoped that his military record along with his good public service performance would be considered, found only discouragement.

Vilaseca's career differed greatly from the other Catalonian officers with whom he had come to New Spain. He was the only one to retire and settle down in accordance with the plan of defense which specified that the Catalonians would eventually become soldier-citizens like their militia counterparts. Callis served the Catalan Company until his death in 1782. Alberni, likewise, continued the Catalonian adventure until his demise in 1802; and Pedo Fages is believed to have died in Mexico City in 1794 after several decades of military service. Thus Vilaseca, the soldier and public servant, faded from the pages of contemporary accounts. An old and infirm man, Vilaseca left no clue to his age other than mention of "advanced age," nor did he mention what illness he suffered. Unlike Callis, Fages, and Alberni, Vilaseca retired from military life and began a second career as public servant in New Spain. His work with the Royal Treasury spanned almost twenty years. It is not known when Vilaseca died; however, in 1788 he felt he was too old and infirm to continue his duties.

Although Vilaseca differed from his fellow Catalonian officers, they had much in common. For example, each one was aggressive and shrewd in money matters and took time to explore and exploit avenues by which reimbursement for their services would be forthcoming. Vilaseca's struggle for additional retirement funds is such an example. Another common characteristic of these four men was the thoroughness and conscientiousness with which they performed their duties. The careers of each of these men attest to the observation that they performed their tasks, no matter how menial, to the best of their capabilities. Vilaseca's contemporaries seemed to recognize his talents in their review comments, which pointed out that Vilaseca left each office in good order. Vilaseca, like his Catalonian-officer friends, was loaned out to jobs that required his special talents. In this sense, Vilaseca remained a Catalonian Volunteer until the end of his working life. Moreover, the significance of Vilaseca's retirement augured changes in the company's chain of command, thus opening the door to advancement for Pedro de Alberni.

11 / *Epilogue*

THE CATALONIAN VOLUNTEERS
AND THE WAR FOR MEXICAN INDEPENDENCE

T he defense of northern New Spain in the latter half of the eighteenth century was only a part of the Bourbon Reforms of the Spanish empire. The Catalonian Volunteers participated in the plan of defense as soldiers, explorers, and settlers. Their importance to the history of northern New Spain lies not only in their presence there but also in their activities. It was in the Elizondo-led Sonora expedition that the Catalonians made their debut. During the course of the Sonora campaigns, the Catalonian Volunteers took part in a number of sorties in the Cerro Prieto range. These Catalonian troopers were used as scouts and skirmishers under the direction of Captain Agustín Callis, Lieutenant Pedro Fages, Sublieutenant Estevan de Vilaseca, and Sublieutenant Pedro de Alberni. These officers from Catalonia, Spain, arrived with one hundred men in Mexico in the late summer of 1767.

Favoring the use of the Catalonian Volunteers in special assignments was José de Gálvez, Visitor General of New Spain. In 1768, the powerful Gálvez commissioned Lieutenant Pedro Fages and twenty-five Catalonian Volunteers to participate in the establishment of Upper California. The significance of the California expedition was the successful founding of San Diego and Monterey, as well as the discovery of San Francisco Bay. These establishments, or outposts, were the beginnings of a continual settlement of California. Simultaneously, Lieutenant Fages and his Catalan troopers were among the first Europeans to penetrate and explore the interior of California, and they are credited with the discovery of California's Central Valley.

Although the Catalonian Volunteers were in California from 1769 to 1774 in their first tour of duty there, they would be associated with the defense of that coastline for the rest of the eighteenth century. Pedro Fages returned to California as governor in 1782; and detachments of Catalan troops under Pedro Alberni, José Font, and Simón Suárez were assigned to San Diego, Monterey, and San Francisco from 1796 to 1803. During that period, Spanish officials hoped that the Catalonian Volunteers would settle there and become soldier-farmers. To that end, Spanish authorities sponsored the founding of the Villa de Branciforte (1796), with the intention that a civilian population made up of retired troops, hopefully Catalonians, would be established there. It was an ill-fated project, and eventually the Catalonian troops were withdrawn from California to Mexico's interior defenses, depriving Branciforte of a potential settler group.

The desirability of Catalonian Volunteers as settlers had been voiced by such authorities as Viceroy Marqués de Croix and José de Gálvez. The eventual settlement of Sonora by retired Catalan troopers was encouraged through land-grant incentives. However, it should be noted that the extent of settlement by the Volunteers was small, because of the number of troops who served in that unit. Moreover, the number of actual Catalonian Volunteers had dwindled to such a small group that by 1790 the company of Catalonian Volunteers had been diluted by Spaniards from various provinces of Spain, other than Catalonia, as well as by the enlistment of American-born recruits.

One of the major uses of the Catalonian Volunteers in the plan to defend the empire was their assignment to Nootka. Led by Pedro de Alberni in 1789, the Volunteers participated in the exploration of the Pacific Northwest and the establishment there of a short-lived outpost. The assignment of the Catalonian Volunteers to Nootka indicates not only their availability for such a special assignment, but the preferment of that unit for such duty by Spanish authorities.

During the course of the late eighteenth century, the officers of the Catalonian Volunteers in New Spain had shown imagination, confidence, and effective leadership in the execution of their assignments. Loyalty to their king and country was manifest in their accomplishments, for the records of Callis, Fages, Vilaseca, and Alberni indicate a conscientious love of duty.

At the beginning of the nineteenth century only one of the original Catalonian Volunteer officers, Pedro de Alberni, was still living. Alberni had been the youngest of the four officers who came to New Spain in 1767. These officers—Callis, Fages, Vilaseca, and, of course, Alberni—had participated in one of Bourbon Spain's imperial dreams: to hold onto its possessions at all costs. But the times were changing.

When these men came to New Spain, the powers of Western Europe, Spain, France, and England were contending for control of the Atlantic seaboard. This struggle spread to the Pacific Ocean, where Spain's claim was further complicated by encroachments by Russia and the United States. Callis, Fages, Vilaseca, and Alberni were prepared to meet the challenge of New Spain's enemies, who by treaties and negotiation wrecked the Spanish dream. Moreover, New Spain was beset with another enemy. From the Gulf of Mexico to the Gulf of California stretched a hostile Indian frontier with which the Spanish also had to contend. The Catalonian officers were professional soldiers who had sought to tame the wild northwest for their king.

The interior enemy was mistakenly thought to be the rebel Indian. Instead, New Spain fell to revolutionaries, but this happened long after the four Catalonian officers were dead. Callis, Fages, Vilaseca, and Alberni did not live to see the times change dramatically. Alberni caught glimpses of a new order, but he too died without fully comprehending the new generation that had grown up around him. Alberni glimpsed Spain's losses in the Pacific Northwest and Spanish weakness in the diplomacy of the Nootka Sound Conventions; and Fages must also have perceived these factors. Alberni lived to see the Free Company of Catalonian Volunteers change in its personnel, for by 1800 very few of the original one hundred men were still in the ranks. After Alberni's death, new officers and men comprised the company, and they were withdrawn to New Spain's interior defenses. There, they were engulfed in the Mexican War for Independence of 1810.

One of the last officers to command the Catalonian Volunteers was Juan Antonio de Viruega from Ceuta, who had served in Oran, in northern Africa. He had been in the Second Company of Catalonian Volunteers since 1790, and held the rank of captain. In 1800 he was stationed at El Perote, between Veracruz and Mexico City. Under Viruega were sublieutenant Agustín de Yslas and First Sergeant Agustín

Malavar. Yslas, born in Horcasitas, Sonora, had been on the Colorado River expedition led by Pedro Fages against the Yumas, and he had fought against the Apaches in 1782. In 1800 Malavar had been transferred to the Catalonian Volunteers from the Dragones de España. He was born in Mérida, Yucatán. At the time of his induction into the Catalonian Volunteers he was stationed with Viruega and Yslas at El Perote.[1]

In 1810, a group of men entered the home of Lieutenant Colonel Juan de Viruega, knelt in prayer for the success of their new battalion, and took an oath of loyalty to their king. The first step of the dissolution of the company of Catalonian Volunteers had taken place. Many of the Volunteers were absorbed in the Batallón de Infantería Provincial Ligero de Querétaro.[2] Its commander was Juan de Viruega, with 439 men.[3]

Between 1790 and 1810, tremors of the coming rebellion against Spain could be felt as colonials evaluated what loyalty to Spain had cost them. Finally, after the French invasion of Spain in 1808, dissidents in the Americas saw an opportunity to break with their mother country. The spontaneous revolt of Father Miguel Hidalgo in Mexico moved the independence movement of 1810 from words to action. Now there would be no turning back.

Aside from a detachment of the First Company of Catalonian Volunteers in San Diego, Alta California,[4] the rest of the unit had been removed to Guadalajara. By that time, the company had been depleted and ordered to reorganize when Hidalgo's revolt began. Like so many other units, the First Company of Catalonian Volunteers would be absorbed into other, much larger units until the company no longer existed.

At the start of hostilities, the Second Company of Catalonian Volunteers, which had been active in assignments near Mexico City, was quickly called to duty against the rebels. However, it was not until Hidalgo's revolt had been put down that Spanish commanders mobilized a large army to quell another, more serious revolt led by Father José María Morelos y Pavón. The Second Company of Catalonian Volunteers, which had been stationed at El Perote and other assignments, was put into the field against Morelos and other insurgents operating south of Mexico City.

On January 14, 1812, troops from Spain arrived at Veracruz; among them, the Primer Batallón de Lobera and the Tercer Batallón de Asturias, which would be used in the campaign against Morelos.[5] The

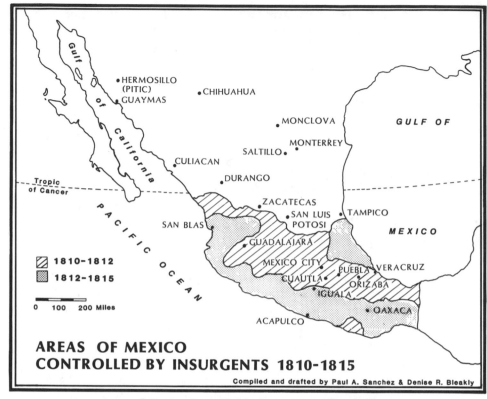

**AREAS OF MEXICO
CONTROLLED BY INSURGENTS 1810-1815**

Compiled and drafted by Paul A. Sanchez & Denise R. Bleakly

Areas of Mexico Controlled by Insurgents, 1810–1815.

Second Company of Catalonian Volunteers would soon be drawn into large troop movements and, like the First Company of Volunteers, would be eventually absorbed into other units.

Following the defeat of Hidalgo at Guadalajara, the royalist army began its concentration of troops in southern and southwestern Mexico. After Hidalgo was captured and executed in 1811 at Ciudad Chihuahua, other rebel leaders emerged to continue the fight against Spain. When Morelos joined his rebel army with that of Miguel Bravo at Cuautla de Amilpas,[6] in the present state of Cuernavaca, Viceroy Francisco Xavier Venegas ordered General Félix María Calleja to move against them. By February 19, 1812, Calleja was camped on the outskirts of Cuautla, and posed for attack. After a six-hour battle that day, Calleja was repulsed by Morelos and his feisty rebels.

In the first battle of Cuautla, the royalist army lost six hundred men—four hundred dead and two hundred wounded. The artillery duel at Cuautla, and Calleja's massive charge to dislodge the barricaded insurgents, had been costly.[7] After their retreat to the nearby Pueblo de Cuautlixco and the Hacienda de Santa Inés, Calleja called a council of war which decided to lay siege to Cuautla and starve out the rebels. Before reinforcements for the siege arrived, Calleja ordered his army to gain control of all trails and roads leading to Cuautla. Next, he cut off the water supply leading to the rebel-held town.[8] Calleja soon moved his command post to a place he called *Campo sobre Cuautla*.

Meanwhile, as the weeks passed, the rebels under Morelos and Bravo were reduced to eating rats, dogs, lizards, and iguanas; and they began to feel the pressure of the siege. As their tightly rationed water supply dwindled, a desperate Morelos broke through a weakly held royalist position to find where the water source to Cuautla had been cut. In late March, Morelos finding that the water had been diverted at Xuchitengo, captured that town.[9] Calleja moved against him. In the end, the rebel fight for water at Xuchitengo was lost, and Morelos retreated to Cuautla. There, the rebels were forced to make a stand.

By then, new royalist reinforcements had arrived and sealed off all routes of escape from Cuautla. Near midnight on April 5, Calleja moved three companies of the Batallón de Lobera into position under Sargento Mayor José Enríques. In order to prevent the insurgents from escaping through the primary line which had established the siege, Calleja ordered Enríques to set up a series of ambuscades behind the royalist troops. At a place called Campo de Sacatepec, an area thick with reeds along a river not far from Cuautla, Enríques set up an ambuscade manned by the Second Company of Catalonian Volunteers. The Volunteers were led by a newly appointed officer, Francisco Castro.[10] By midnight all troops were in place.

The royalists knew the rebels would come out fighting. Calleja had tested their strength in several sorties against them during March. Each time, the rebels had repulsed the royalist advances with a sharp sting, and their desperate plight had strengthened their resolve. Under the strong leadership of Morelos and Bravo, the rebel will to fight could not be broken by the siege. Shortly before the battle, Calleja wrote to Viceroy Venegas: "The enemy never stops, not in daytime nor at night; they are acclimated to resist heat, and their fanaticism fans their spirit."[11]

In the wee hours of the morning, before dawn, on April 6, 1812,

Calleja ordered the assault on Cuautla. Morelos and Bravo were ready, but the royalists gained the walls, barricades, and redoubts of the dusty colonial town. Fighting hard, the rebels broke through the royalist attack and overran their artillery positions in their desperate attempt to break the siege. But the reinforced royalist army led by Calleja had the better plan. Realizing the strength of the royalists, the rebels turned to escape. In the fury of the battle, the rebels who survived the charge against Calleja's artillery fled to the reeds for cover. They were met by the Catalonian Volunteers, who set up such a lively and deadly fire that the rebels were hardly able to withstand the initial shock. Caught between the ambuscade and the pursuit of royalist troops, the intrepid rebels launched two or three attacks against the Catalonian Volunteers before they were able to escape. Although the Second Company of Catalonian Volunteers was badly mauled in the battle of Cuautla, they managed to survive as a unit. General Calleja praised them for their "valiant" stand against a resourceful rebel army.[12] Both sides learned valuable lessons at Cuautla, but in the end the independence movement proved to be a strong historical force.

The Mexican War for Independence swept New Spain like a wind. From time to time glimpses of the Second Company of Catalonian Volunteers could be caught in battles named after towns like Tuxpango (1813), Tlacótepe (1814), and Ajuchitlán (1815).[13] As the unit lost men to battle, it was absorbed into other companies; a pattern experienced by all the companies which came to New Spain in 1766 with Juan de Villalba's Regimiento de America. Finally, when Viceroy Juan O'Donojú signed the Treaty of Cordóba with the insurgents on August 24, 1821, Bourbon Mexico was no more, and the Catalonian Volunteers, which had been formed to defend Bourbon interests, had long ceased to exist.

Appendix

NAMES OF KNOWN CATALONIAN VOLUNTEERS
WHO SERVED IN NEW SPAIN

Note: Numbers following name indicate the following:

1. Original Catalonian Volunteer who sailed from Cádiz, May 27, 1767, commanded by Agustín Callis.

2. Catalonian Volunteer who participated in the Sonora expedition of 1767 under Agustín Callis.

3. Catalonian Volunteer who was with Pedro Fages in California, 1769–74.

4. Catalonian Volunteer who was assigned to Nootka under Pedro Alberni, 1789–92.

5. Catalonian Volunteer with Alberni in California, 1796–1802.

6. Catalonian Volunteers with Fages in Sonora, 1781.

José Acosta, 5.
José Alari, 5.
Domingo Albarez, 4.
Pedro de Alberni, 1, 2, 4, 5.
Vicente Alemán, 1, 2.
Pablo Argenter, 1, 2.
Domingo Arús (Ariús), 1, 2, 3.
Andrés Auguet, 1, 2, 3.
Antonio Bacilio, 5.
Antonio Baldes, 4.
Matheo Baldonia, 1, 2.
Gabriel Balsells, 1, 2.
José Barrientos, 5.
Lorenzo Bentuna, 4.

Antonio Berbens, 1, 2.
Antonio Bonilla, 4.
Ramón Bonnél, 3.
Bautista Bosch, 4.
Pedro Bruél, 1, 2.
Francisco María Bucareli, 4.
Saturnino Budet, 4.
Geronimo Bulferig (Bulferic), 1, 2, 3.
Francisco Bumbáu, 3.
Gerónimo Burón, 4.
Juan Busquéts, 1, 2.
Manuel Butrón, 1, 2.
José Caballero, 4, 5.

Estévan Cabre, 4.
Agustín Callis, 1, 2.
José Campo, 4, 5.
Antonio Cañizares, 4.
Pedro Capallera, 1, 2.
José Carcamo, 5.
Joseph Cardó, 1, 2.
Joseph Casas, 1, 2.
Simón Casasallas, 5, 4.
Francisco Cayuelas, 3.
Miguel Civera, 1, 2.
Domingo Clua, 1, 2, 3.
Rafael Coca, 4.
Juan Colom, 1, 2.
Féliz Comans, 1, 2.
Ramón Conejo, 1, 2.
Francisco Corbella, 4.
Joseph Corominas, 1, 2.
Caietano Cubells, 1, 2.
Joseph Culi, 1, 2.
Jacinto Dalmau, 1, 2.
Jaime Dalmau, 1, 2.
Alonzo Delgado, 5.
Joseph Demeus, 1, 2.
Mariano Domenic, 1, 2.
Antonio Domínguez, 4.
Ygnacio Domínguez.
Raimundo Donato, 1, 2.
Antonio Dubesac, 1, 2.
Sebastian Ducil, 4, 5.
Baptista Escoda, 4.
José Pió Espinosa, 5.
Pedro Espinosa, 5.
Sebastián Escribano, 5.
Ynacio Estovanell, 1, 2.
Francisco Fabregatt, 4.
Pedro Fages, 1, 2, 3, 6.
Mauricio Faulia, 1, 2, 4.
Víctor Fernández, 5.
Joseph Ferrar, 1, 2.
José Antonio Ferre, 4.
Pablo Ferrer, 1, 2, 3, 4.

Estevan Figueredo, 4.
Pablo Filba, 1, 2.
Francisco Flores, 4.
Juan Flutas, 1, 2.
José Font y Bermúdes, 5.
Joseph Font, 1, 2.
Rafael Fragoso, 5.
Agustín Freylas, 1, 2.
Diego Gálves, 4, 5.
Claudio Galindo, 4, 5.
Francisco Garcés, 1, 2.
Francisco García, 1, 2, 6.
Joseph García, 1, 2.
Nicolas García, 5.
Sebastian García, 1, 2.
Pedro Garreta, 1, 2.
Baldirio Ginabreda, 1, 2.
Francisco Gombari, 3.
José Gómes, 4.
José Antonio Gómez, 5.
Sevastian Gonbara, 4.
Alejo González, 5.
Blas Gonzáles, 4.
José Gonzáles, 5.
Simon Gonzáles, 4.
Joseph Gorden, 1, 2.
Joseph Granena, 1, 2.
Segismundo Gras, 1, 2.
José Guerrero, 4.
Sebastián Guevara, 5.
Tadeo Guias, 4.
Felipe Gutiérrez, 4.
Francisco Gutiérrez, 4, 5.
Francisco Gumball, 1, 2.
Felipe Haro, 5.
Francisco Herrera, 4.
Juan Hortel, 5.
Juan Iñiguez (Yñiguez), 5.
Miguel Pedro Jarro, 1, 2.
Francisco Jiménez, 5.
Jaime Joven, 1, 2.
Carlos Lamarge, 1, 2.

Melchor Leoni, 1, 2.
Miguel Lineza, 3.
Antonio Llamas, 3.
Jaime Llentas, 1, 2.
Andres López, 4.
Pedro Lozano, 5.
José Lugo, 5.
Domingo Malaret, 1, 2, 3.
Juan Maldonado, 4, 5.
Manuel Mallen, 4, 5.
Joseph Mana, 1, 2.
Pedro Manurrit, 1, 2.
Miguel Manzana, 3.
Juan Manzanilla, 4.
Silvestre Mares, 1, 2.
Antonio Marín, 4, 5.
Juan Marine, 4.
Carlos Marqués, 1, 2.
Francisco Martí, 4.
José Martínez, 5.
Manuel Martínez, 4, 5.
Antonio Masclans, 1, 2.
Manuel Mendoza, 5.
Miguel Mendoza, 5.
José Mercader, 4.
Pedro Mías, 1, 2.
Raphael Miragle, 1, 2.
José Mariano Miranda, 5.
Joseph Molas, 1, 2, 3.
Luis Monman (Moumarus), 1, 2, 3.
Antonio Montaña, 1, 2, 3.
Vicente Montenegro, 4.
Francisco Murguía, 4.
Juan Murla, 1, 2.
José Muruato, 5.
José Navarro, 4.
Domingo Nefrerias, 4.
Joseph Nogues, 1, 2.
Antonio Noriega, 6.
Faustino Oceguera, 5.
Pedro Oliver, 1, 2.
Miguel Ortega, 5.

Juan Ortel, 4, 5.
José María Osio, 5.
Francisco Pacheco, 4, 5.
Jacinto Padilla, 5.
José Palafox, 5.
Teodoro Peña, 5.
Miguel Sobrevía Pengues, 3.
Francisco Pérez, 4.
Francisco Pérez (another), 4.
Juan Bautista Pérez, 5.
Miguel Pericas, 1, 2, 3, 6.
Cipriano Pexals, 1, 2.
Francisco Pich, 1, 2.
Joseph Piguex, 1, 2.
Valentín Planello, 1, 2, 3.
Gerónimo Planes, 1, 2, 3.
Miguel Pomaneda, 1, 2.
Francisco Portella, 1, 2, 3.
Joseph Puig, 1, 2.
Juan Puig, 1, 2, 3.
Pedro Puyol, 1, 2.
Juan Puyol, 1, 2.
Manuel Quesada, 5.
Francisco Quintana, 1, 2.
Cayetano Ramos, 4.
José Ramos, 4.
Miguel Ramos, 4, 5.
Juan Recio, 1, 2.
Raimundo Ribas, 1, 2.
Cristóbal Rey, 5.
José Rey, 4, 5.
Pedro Racamora, 1, 2.
José Rocha, 5.
Francisco Rodríguez, 4.
Francisco Roig, 1, 2.
Luís Rojas, 2.
Rafael Romero, 4, 5.
Francisco Rubiol, 4.
José Rubin, 4.
Juan Ruiz, 4.
Bartolomé Sala, 1, 2.
Francisco Salas, 5.

Francisco Salbat, 1, 2.
José Sánchez, 4.
Juan Sánchez, 4.
Celido San Cristóbal, 1, 2.
Francisco Sarmiento, 4, 5.
Damián Seguera, 4.
Miguel Seguera, 4.
Miguel Serera, 4.
Joseph Serra, 1, 2.
José María Serrano, 5.
José Isidro Servín, 5.
Estévan Solá, 2, 6.
Manuel Soler, 1, 2.
José Sorde, 3.
Estéban Stá, 1, 2.
Simón Suárez, 5.
Ygnacio Tejo (Ignacio Antonio Texo), 4.
Francisco Terricabres, 4.
Joaquín Tico, 4, 5.
Esteven Tigell, 1, 2.
Juan Torrell, 1, 2.
José Tórres, 4.
Narciso Tórres, 5.

Antonio Torva (see Antonio Yorba).
Francisco Trillas, 1, 2.
José Trujillo, 5.
Francisco Váldes, 5.
Cayettano Valls, 4.
José Manuel Vega, 5.
José Velis, 5.
Lorenzo Ventura, 1, 2.
Agustín Vicens, 1, 2, 4.
Antonio Vidal, 1, 2.
Francisco Vidal, 1, 2.
Estévan de Vilaseca, 1, 2.
Antonio Vilax, 1, 2.
Onofre Villalba, 4, 5.
Francisco Villaubi, 4.
Pedro Nata Viñolas, 6.
José Vino, 4.
Francisco Ydalgo, 4.
Juan Yñiguez, 4.
Agustín de Yslas, 6.
Antonio Yorba, 1, 2, 3 (see Antonio Torva).
Antonio Yusmet, 1, 2.

Sources: Bancroft, *California,* I, 732–44; Tibesar, *Writings of Serra,* 2, 149; Rómulo Velasco Ceballos, "La Administración de Bucareli, *PAGN,* 29, 281; Hoja de Servicios found in AGS, Guerra Moderna 7275 and 7277; Hoja de Servicios found in AGI, México 1379; Revista de Comisario, Nootka, signed by Pedro de Alberni, December 1, 1790, AGI, Guadalajara 509; Pié de lista de la Compañía, signed by Alonso Cavallero, Sevilla, May 13, 1767, AGI, México 2455; and, Ives, "The Fages expedition, 1781," *AW.*

Abbreviations

AGI	Archivo General de Indias, Sevilla
AGN	Archivo General de la Nación, México, D.F.
AGS	Archivo General de Simancas, Simancas
AHN	Archivo Histórico Nacional, Madrid
AW	*Arizona and the West*
BNM	Biblioteca Nacional de Madrid
BN de M	Biblioteca Nacional de México
CHSQ	*California Historical Society Quarterly*
HLM	Huntington Library Manuscript
HSSCQ	*Historical Society of Southern California Quarterly*
MN Ms.	Museo Naval (Madrid) Manuscript
NMHR	*New Mexico Historical Review*
RAH	Real Academia de la Historia, Madrid
PAGN	*Publicaciones del Archivo General de la Nación*
UT-WBS	University of Texas Library, Austin, W. B. Stephens Collection

Notes

PREFACE

1. Hubert Howe Bancroft, *History of California* (San Francisco: A. L. Bancroft Company, 1884–1890), 7 vols.

2. Herbert I. Priestley, *José de Galvez, Visitor-General of New Spain, 1765–1771* (Berkeley: University of California Press, 1916).

3. Donald W. Roland, "The Elizondo Expedition against the Indian Rebels of Sonora, 1765–1771" (Ph.D. diss., University of California, 1930).

4. Donald A. Nuttall, "Pedro Fages and the Advance of the Northern Frontier of New Spain, 1767–1782" (Ph.D. diss., University of Southern California, 1964).

5. Oakah L. Jones, "The Spanish Occupation of Nootka Sound, 1790–1795" (Master's thesis, University of Oklahoma, 1960).

6. Donald C. Cutter, "Pedro Alberni and the First Scientific Agriculutral Experiments in the Northwest" (unpublished ms., 1973).

7. Ronald Ives, *José Velasquez: Saga of a Borderland Soldier* (Tucson: Southwestern Mission Research Center, 1984).

CHAPTER I

1. Arthur Aiton, "Spanish Colonial Reorganization under the Family Compact," *Hispanic American Historical Review,* 12 (August 1932), 273–74.

2. Lyle McAlister, "The Reorganization of the Army of New Spain, 1763–1766," *Hispanic American Historical Review,* 32 (February 1953), 9.

3. Plan de compañias para la formación de los dos Battallones que pasan a Nueva España, November 10, 1764, Archivo General de Simancas; hereinafter cited as AGS, followed by section and legajo number, Guerra Moderna, 2811.

4. María del Carmen Velásquez, *El Estado de Guerra en Nueva España, 1760–1808* (México: El Colegio de México, 1950), 64.

5. Ibid., 59.

6. Viceroy Marqués de Cruillas to Rubí, Instrucciones, México, March 10, 1766, AGI, Guadalajara 511. Villalba to Cruillas, México, December 27, 1764; and unsigned letter to Marqués de Rubí, August 7, 1765, AHN, Estado, 3882.

7. Reglamento e Instrucción para los Presidios que se han de formar en la linea de frontera de la Nueva España. Resuelto por el Rey N.S. en Cedula de 10 de Septiembre de 1772; hereinafter cited as Reglamento de 1772 De orden de su Magestad. Madrid: Por Juan de San Martín, Impresor de la Secretaria del Despacho Universal de Indias, Año de 1772, AHN, Estado 3882, Expediente 16.

8. Relación de la expedición de las Provincias de Sinaloa, Ostimuri, y Sonora en el Reino de Nueva España; hereinafter cited as Relación de la expedición, México, September 1, 1771, AGI, Guadalajara 416.

9. Ibid.

10. Junta de Guerra de Generales, signed by Croix, Gálvez, Palacio, Ricardos, Cornide, and Joseph de Gorraez, México, January 8, 1767, AGI, México 2455.

11. Unsigned letter addressed to Juan Gregorio Muniain, Aranjuez, April 26, 1767, AGI, México 2455.

12. Arriaga to Croix, Aranjuez, May 12, 1767, AGI, México 2455.

13. Muniain to Arriaga, Aranjuez, May 19, 1767, AGI, México 2455.

14. Abelardo Carillo y Gariel, *El Traje en la Nueva España* (México: Instituto Nacional de Antropología e Historia, 1959), 178–79. Detmar H. Finke, "La Organización del Ejército en Nueva España," *Boletín del Archivo General de la Nación*, Mexico City, 11, 636.

15. Noticia del armamento que esta compañía tiene hoy dia de la fecha, con expresión del tiempo de su uso y el estado en que se halla, signed by Pedro de Alberni, Tepic, January 1790, Huntington Library, San Marino, California, Ms. 327. Signed statements by Antonio Pol, México, May 23, 1772, AGI, México 1392 indicates that .19 caliber fusil was used. However, Sidney B. Brinckerhoff and Pierce A. Chamberlain, *Spanish Military Weapons in Colonial America, 1700–1821* (Pennsylvania: Stackpole Books, 1972), 24–25, note that the fusil was .69 caliber.

16. Pié de lista de la Compañía que se orden de S.M. se ha formado con destino al Virreynato de México por saca voluntaria en la tropa de el Segundo

Regimiento de Infantería Ligeria de Cataluña; hereinafter cited as Pié de lista de la compañía signed by Alonso Cavallero, Sevilla, May 13, 1767, AGI, México 2455.

17. Partido del Casamiento, Testimonio del expediente formado en virtud de instancia hecha por Doña Rosa Callis, viuda del Theniente Coronel Graduado Don Agustín Callis, capitán de la Compañía franca de Voluntarios de Cataluña, solicitando la pensión del Monte Pio, que le corresponde por razón de viudad; hereinafter cited as Testimonio del expediente Superior Govierno, año de 1782 con sello, AGI, México 1395.

18. Agustín Callis, Hoja de Servicios, December 1776, AGI, México 1379.

19. Ibid.

20. Signed statement by Miguel Boix, September 14, 1763, AGI, México 2458.

21. Ibid.

22. Testimonio del expediente, AGI, México 1395.

23. Testimonio del expediente, AGI, México 1395.

24. Croix to Arriaga, México, September 11, 1767, AGI, México 1355.

25. Muniain to Arriaga, Aranjuez, May 22, 1767, AGI, México 2455.

26. Unsigned letter to Muniain, May 19, 1767, AGI, México 2455.

27. Signed note by Juan Antonio de la Colina, May 12, 1767; and unsigned letter to Gregorio Muniain, Aranjuez, May 19, 1767, both in AGI, México 2455.

28. Unsigned letter to Marqués del Real Thesorero, Aranjuez, May 19, 1767, AGI, México 2455.

29. Bancroft, *History of California* (1866), I:116.

30. Marqués de Croix to Arriaga, México, August 27, 1767, AGI, Guadalajara 416.

31. Estado que manifiesta el número de Tropa que tiene esta compañía con individualidad de los desertores, muertos, y ausentes, que han acaesido desde su embarco en Cádiz hasta el arribo a esta ciudad, signed by Agustín Callis, México, September 24, 1767, AGI, México 2429.

32. Marqués de Croix, to Muniain, México, September 26, 1767, AGI, México 2429.

33. José de Gálvez to Julian de Arriaga, Guanajuato, October 25, 1767, AGI, Guadalajara 416.

34. Marqués de Croix to Arriaga, México, August 27, 1767; and Gálvez to Arriaga, México, October 25, 1767, both in AGI, Guadalajara 416.

35. Relación de la expedición, México, September 1, 1771, AGI, Guadalajara 416.

36. Gálvez to Arriaga, Guanajuato, October 25, 1767, AGI, Guadalajara 416.

37. Relación de la expedición, México, September 1, 1771, AGI, Guadalajara 416.
38. Ibid.
39. Ibid.
40. Ibid.
41. Ibid.
42. Ibid.

CHAPTER 2

1. Marqués de Croix to Arriaga, México, May 22, 1768; and Relación de la Expedición de las Provincias de Sinaloa, Ostimuri, y Sonora en el Reino de la Nueva España; hereinafter cited as Relación de las expedición, Mexico, September 1, 1771, AGI, Guadalajara 416.
2. Capellán Thomás Ignacio Lizasoin to Marqués de Cruillas (n.d.) in *Documentos para la Historia de México* (México, 1856), tercera serie, 692.
3. Relación de los sucesos acaecidos en la partida que a mis ordenes, salió de este quartel, a socorrer la que se hallaba en campaña, a las de Don Juan Román, Teniente de la segunda Compañía Volante, de la que es capitan Don José Antonio Vildosola, 1771, signed by Agustín Callis, AGN, Historia, Tomo 24, Expediente 12.
4. Breve Ynforme sobre la guerra que ha echo en la Provincia de Sonora del Reyno de la Nueva España, y como se devio haver echo, signed by Matías de Armona, México, January 2, 1771, AGI, México 2477.
5. Relación de la expedición, México, September 1, 771, AGI, Guadalajara 416.
6. Ibid.
7. "Estado de las tropas," signed by Pineda, Pitic, September 15, 1768, AGI, Guadalajara 416.
8. Relación de la expedición, México, September 1, 1771, AGI, Guadalajara 416.
9. Croix to Arriaga, México, October 27, 1768, AGI, Guadalajara 416.
10. Relación de la expedición, México, September 1, 1771, AGI Guadalajara 416.
11. Ibid.
12. Ibid.
13. Ibid.
14. Extracto signed by Marqués de Croix, México, December 31, 1768; and Relación de la expedición, México, September 1, 1771, both in AGI, Guadalajara 416.

15. Relación de la expedición, México, September 1, 1771, AGI Guadalajara 416.

16. Ibid.

17. Ibid.

18. Pedro de Alberni, Hoja de Servicios, July 1798, AGI, México 1446.

19. Relación del ataque general que las tropas de S. M. dieron a los yndios rebeldes de las tres naciones Piatos, Seris, y Sibubapas en el Caxón de la Palma de la Serranía del Cerro Prieto, el día veinte cinco de noviembre de 1768; hereinafter cited as Relación del ataque, AGI, Guadalajara 416.

20. Relación del ataque, November 25, 1768, AGI, Guadalajara 416.

21. Plano y detalle de la Tropa destinada al proiectado ataque general de los enemigos en el cajón de la Palma de Cerro Prieto para el día veinte y cuatro de Noviembre de 1768, AGI, Guadalajara 416.

22. Relación de la expedición, México, September 1, 1771, AGI, Guadalajara 416.

23. Relación del ataque, November 25, 1768, AGI, Guadalajara 416.

24. Ibid.

25. Ibid.

26. Pineda to Croix, Pitic, December 20, 1768, AGI, Guadalajara 416.

27. Relación del ataque, November 25, 1768, AGI, Guadalajara 416.

28. Relación de los subcessivos destacamentos en que desde 1 de agosto proximo passado se ha exercitado la tropa del Rey . . . (hereinafter cited as Relación de los subcessivos) signed by Domingo Elizondo, Pitic, December 20, 1768, AGI, Guadalajara 416.

29. Relación de los subcessivos, Pitic, December 20, 1768, AGI, Guadalajara 416.

30. Solá to Teodoro de Croix, Arizpe, January 20, 1783, AGN, Californias 31 Estevan Solá, Hoja de Servicios, December 1776, AGI, México 1379.

31. Luís Rojas, Hoja de Servicios, December 1776, AGI, México 1379.

32. Mauricio Faulia, Hoja de Servicios, December 1776, AGI, México 1379.

33. Estevan Stá, Hoja de Servicios, June 1777, AGI, México 1382.

34. Relación de los subcessivos, Pitic, December 20, 1768, AGI, Guadalajara 416.

35. Relación de la expedición, México, September 1, 1771, AGI, Guadalajara 416.

36. Plano y detalle de la Tropa destinado al proiectado ataque en el Cajón de la Palma, November 24, 1768, AGI, Guadalajara 416.

37. Pineda to Marqués de Croix, Pitic, December 20, 1768, AGI, Guadalajara 416.

38. Relación de los subcessivos, Pitic, December 20, 1768, AGI, Guadalajara 416.

39. Ibid.
40. Ibid.
41. Ibid.
42. Ibid.
43. Ibid.
44. Plano y detalle para el proiectado ataque general de el caxón, o cañada de Cara Pintada de Cerro Prieto. February 25, 1769, AGI, Guadalajara 416.
45. Bucareli to Arriaga to Arriaga, México, May 26, 1772, AGI, México 2458.
46. Noticia del armamento que esta compañía tiene oy día de la fecha, con expresión del tiempo de su uso, el estado en que se halla y número que falta para su completo, Agustín Callis, Real del Monte, September 8, 1777, AGN, Historia 207.
47. Signed statement by Domingo Elizondo, Pitic, April 28, 1771, AGN, Marina 77.
48. Signed statement by Francisco Hixosa, San Blas, July 8, 1788 (con sello) AGN, Marina 77.

CHAPTER 3

1. Bancroft, *History of California,* I:116.
2. Gálvez to Marqués de Croix, December 16, 1768, AGI, Guadalajara 416.
3. Ibid.
4. Compendio Histórica de las navegaciones practicadas por oficiales y pilotos, en Buques de la Real Armada, sobre las costas septentrionales de las Californias, con el objeto de descubrir, y determinar la extensión, y posición de sus distritos, e yslas adyacentes, ordenado por un oficial de la Marina Real Española, Año de 1799, Museo Naval, Madrid, manuscript (hereinafter cited as MN, Ms. followed by number) 575 bis. This document mentions the arrival of the Catalonian Volunteers in La Paz in December 1768.
5. Instrucción que ha de observar el Theniente de Ynfantería don Pedro Fages como comandante de la Partida de veinte y cinco Hombres (n.d.), (hereinafter cited as Instrucción, que had de observar el teniente de infantería), AGI, Guadalajara 416. Fages received his instructions on January 5, 1769; see Bancroft, *History of California,* I:131, n. 11.
6. Ibid.
7. Ibid.
8. Ibid.
9. Ibid.

10. Bancroft, *History of California,* I:120.

11. Ibid.

12. Diario de Fray Junípero Serra en su viaje de Loreto a San Diego, in Lino Gómez Canedo, *De Mexico a la Alta California: Una Gran Epopeya Misional* (México, 1969), 18.

13. Zoeth S. Eldredge and E. J. Molera, *The March of Portolá and the Log of the San Carlos* (San Francisco: California Promotion Committee, 1909), 26.

14. Bancroft notes those who were with Fages in those early years (1769–74) in California. Bancroft's list helped the author distinguish some of the original Catalonian Volunteers from the others by using Alonso Cavallero's Sevilla *comisario* list of 1767. See Bancroft, *History of California,* 1:732–44, and Pié de la lista de la compañía, signed by Alonso Cavallero, Sevilla, May 13, 1767, AGI, México 2455. See also Herbert Eugene Bolton, ed., *Historical Memoirs of New California by Fray Francisco Palou, O.F.M.* (hereinafter cited as Bolton, *Palou's New California*) (Berkeley: University of California Press, 1926), III:230; and Velasco, "La Administración de Bucareli," *PAGN,* 29, 227; and Antoine Tibesar, O.F.M., ed., *The Writings of Fray Junipero Serra* (Washington, D.C.: Academy of American Franciscan History, 1955), VI:149. Yorba and Torba appear not to be two distinct individuals in the above sources.

15. Instrucciones que ha de observar el teniente de infantería (January 5, 1769), AGI, Guadalajara 416.

16. Ibid.

17. Ibid.

18. Ibid.

19. Ibid.

20. Ibid.

21. Ibid.

22. Ibid.

23. Ibid.

24. Ibid.

25. Don Miguel Costansó, *Diario Histórico de los viages de mar, y tierra hechos al norte de la California de orden del Excelentíssimo Marqués de Croix, Virrey, Governador, y Capitan General de la Nueva España y por dirección del Illustríssimo Señor D. Joseph de Gálvez, del consejo, y cámara de S. M. en el Supremo de Indias de Ejército, Visitador General de este Reyno* (hereinafter cited as Costansó, *Diario Histórico*) (De la Imprenta del Superior Gobierno), October 24, 1770, MN, Ms. 334.

26. Ibid.

27. Bancroft, *History of California,* I:129.

28. Costansó, *Diario Histórico,* October 24, 1770, MN, Ms. 334.

29. Ibid.

30. Ibid.

31. Vicente Vila, Diario de Navegación del Paquebot de S. M. nombrado el San Carlos, Alias el Toyson, su comandante Don Vicente Villa . . . 1769 (hereinafter cited as Vila, Diario), MN, Ms. 575.

32. Ibid.

33. Ibid.

34. Costansó, *Diario Histórico*, October 24, 1770, MN, Ms. 334.

35. Ibid.

36. Costansó, *Diario Histórico*, October 24, 1770, MN, Ms. 334. Vila, Diario, 1769, MN, Ms. 575.

37. Ibid.

38. Ibid.

39. Vila, Diario, 1769, MN, Ms. 575.

40. Ibid.

41. Bancroft, *History of California*, I:28. Pedro Prat died in 1773. Prior to his death, he went insane. See Minutes of Junta de Guerra, signed by Bucareli, Barcarcel, Toro, Areche, Barrueta, Abad, Valdes, Gutiérrez, Magino, Arce, José de Gorraez, Mexico, May 6, 1773, in Velasco, "La Administración de Bucareli," *PAGN*, 29, 135.

42. Gálvez to Marqués de Croix, Cabo San Lucas, February 16, 1769; Estado, Memorias, e Inventorio de los que had llevado el paquetbot de S. M. San Joseph, alias el Descubridor al los Puertos de San Diego, y Monterey . . . Hecho de orden del governador interino Don Juan Gutiérrez Ensenada de Loreto, June 5, 1769; both in AGI, Guadalajara 416. The San Joseph was lost at sea.

43. Costansó, *Diario Histórico*, October 24, 1770, MN, Ms. 334.

44. Ibid.

45. Ibid.

46. Bancroft, *History of California*, I:130.

47. Costansó, *Diario Histórico*, October 24, 1770, MN, Ms. 334.

48. Vila, Diario, 1769, MN, Ms. 575.

49. Ibid.

50. Ibid.

51. Costansó, *Diario Histórico*, October 24, 1770, MN, Ms. 334.

52. Ibid.

53. Ibid.

54. Fray Juan Crespi to Fray Juan Andrés, Guardian of San Fernando, Puerto de San Diego, June 22, 1769, in Lino Gómez Canedo, *De México a la Alta California*, 72.

55. Father Junípero Serra to Fray Juan Andrés, San Diego, July 3, 1769, in Lino Gómez Canedo, *De México a la Alta California*, 77.

56. Costansó, *Diario Histórico*, October 24, 1770, MN, Ms. 334.

57. Ibid.

58. Bancroft, *History of California*, I:134.

59. Costansó, *Diario Histórico*, October 24, 1770, MN, Ms. 334.

60. Ibid.

61. Ibid.

62. Portolá to Marqués de Croix, Monterey, June 15, 1770, AGN, Californias 76. The San Joseph left San Blas in May 1769, and was never heard from again.

63. Costansó, *Diario Histórico*, October 24, 1770, MN, Ms. 334.

64. Vila, Diario, 1769, MN, Ms. 575.

65. Crespi to Palou, San Diego, June 9, 1769, in Herbert Eugene Bolton, *Fray Juan Crespi, Missionary Explorer on the Pacific Coast, 1769–1774* (hereinafter cited as Bolton, *Crespi*) (New York: AMS Press, 1971), 2.

66. Crespi to Palou, San Diego, June 9, 1769, in Bolton, *Crespi*, 2.

67. Crespi to Fray Juan Andrés, San Diego, June 22, 1769, in Bolton, *Crespi*, 2.

68. Serra to Andrés, San Diego, July 3, 1769, in Lino Gómez Canedo, *De México a la Alta California*, 77.

69. Donald Andrew Nuttall, "Pedro Fages and the Advance of the Northern Frontier of New Spain, 1767–1782" (hereinafter cited as Nuttall, "Pedro Fages") (Ph.D. diss., University of Southern California, 1964), 52, n. 52.

70. "Copy of a report which I received, enclosed in a letter, coming on board the *El Príncipe*, from Monterey—which I am keeping in my possession—and which the Corporal of the Volunteer soldiers of that presidio, Miguel Periquez, assures me to be the substance of what he is writing to his captain, Don Agustín Callis, about the treatment that Don Pedro has accorded them (n.d.)," signed by Father Junípero Serra, in Antoine Tibesar, O.F.M., *Writings of Serra*, I:402.

71. Nuttall, "Pedro Fages," 56, n. 57. Father Crespi reported that seven Catalan Volunteers marched with Fages; Bolton, *Crespi*, 120. However, Costansó mentions only six Catalonians, Costansó, *Diario Histórico*, October 24, 1770, MN, Ms. 334; and Portolá noted eight Volunteers in his group, Portolá to Marqués de Croix, San Diego, July 4, 1769, AGN, Californias 76.

72. Maynard Geiger, O.F.M., translator and editor, *Palou's Life of Fray Junípero Serra* (hereinafter cited as Geiger, *Palou's Life of Serra*) (Washington, D.C.: Academy of American Franciscan History, 1955), 74. Palou wrote in reference to the Catalonian that "many had died."

73. Bolton, *Crespi*, 122.

74. Costansó, *Diario Histórico*, October 24, 1770, MN, Ms. 334.

75. Bolton, *Crespi*, 123. Bolton noted that this camp was not far from

Ladrillo, California. All modern place names cited in this chapter are from footnotes in Bolton, *Crespi*.

76. Bolton, *Crespi*, 124–35 passim.
77. Ibid., 136.
78. Ibid., 138.
79. Ibid., 142.
80. Ibid., 144.
81. Ibid., 145.
82. Ibid., 152.
83. Ibid., 152.
84. Ibid., 150–65 passim.
85. Ibid., 170.
86. Ibid., 179.
87. Ibid., 162.
88. Ibid., 164.
89. Ibid., 172.
90. Ibid., 174.
91. Ibid., 176.
92. Ibid., 205.
93. Ibid., 206.
94. Bancroft, *History of California*, I:152–53, n. 11.
95. Bolton, *Palou's New California*, II:278.
96. Extract of the report from the Port of Monterey, about the mission and presidios established there with the name and sea expeditions which were dispatched for this purpose in the past year, 1769, Mexico City, August 16, 1770, in Geiger, *Palou's Life of Serra*, 98.
97. Bancroft, *History of California*, I:168.
98. Informe a S. M. en que el Colegio de San Fernando de México, da cuenta de los nuevos descubrimientos hechos en California desde 1769 hasta el presente de 1776 y de las Misiones que a su cargo se han fundado, signed by Fray Esteban Antonio de Arenaza, Fray Juan Ramos Lora and Fray Domingo de Bengoechea, Colegia de San Fernando de México, February 26, 1776, AGI, Guadalajara 515.
99. Signed statement Pedro Fages, June 11, 1770, AGN; Californias 76.
100. Miguel Pericas, Hoja de Servicios, April 15, 1789; and signed application for retirement by Pericas, April 15, 1789, in AGN, Provincias Internas 266.
101. Juan Puig and Miguel Pericas to Viceroy Bucareli, Real del Monte, March 11, 1775, in Velasco, "La Administración de Bucareli," *PAGN*, 29, 227.

CHAPTER 4

1. Bolton, *Crespi,* 63.
2. Nuttall, "Pedro Fages," 49.
3. Ibid., 50.
4. "Expedition which was made by Don Pedro Fages, Lieutenant of the Catalonian Volunteers, with six soldiers and a muleteer," translated by Emma Helen Blair in Irving Berdine Richman, *California Under Spain and Mexico, 1535–1847* (New York: Houghton Mifflin Company, 1911), 514 (hereinafter cited as Richman, Fages Diary, 1770).
5. Bolton, *Crespi,* xxxiv.
6. Modern place names as found in ibid.
7. Ibid.
8. Richman, "Fages Diary, 1770," 517–18.
9. Bancroft, *History of California,* I:160, n. 20.
10. Nuttall, "Pedro Fages," p. 165.
11. Richman, "Fages Diary, 1770," 518.
12. Ibid., 518.
13. Diario que hizo desde la Mision y Real Presidio del Señor Don Carlos del Puerto de Monte-Rey en busca del Puerto de San Francisco, y se compusó el cuerpo de esta Expedición del Reverendo Padre Fray Juan Chrespy. Capitán Don Pedro Fages, Catorze soldados y un Yndio Christiano Paje del Reverendo Padre, signed by Pedro Fages (hereinafter cited as Fages, Diario, 1772). Real Presidio de San Carlos de Monterey, November 27, 1773, AGN, Californias 66. See also Bolton, *Crespi,* in which Father Crespi's diary on the same expedition is printed under "Diary kept during the Exploration that was made of the Harbor of our Father San Francisco," 277–303. Crespi states that there were six Catalonian Volunteers in the party.
14. Bolton, *Crespi,* 284n.
15. Fages, Diario, 1772, AGN, Californias 66.
16. Bolton, *Crespi,* 287n.
17. Bolton, *Crespi,* 290. Fages's version reads that they were traveling in a north–northwest direction; Fages, Diario, 1772, AGN, Californias 66.
18. Fages, Diario, 1772, AGN, Californias 66.
19. Ibid.
20. Bolton, *Crespi,* 293n.
21. Ibid., 292.
22. Ibid., 293n.
23. Fages, Diario, 1772, AGN, Californias 66.
24. Bolton, *Crespi,* 295.
25. Ibid., 295n.
26. Fages, Diario, 1772, AGN, Californias 66.

27. Ibid., and Bolton, *Crespi,* 295n.

28. Donald C. Cutter, "Spanish Exploration of California's Central Valley" (Ph.D. diss., University of California, 1950), 32.

29. Ibid., 32.

30. Herbert E. Bolton, "In the South San Joaquín Ahead of Garcés," *California Historical Society Quarterly,* 10 (September 1931), 214.

31. Ibid., 216.

32. Ibid., 213.

33. Cutter, "Spanish Exploration," 33.

CHAPTER 5

1. Ives, "The Fages expedition, 1781," *AW,* 8, 159.

2. Ibid., 159.

3. Ibid., 160.

4. Ibid., 170.

5. Pedro Fages, Hoja de Servicios, December 1776, AGI, México 1379.

6. Ibid.

7. Ibid.

8. Fages to Juan Gregorio Muniain, Cuartel de Guaymas, June 28, 1768, AGI, México 2429.

9. Fages to Muniain, Cuartel de Guaymas, June 28, 1769, AGI, México 2429.

10. Ynforme del Real Tribunal de Cuentas, signed by Barroeta, Abad, and Gallardo, December 19, 1776, AGI, Guadalajara 515.

11. Nuttall, "Pedro Fages," 167–69.

12. Ibid.

13. Ibid.

14. Bancroft, *History of California,* I:191.

15. Copy of a report which I received, enclosed in a letter, coming on board the *El Príncipe,* from Monterey—which I am keeping in my possession—and which the Corporal of the Volunteer soldiers of that presidio, Miguel Periquez, assures me to be the substance of what he is writing to his Captain, Don Agustín Callis, about the treatment that Don Pedro Fages has accorded them, n.d., signed by Father Serra (hereinafter cited as Serra, Copy of a report), in Tibesar, *Writings of Serra,* I:403.

16. Serra, Copy of a report in Tibesar, *Writings of Serra,* I:403.

17. Ibid., 404.

18.	Serra to Bucareli, College of San Fernando de Mexico, June 4, 1773, in Tibesar, *Writings of Serra,* I:375.

19.	Maynard Geiger, O.F.M., *The Life and Times of Junípero Serra* (Washington, D.C.: Academy of American Franciscan History, 1950), I:379.

20.	Geiger, *The Life and Times of Serra,* I:379.

21.	Ibid., 380.

22.	Puig and Pericas to Bucareli, Real del Monte, March 11, 1775, in Velasco, "La Administración de Bucareli," *PAGN,* 29, 280.

23.	Ibid., 279.

24.	Ibid.

25.	Ibid., 280.

26.	Ibid.

27.	Ibid., 281.

28.	An account of some things that have happened during the new conquest of Monte-Rey since the beginning of its foundation, which took place on the fifth day of June in the year of our Lord one thousand seven hundred and seventy; the manner in which the soldiers have been dispersed; also the way the work has been carried on, and how these same soldiers have been compelled to labor by force, signed by Mariano Carillo, Presidio of Monterey December 21, 1772, in Thomas Workman Temple II, trans. and ed., "Three Early California Letters," *Historical Society of Southern California Quarterly* (hereinafter cited as Temple, "Three Early California Letters," *HSSCQ*) 15, pt. 4 (1931), 31.

29.	Temple, "Three Early California Letters," *HSSCQ,* 15, 32.

30.	Ibid.

31.	Miguel Pericas, Hoja de Servicios, April 15, 1789, AGN, Provincias Internas 266.

32.	Nuttall, "Pedro Fages," 168–69.

33.	Bancroft, *History of California,* I:188.

34.	Temple, "Three Early California Letters," *HSSCQ,* 15, 45.

35.	Geiger, ed., *Palou's Life of Serra,* 123.

36.	Serra to Gálvez, Monterey, July 2, 1770 in Tibesar, *Writings of Serra,* I:185.

37.	Bucareli to Arriaga, México, February 24, 1773, in Velasco, "La Administración de Bucareli," *PAGN,* 29, 126.

38.	El Virrey de N.E. acompaña 5 testimonios del expediente formado para el arreglo de la peninsula de Californias y Departmento de San Blas, signed by Bucareli, Barcarel, Toro, Areche, Barrueta, Abad, Valdez, Gutiérrez, Mangino, Arce, José de Gorraez, Mexico, May 6, 1773, in Velasco, "La Administración de Bucareli," *PAGN,* 29, 130.

39.	Bucareli to Arriaga, México, February 25, 1776, AGI, Guadalajara 515.

40. Tibesar, *Writings of Serra,* I:421, n. 133.

41. Ibid.

42. Geiger, *Life and Times of Serra,* I:385.

43. Nuttall, "Pedro Fages," 417.

44. For reports made by Fages, see Relación hecho y firmado por Pedro Fages sobre los establecimientos en California, desde el de San Diego de Alcala hasta el Puerto de San Francisco, México, November 30, 1775; and Don Pedro Fages incluyendo relación y testimonio de los asuntos de la California Septentrional, México, March 25, 1776; both in AGI, Guadalajara 515. See also Herbert I. Priestley, ed., *A Historical, Political and Natural Description of California by Pedro Fages, Soldier of Spain* (Berkeley: University of California Press, 1937).

45. Nuttall, "Pedro Fages," 433.

46. Ibid., 434.

47. Bucareli to Gálvez, México, December 27, 1777, enclosed in this correspondence are signed statements by Fages (n.d.), Pasqual de Cisneros, México, December 20, 1777; and Agustín Callis, Real del Monte, December 6, 1777, in AGI, México 1380.

48. Pedro Fages, Hoja de Servicios, December 1776, AGI, México 1379.

49. Copy of baptismal record for Eulalia Callis signed by Agustín Alvarez, Real y Minas del Monte, December 4, 1777, AGI, México 1380. This record indicates that Eulalia Francisca y Josepha Callis was baptized on October 4 [1751?]. Her godparents were Felix Cerra, retired sergeant, and Eulalia Cerra (before Eulalia Puig), both of the city of Vich. The priest was Joseph Antich, priest and vicar of the church of San Andreu de Palomar in the diocese of Barcelona. It should be noted that her parents, Agustín Callis and Rosa Casañas de Callis were married in 1750; see copy of Partido de Casamiento in AGI, México 1395. Eulalia's brother, Antonio Callis, was born sometime in 1760; see Antonio Callis, Hoja de Servicios, December 1776, AGI, México 1379.

50. Pedro Fages, Hoja de Servicios, December 1776, AGI, México 1379. Fages had been captain since November 4, 1774.

51. Nuttall, "Pedro Fages," 448.

52. Ibid., 449.

53. Thomas, *Teodoro de Croix,* 144. Pedro Fages, Hoja de Servicios, December 1790, AGI, México 3186.

54. Pedro Fages, Hoja de Servicios, December 1790, AGI, México 3186.

55. Thomas, *Teodoro de Croix,* 152–53.

56. Mugártegui to the Guardian of the College of San Fernando, San Juan Capistrano, March 15, 1779, Biblioteca Nacional, Mexico City, section Documentos relativos a las misiones de California, Lancaster Jones Papers, Vol. 2, ff. 172–73. Translation by Cheryl Rowe Foote.

57. Thomas, *Teodoro de Croix,* 65 and 153.

58. Ibid. See also Richman, *California under Spain and Mexico,* 156.
59. Richman, *California under Spain and Mexico,* 156.
60. Thomas, *Teodoro de Croix,* 51–52, 154, and 216–17.
61. Relación por antiguidad de los oficiales, December 1794, AGI, Audiencia de México 1438. Also, see Donald A. Nuttall, "The Gobernantes of Spanish Upper California: A Profile," *California Historical Society Quarterly,* 51, no. 3 (Fall 1972), 268.

CHAPTER 6

1. Bucareli to Teodoro de Croix, México, August 27, 1777, in Velasco, "La Administración de Bucareli," *PAGN,* 29, 371.
2. Warren Cook, *Flood Tide of Empires: Spain and the Pacific Northwest, 1543–1819* (New Haven: Yale University Press, 1973), 70.
3. Cook, *Flood Tide of Empire,* 81.
4. Ibid., 88.
5. Spanish authorities referred to Nootka as the Puerto de Santa Cruz de Nootka (Nootka spelled in various ways: Nuca, Nuka, Nutca, Nutka). Juan Pérez named it Puerto de San Lorenzo de Nootka; and James Cook referred to it as Friendly Cove; see Vito Alessio Robles, ed., *Alejandro de Humboldt, Ensayo Político Sobre el Reino de Nueva España* (México, D.F., 1941), II:368.
6. Cook, *Flood Tide of Empire,* 93.
7. Ibid., 122–23.
8. Ibid., 125.
9. Ibid., 147.
10. Mario Hernández Sánchez-Barba, *La Ultima Expansión Española en America* (Madrid, 1957), 295. Hernández notes Colnett was taken to San Blas.
11. Cook, *Flood Tide of Empire,* 247–49 and 544–48.
12. Ibid., 226.
13. Unsigned letter to Antonio Villa Urrútia, México, August 29, 1789, Huntington Library Manuscript (hereinafter cited as HLM), San Marino, Calif., 327.
14. Antonio Villa Urrútia to Viceroy Manuel Antonio Flores, Guadalajara, September 4, 1789, HLM 327.
15. Unaddressed letter signed by Tomás Rodríguez, México, September 15, 1789, HLM 327.
16. Ibid.
17. Relación de los Yndibiduos de mi compañía que se hallan cansados, y enfermedades incurables, inabiles para el servicio de armas, signed by Pedro de Alberni, September 26, 1789, HLM 327.

18. Miguel Pericas to Flores, Guadalajara, September 25, 1789, HLM 327.

19. Signed letter by Pedro Alberni, October 6, 1789, HLM 327.

20. Alberni to Revillagigedo, Guadalajara, December 18, 1789, HLM 327.

21. Ibid.

22. Villa Urrútia to Revillagigedo, Guadalajara, December 18, 1789, HLM 327.

23. Flores to Antonio Váldez, México, February 25, 1788, AGI, México 1515.

24. Unaddressed letter signed by Juan de Dios Morelos, January 22, 1790, HLM 327.

25. Alberni to Bodega y Quadra, Tepic, January 21, 1790, HLM 327.

26. Bodega y Quadra to Revillagigedo, Tepic, January 22, 1790, HLM 327.

27. Alberni to Revillagigedo, Tepic, January 22, 1790, HLM 327.

28. Villa Urrútia to Revillagigedo, Guadalajara, February 26, 1790, HLM 327.

29. Unsigned letter addressed to Señor Intendente de Guadalajara, March 9, 1790.

30. Revista de Comisario, signed by Pedro Alberni, Nootka, April 1, 1791, AGI, Guadalajara 509.

31. Noticia del armamento que esta compañía tiene oy día de la fecha, con expresión del tiempo de su uso y el estado en que se halla, signed by Pedro de Alberni, Tepic, January 22, 1790, HLM 327.

32. Alberni to Revillagigedo, Tepic, January 22, 1790, HLM 327.

33. Letter addressed to Señor Comandante de San Blas, February 12, 1790, HLM 327.

34. Bodega y Quadra to Revillagigedo, San Blas, March 5, 1790, HLM 327.

35. Con fecha de 7 de diciembre de 89 ordenó el Excelentíssimo Señor Virrey de Conde Rebilla Gigedo al Comandante del Departamento de San Blas Don Juan Francisco de la Quadra, que la Fragata Concepción, el Paquebot Argonauta y la Balandra Princesa Real debian salir sin falta en todo Enero para el Puerto de Nutka a relevar la Fragata Princesa, que lo ocupaba (hereinafter cited as Orders of December 7, 1789), MN, Ms. 575 bis.

36. Orders of December 7, 1789, MN, Ms. 575 bis.

37. Henry R. Wagner, *Spanish Explorations in the Strait of Juan de Fuca* (New York: AMS Press, 1971), 85 n.

38. Orders of December 7, 1789, MN, Ms. 575 bis.

39. Unsigned letter to Alberni, Mexico, December 7, 1789, HLM 327.

40. Villa Urrútia to Revillagigedo, Guadalajara, January 1, 1790, HLM 427.

41. Villa Urrútia to Revillagigedo, Guadalajara, January 8, 1790, HLM 327. Revista de Comisario, signed by Pedro Alberni, Nootka, October 1, 1790, AGI, Guadalajara 509.

42. Villa Urrútia to Revillagigedo, Guadalajara, January 8, 1790, HLM 327.

43. Cook, *Flood Tide of Empire*, 275–76.

44. Instrucciones secretas dadas por el comandante de San Blas Don Juan Francisco de la Bodega y Quadra al teniente de Navio Don Francisco Eliza, Comandante de la Fragata Concepción y de los buques Filipino y Princesa Real; como asi mismo comandante de Nutka (hereinafter cited as Instrucciones secretas dadas al teniente Eliza), signed by Juan Francisco de la Bodega y Quadra, San Blas, January 28, 1790, MN, Ms. 575 bis.

45. Francisco Eliza, Hoja de Servicios, 1816, MN, Ms. 2305.

46. Instrucciones secretas dadas al teniente Eliza, San Blas, January 28, 1790, MN, Ms. 575 bis.

47. Ibid.

48. Ibid.

49. Ibid.

50. Ibid.

51. Cook, *Flood Tide of Empire*, 276.

52. Vito Alessio Robles, ed., *Alejandro de Humboldt, Ensayo Político sobre el Reino de la Nueva España* (México, D.F., 1941), II:369. Further discussion of Alberni's garden appears here in Chapter 7. See also Bodega y Quadra to Revillagigedo, Nootka, June 22, 1792, HLM 327.

53. Figures for 1793 compiled from Revista de Comisario, Tepic, January 30, 1793; Revista de Comisario, Tepic, February 22, 1973; Revista de Comisario, Guadalajara, March 15, 1793, all signed by Pedro Alberni in AGI, Guadalajara 509. See also Ajustamiento que forma la Contaduria Principal de Real Hacienda de la Provincia de Guadalajara en complimiento de orden del Excelentisímo Señor Virrey Conde de Revillagigedo de . . . la Compañía de Voluntarios de Cataluña del mando del Teniente Coronel su Capitán Don Pedro Alberni desde 1 de Enero de 1790 hasta fin de diciembre de 1792 . . . signed by José Manuel Gonzales Calrada and Juan Ortiz de (Rosas?), Guadalajara, August 27, 1793, AGI, Guadalajara 509.

54. Revista de Comisario signed by Pedro de Alberni, Nootka, April 1, 1792, AGI, Guadalajara 509.

55. Extract of the navigation made by the pilot Don Juan Pantoja y Arriaga in His Majesty's packetboat *San Carlos,* under the command of the ensign of the royal navy Don Ramón Saavedra, which sailed from the department of San Blas February 4, 1791, destined to carry supplies to the

establishment of San Lorenzo de Noca; and of the expedition in this vessel upon the northern coast of California under the command of First Lieutenant Don Francisco Eliza, the commandant of that establishment, which is situated in lat. 49° 35′ N and long. 21° 20′ W of San Blas by astronomical observation (hereinafter cited as "Pantoja's Extracto"), in Wagner, *Spanish Explorations,* 155. Manuscript copy of "Pantoja's Extracto" 1791, may be found in Museo Naval, Madrid, MN, Ms. 331.

56. Bodega y Quadra to Revillagigedo, January 26, 1792, HLM 327.

57. "Pantajo's Extracto," in Wagner, *Spanish Explorations,* 163.

58. Pedro Gorostiza to Revillagigedo, México, June 17, 1791, HLM 327.

59. Luís Gutiérrez and Juan Aranda to Revillagigedo, México, March 10, 1792, HLM 327.

60. Gutiérrez and Aranda to Revillagigedo, México, March 10, 1792, HLM 327.

61. Revista de Comisario, signed by Pedro de Alberni, Tepic, December 31, 1792, AGI, Guadalajara 509.

62. Relación de la fuerza con que se halla la compañía hoy día de la fecha, signed by Pedro Alberni, Puerto de San Lorenzo de Nootka, August 23, 1790, MN, Ms. 330.

63. Revista de Comisario, signed by Pedro de Alberni, Fragata Concepción a la vela con rumbo para Nootka, March 1, 1790, AGI, Guadalajara 509.

64. Extracto de lo mas esencial del Diario de Teniente de Navio de la Real Armada don Salvador Fidalgo, Comandante de Paquebot de S.M. nombrado *San Carlos,* con el que tubo la Comisión de pasar a Notka en conserva de la Fragata Concepción, y Balandra Inglesa Princesa Real, esta al mando del Alferez de Navio don Manuel Quimper, y la Fragata al del Teniente de Navio don Francisco Eliza; y despues de dejados posesionados, y fortificados en aquel Puerto, la de seguir al escrupulaso reconocimiento del Principe Guillermo, y Rivera de Cook, para saber si en aquellos partes se hallaban establecidos los Rusos (hereinafter cited as Extracto del diario del Fidalgo) 1790, MN, Ms. 271.

65. Revista de comisario signed by Pedro de Alberni, Nootka, June 1, 1790, AGI, Guadalajara 509.

66. Cook, *Flood Tide of Empire,* 277. Modern place names cited in the remainder of this chapter are taken from Warren Cook's *Flood Tide of Empire,* in which they are appropriately indexed.

67. Extracto del diario del Fidalgo, 1790, MN, Ms. 271.

68. Ibid.

69. Cook, *Flood Tide of Empire,* 278.

70. Ibid., 278.

71. Ibid., 280.

72. Ibid., 281.

73. Ibid., 283.

74. Revista de Comisario, signed by Pedro de Alberni, Nootka, June 1, 1790, AGI, Guadalajara 509.

75. Cook, *Flood Tide of Empire*, 283.

76. Revista de Comisario, signed by Pedro de Alberni, Nootka, January 1, 1792, AGI, Guadalajara 509. Ultimately twenty-eight men were sent to San Blas from Nootka.

77. Revista de Comisario, signed by Pedro de Alberni, Nootka, May 1, 1792, AGI, Guadalajara 509.

78. Miguel Salva and Pedro Sainz de Baranda, *Colección de Documentos Inéditos para la História de España* (Madrid, 1849), 15, 105–12.

79. Instrucciones secretas dadas al teniente Eliza, San Blas, January 28, 1790, MN, Ms. 575 bis.

80. Ibid.

81. Salva and Sainz, *Documentos Inéditos para la historia de España*, 15, 116. Also, Extracto de la navegación, Reconocimientos y descubrimientos hechos de orden del Excelentísimo Señor Conde Revilla Gigedo, Virrey de N. E. comunicada por el capital de Navío de la Real Armada don Juan Francisco de la Bodega y Quadra, comandante del Departamento de San Blas ala costa septentrional de California desde 48° 26′ hasta los 49° 50′ ambos del norte con el paquebot San Carlos . . . y la goleta San Saturnina, Alias la Orcasitas construida en Nuca . . . mandada esta Expedición por el Teniente de Navio de la Real Armada y comandante de este Establecimiento de San Lorenzo de Nuca don Francisco de Eliza en el Año de 1791 (hereinafter cited as Eliza, Extracto de Navegación), signed by Francisco Eliza, Fragata Concepción al Ancla en el Puerto de la Santa Cruz de Nuca, October 10, 1791, MN, Ms. 332.

82. Eliza, Extracto de Navegación, October 10, 1791, MN, Ms. 332.

83. Ibid.

84. Revista de Comisario, signed by Pedro de Alberni, Nootka, June 1, 1791, AGI, Guadalajara 509. Eliza mentioned that he had with him ten men; see Eliza, Extracto de Navegación, October 10, 1791, MN, Ms. 332.

85. Eliza, Extracto de Navegación, October 10, 1791, MN, Ms. 332.

86. Ibid. Cook, *Flood Tide of Empire*, 304.

87. Eliza, Extracto de Navegación, October 10, 1791, MN, Ms. 332.

88. Ibid.

89. "Pantoja's Extracto," in Wagner, *Spanish Explorations in Juan de Fuca Strait*, 172.

90. Cook, *Flood Tide of Empire*, 305.

91. Ibid.

92. Eliza, Extracto de Navegación, October 10, 1791, MN, MS. 332.

93.　Ibid.

94.　Revista de Comisario, signed by Pedro de Alberni, Nootka, September 1, 1791, AGI, Guadalajara 509. Alberni spelled the name Serera; Eliza spelled it Zireras, and Wagner translated the name to be Zieras; see Eliza, Extracto de Navegación, October 10, 1791, MN, Ms. 332, and Wagner, *Spanish Explorations*, 154.

95.　Secret Instructions to Eliza from Bodea y Quadra, February 4, 1791, in Wagner, *Spanish Explorations*, 138.

96.　Ibid.

97.　Revista de Comisario, Fragata Concepción a la vela con el rumbo a Monterey, signed by Pedro de Alberni, July 1, 1792, AGI, Guadalajara 509.

98.　Revista de Comisario, signed by Pedro de Alberni, Nootka, March 1, 1792; Revista de Comisario, signed by Pedro de Alberni, Nootka, April 1, 1792; Revista de Comisario, signed by Pedro de Alberni, Nootka, June 1, 1792; Revista de Comisario, signed by Pedro de Alberni, Fragata Concepción al la vela con el rumbo a Monterey, July 1, 1792, all in AGI, Guadalajara 509.

99.　Warren Cook maintains that there were thirteen Catalonian troopers with Fidalgo; see Cook, *Flood Tide of Empire*, 349. Alberni's revistas cited above name fifteen Volunteers on the *Princesa;* see n. 98, above, for source.

100.　Cook, *Flood Tide of Empire*, 350.

101.　Ibid., 427.

102.　Revista de Comisario, signed by Pedro de Alberni, Fragata Concepción a la Ancla en la Bahia de Monterey, August 1, 1792, AGI, Guadalajara 509.

103.　Ibid.

104.　Revista de Comisario, signed by Pedro de Alberni, Guadalajara, March 15, 1793, AGI, Guadalajara 509.

105.　Ibid.

106.　Ibid.

107.　Ibid.

108.　Alberni to Revillagigedo, Puerto de San Blas, November 22, 1792, HLM 327.

109.　Ibid.

110.　José Font to Excelentisimo Señor, Tepic, January 5, 1793, HLM 327.

111.　Bodega y Quadra to Revillagigedo, Tepic, February 28, 1793, HLM 327.

112.　Jacobo Ugarte y Loyola to Revillagigedo (Guadalajara) March 14, 1793, HLM 327.

113. Pedro Gorostiza to Revillagigedo, México, March 30, 1793, HLM 327.

114. Alberni to Revillagigedo, Guadalajara, March 22, 1793, HLM 327.

CHAPTER 7

1. Antonio Villa Urrútia to Viceroy Manuel Antonio Flores, Guadalajara 25, 1789 in Expediente sobre queja interpuesta por el Regente de Guadalajara contra el Capitán de la primera compañía de Voluntarios de Cataluña don Pedro Alberni (hereinafter cited as Expediente sobre queja) Año/1790, Huntington Library Manuscript (hereinafter cited as HLM) 327.

2. Alberni to Flores, Guadalajara, September 25, 1789; Antonio Villa Urrútia to Manuel Antonio Flores, Guadalajara, September 25, 1789; both in Expediente sobre queja, Año 1790, HLM 327. Villa Urrútia cites the day in question as September 23, 1789.

3. Ibid.

4. Ibid.

5. Ibid.

6. Ibid. The scribe's words to Alberni were "Callece (*sic*) y vallase."

7. Villa Urrútia to Flores, Guadalajara, September 25, 1789 in Expediente sobre queja, Año 1790, HLM 327.

8. Ibid.

9. Ibid.

10. Ibid.

11. Alberni to Flores, Guadalajara, September 15, 1789, in Expediente sobre queja, Año 1790, HLM 327.

12. Expediente, México 16, November 1789 in Expediente sobre queja, Año 1790, HLM 327.

13. Villa Urrútia to Revillagigedo, Guadalajara, December 18, 1789, in Expediente sobre queja, Año 1790, HLM 327.

14. Unsigned letter to Bodega y Quadra, México, December 30, 1789; also, unsigned letter to Bodega y Quadra, February 24, 1790. Alberni was advised of his arrest in an unsigned letter to Alberni, February 24, 1790. All three letters may be found in Expediente sobre queja, Año 1790, HLM 327.

15. Alberni to Revillagigedo, Puerto de San Lorenso de Nuca, July 5, 1790, in Expediente sobre queja, Año 1790, HLM 327.

16. Alberni to Revillagigedo, July 6, 1790, in Expediente sobre queja, Año 1790, HLM 327.

17. Bodega y Quadra to Revillagigedo, Nootka, June 22, 1792, HLM 327.

18.   Pedro de Alberni, Hoja de Servicios, December 1776, AGI, México 1379. This record shows Alberni to be thirty-one years old in 1776.

19.   Bancroft, *History of California*, II:5n.

20.   Signed statement by Inspector Pasqual de Cisneros, México, August 31, 1782, AGI, México 1395.

21.   Alberni, Hoja de Servicios, December 1776, AGI, México 1379.

22.   Signed statement by Inspector Pasqual de Cisneros, México, August 31, 1782, AGI, México 1395.

23.   As an example of early enlistment, Antonio Callis, son of Agustín Callis was thirteen years old when he enlisted in 1773; Antonio Callis, Hoja de Servicios, December 1776, AGI, México 1379.

24.   Signed statement by Inspector Pasqual de Cisneros, México, August 31, 1782.

25.   Bancroft, *History of California*, II:5.

26.   Martín de Mayoraga to Gálvez, México, September 5, 1782, AGI, México 1395.

27.   Signed statement by Inspector Pasqual Cisneros, México, August 31, 1782; and signed statement by Martín Mayoraga, México, September 3, 1782; both in AGI, México 1395.

28.   Cook, *Flood Tide of Empire*, 275.

29.   Donald C. Cutter, "Pedro Alberni and the First Scientific Agricultural Experiments in the Northwest" (hereinafter cited as Cutter, "Pedro Alberni") unpublished ms., 3.

30.   Mariano Moziño, "Noticias de Nutka," 1792, MN, Ms. 468.

31.   Cutter, "Pedro Alberni," 5.

32.   Moziño, "Noticias de Nutka," 1792, MN, Ms. 468.

33.   Cutter, "Pedro Alberni," 6. Moziño wrote that Alberni "lo enseño a cantar la tropa por el tono de Malbrúch," Moziño, "Noticias de Nutka," 1792, MN, Ms. 468.

34.   Moziño, "Noticias de Nutka," 1792, MN, Ms. 468.

35.   Ibid.

36.   Bodega to Revillagigedo, Nootka, June 22, 1792, HLM 327.

37.   Moziño, "Noticias de Nutka," 1792, MN, Ms. 468.

38.   Moziño, "Noticias de Nutka," 1792, MN, Ms. 468. Reflexiones sobre los reconocimientos de los canales por donde hicieron esta navegación, y recolección de algunas producciones, signed by Dionisio Alcalá Galiano, México, October 18, 1793, MN, Ms. 468.

39.   Moziño, "Noticias de Nutka," 1792, MN, Ms. 468. Bodega to Revillagigedo, Nootka, June 22, 1792, HLM 327.

40.   Noticia de las Semillas que se dan en Nootka, document 18, folio 51, MN, Ms. 330.

41.   Ibid.

42. Examen Político de las Costas del No. de America, document 29, folio 101, MN, Ms. 330.

43. Descripción Física de las costas del Norte de la America visitadas por nosotros o por los navegantes anteriores (hereinafter cited as "Descripción Física"), document 30, folio 121, MN, Ms. 330. This brief work is attributed to Malaspina.

44. Ibid.

45. In the Museo Naval, Madrid, are two unsigned documents in original form, which appear to be in Alberni's handwriting. The first is datelined "Nutka, Noviembre del 1790," document 15, folio 47, MN, Ms. 330, and contains notes on the weather at Nootka from November 1790 to April 1971. The second document, "En el Año de '90, Abril, Mayo, Junio . . . ," document 22, folio 76, MN, Ms. 330, contains more notes on the weather. These two documents corroborate information contained in Malaspina's chart.

46. "Descripción Física" document 30, folio 121, MN, Ms. 330. Note that the month of June is omitted.

47. *Gaceta de México, Compendio de Noticias de Nueva España, México,* Tomo Quinto que se comprehenden los años de 1792 y 1793, 171.

48. Bancroft, *History of California*, I:535.

49. Ibid., I:530.

50. Ibid., I:539n.

51. Ibid., I:539.

52. Ibid.

53. Ibid., I:539, 540n.

54. Ibid., I:693.

55. Ibid., I:541.

56. Ibid., I:679.

57. Felix Berenguer de Marquina to José Antonio Caballo, México, July 27, 1802, AGI, México 1464. Alberni's health had been deteriorating since 1801. Father Fermin Francisco de Lasuén noted Alberni's illness; "For the past three days the good Don Pedro de Alberni has been here. He came to relax in the hope that he may be able to rid himself of a severe form of melancholy which he could not shake off as a result of some form of insult given him at the presidio." Lasuén to Fray José Gasol, San Carlos, March 6, 1801, in Finbar Keneally, O.F.M., ed., *Writings of Fermin de Lasuén* (hereinafter Keneally, *Lasuén*) (Washington, D.C.: Academy of American Franciscan History, 1965), II, 184. Lasuén continued a progress report of Alberni, writing "for the past five days Señor Don Pedro Alberni who has been staying at this mission, has been suffering from a severe pain in the side. He seems to be on the road to recovery for his is feeling better just now." Lasuén to Gasol, San Carlos, July 3, 1801, in Keneally, *Lasuén*, II, 234. Lasuén further commented that "I left the Honorable Don Pedro de Alberni at the mission of San Carlos well on the

way to convalescence after having had one foot in the grave." Lasuén to Gasol, Santa Clara, July 17, 1801, in Keneally, *Lasuén,* II:238.

58. Pedro de Alberni, Hoja de Servicios, December 1800, AGS, Guerra Moderna 7277, c:8. Alberni was at San Juan de Ulúa, Vera Cruz in 1793.

CHAPTER 8

1. See Finke, "La organización del ejército," *BAGN,* 11, 636.

2. Finke, "La organización del ejército," *BAGN,* 11, 636. See also Abelardo Carrillo y Gariel, *El Traje en la Nueva España* (México: Instituto Nacional de Antropología e Historia, 1959), 178–79.

3. Sidney B. Brinckerhoff and Pierce A. Chamberlain, *Spanish Military Weapons in Colonial America 1700–1821* (Pennsylvania: Stackpole Books, 1972), 24–25. The above is a description of the weapon identified as that used by the Catalonian Volunteers.

4. Brinckerhoff and Chamberlain, *Spanish Military Weapons,* 25.

5. Signed statement by Antonio Pol, México, May 23, 1772, AGI, México 1392.

6. Noticia del armamento que esta compañía tiene oy día de la fecha, con expresión del tiempo de su uso y el estado en que se halla, signed by Pedro Alberni, Tepic, January 1790, HLM 327.

7. Josef Rafadel to Revillagigedo, Real Fuerte de San Carlos de Perote, February 26, 1790, HLM 327.

8. Bodega y Quadra to Revillagigedo, San Blas, March 5, 1790, HLM 327.

9. Teodoro de Croix to Bucareli, Chihuahua, April 3, 1771, AGI, Guadalajara 416.

10. Relación de la expedición, México, September 1, 1771, AGI, Guadalajara 416.

11. El capitán de esta compañía existe mandando el castillo de el Puerto de Nutka, and Relación de la Fuerza con que se halla la compañía hoy en día, signed by Pedro de Alberni, Puerto de San Lorenzo de Nuca [*sic*], 23 de agosto de 1790, MN, Ms. 330. See also Compañía Franca de Voluntarios de Cataluña del mando de su capitán don Pedro de Alberni, Guadalajara, 11 de diciembre de 1787, in Extracto de la Revista pasada por los Ministros Principales de Real Hacienda de esta capital, signed by Nicolas Garcia, AGI, México 1515; Juan Gregorio Muniain to Julian de Arriaga, Aranjuez, 22 de mayo de 1767, AGI, México 2455; and, Reglamento e Instrucción para los Presidios que se han de formar en la linea de frontera de la Nueva España. Resuelto por el Rey N. S. en Cedula de 10 de septiembre de 1772 (hereinafter cited as

Reglamento de 1772 De orden de su Magestad). Madrid: Por Juan de San Martín, Impresor de la Secretaria del Despacho Universal de Indias, Año de 1773, AHN, Estado 3882, Expediente 16. Max L. Moorehead, *The Presidio: Bastion of the Spanish Borderlands* (Norman: University of Oklahoma Press, 1975), pp. 201–21.

12. Vilaseca to Flores, San Blas, February 16, 1788, AGN, Marina 77.

13. Luís Rojas, Hoja de Servicios, June 1777, AGI, México 1382. Rojas retired from military service in 1783; Matías de Galvez, México, June 29, 1783, AGI, México 1405.

14. Donald C. Cutter, "Pedro Alberni and the First Scientific Agricultural Experiments in the Northwest" (unpublished ms.), 4; hereinafter cited as Cutter, "Pedro Alberni."

15. Reglamento de 1772, September 10, 1772, AHN, Estado 3882, Expediente 16.

16. Bucareli to Arriaga, México, May 26, 1772, AGI, México 2458.

17. Signed statement by Antonio de Pol, México, May 23, 1772, AGI, México 2458.

18. Bucareli to Arriaga, México, March 27, 1772, AGI, México 2459.

19. Bucareli to Arriaga, México, March 27, 1773, and Bucareli to Arriaga, México, May 26, 1772, both in AGI, México 2459.

20. Bucareli to Arriaga, México, March 27, 1773, AGI, México 2459.

21. Ibid.

22. Plan que manifiesta el número de Plazas de Dotación de que deve componerse actualmente cada una de las Compañía Francas de Voluntarios de Cataluña, y de la fuerza en que quedaran reduciendolas al Estado que a continuación se expresa y se propone en la carta 385, México, May 25, 1772, AGI, México 2459. Another company of Catalonian Volunteers was formed and stationed at El Perote.

23. In 1808 both companies of Catalonian Volunteers numbered 160 men, 80 each; see *Documentos Históricos Obra Comemorativa del Primer Centenario de la Independencia de México* (México: Museo de Arqueología, Historia y Etnología, 1910), II:42.

24. Bucareli to Arriaga, México, May 26, 1772, AGI, México 2459.

25. Finke, "La organización del ejército," *BAGN,* 11, 635.

27. Croix to Gálvez, Chihuahua, April 3, 1778, AGI, Guadalajara 276.

27. Ibid.

28. Reglamento de 1772, September 10, 1772, AHN, Estado 3882, Expediente 16.

29. Bucareli to Arriaga, México, February 24, 1773; and Bucareli to Arriaga, México, May 26, 1772, in AGI, México 2459.

30. Bucareli to Arriaga, México, March 27, 1773, AGI, México 2459.

31. Ibid.

32. Bucareli to Arriaga, México, February 24, 1773, AGI, México 2459. See also Reglamento de 1772, September 10, 1772, AHN, Estado 3882, Expediente 16.

33. Bucareli to Arriaga, México, May 26, 1772, AGI, México 2459.

34. El Virrey de Nueva España da cuenta, México, February 1771, in Velasco, "La Administración de Bucareli," *BAGN,* 30, 375.

35. Bolton, *Palou's New California,* III:130.

36. Ibid.

37. Ibid.

38. Puig and Pericas to Bucareli, Real del Monte, March 11, 1775, in Velasco, "La Administración de Bucareli," *PAGN,* 39, 227.

39. Ibid.

40. Estado que manifiesta la fuerza en que se hallan los cuerpos veteranos de Infantería y Dragones de este Reyno, con distinción de clases, número que les falta para su completo, y destino actual de dicho cuerpo (hereinafter cited as Estado que manifiesta la fuerza) México, July 26, 1777, AGI, México 1382. Another Estado que manifiesta la fuerza, México, December 1777, AGI, México 1380.

41. Estado que manifiesta la fuerza, México, July 26, 1977, AGI, México 1382.

42. Estado que manifiesta la fuerza, México, January 27, 1778, AGI, México 1383; Estado que manifiesta la fuerza, México, May 27, 1778, AGI, México 1380.

43. Estado que manifiesta la fuerza, México, January 27, 1778, AGI, México 1383, Estado que manifiesta la fuerza, México, April 27, 1778, AGI, México 1384; and Estado que manifiesta la fuerza, México, May 27, 1778, AGI, México 1380.

44. Croix to Bucareli, Querétaro, August 22, 1777, in Velasco, "La Administración de Bucareli," *PAGN,* 29, 371.

45. Bucareli to Croix, México, August 27, 1777, in Velasco, "La Administración de Bucareli," *PAGN,* 29, 353–68.

46. Croix to Bucareli, México, November 26, 1777, in Velasco, "La Administración de Bucareli," *PAGN,* 29, 378.

47. Croix to Bucareli, Hacienda de Abinito, October 16, 1777, in Velasco, "La Administración de Bucareli," *PAGN,* 29, 380.

48. Croix to Bucareli, Chihuahua, April 3, 1778, AGN, Provincias Internas 246.

49. Anza to Croix, Chihuahua, June 20, 1778, AGI, Guadalajara 276.

50. Croix to Gálvez, Chihuahua, June 29, 1778, AGI, Guadalajara 276.

51. Eugenio del Hoyo, Malcom D. McLean, eds., *Diario y Derrotero (1777–1781) por Fray Juan Agustín de Morfí* (Monterrey, 1767) (hereinafter cited as

Hoyo and McLean, *Morfí, Diario y Derrotero*), 218. The entry in Morfí's diary describing the incident was for September 11, 1779.

52. Ibid.

53. Alfred Barnaby Thomas, ed., *Teodoro de Croix and the Northern Frontier of New Spain, 1776–1783* (Norman: University of Oklahoma Press, 1941), 152.

54. Thomas, *Tedoro de Croix,* 153.

55. Fages to Morfí, Pitic de Caborca, February 12, 1782, AGN, Historia 24.

56. Ronald L. Ives, ed., "Retracing the Route of the Fages Expedition of 1781," *Arizona and the West;* hereinafter cited as Ives, "The Fages expedition, 1781," *AW,* VIII, no. 1 (1966), 58.

57. Ibid., 58.

58. Ibid.

59. Ibid.

60. Ibid., 163.

61. Ibid.

62. Fages to Morfí, Pitic de Caborca, February 12, 1782, AGN, Historia 24.

63. Ives, "The Fages expedition, 1781," *AW,* VIII, 166.

64. Ibid.

65. Ronald L. Ives, "From Pitic to San Gabriel in 1782: The Journey of Don Pedro Fages," *The Journal of Arizona History,* 9, no. 4 (Winter 1968), 225. See also Hero Euguene Rensh, "Fages' Crossing of the Cuyamacs," *California Historical Society Quarterly,* 34, no. 2 (June 1955), 193–208. Rensch describes Fages's return to California, detailing the route taken and the valuable information acquired by Fages on that exploratory trip.

66. Solá to Croix, Presidio del Pitic, November 8, 1772, AGN, Californias 31, contains Solá's application, Martín de Mayoraga to Gálvez, México, September 5, 1782, AGI, México 1395 contains Alberni's application.

67. Vicente de Herrera to Gálvez, México, April 26, 1785, AGI, México 1416.

68. Manuel Flores to Antonio Valdez, México, February 28, 1788, AGI, México 1515.

69. Ibid.

70. Patente de Capitán de la Compañía de Caballería del Presidio de San Bernardino de la Provincia de Sonora, signed by Manuel de Negrete y de la Torre, Madrid, October 18, 1790, AGI, Guadalajara 506.

71. Pedro Alberni, Hoja de Servicios, July 1798, AGI, México 1446.

72. Pedro Antonio Cossio to Gálvez, México, September 5, 1782, AGI, México 1395. Matías de Gálvez to José de Gálvez, Mexico, June 26, 1783, AGI, México 1405.

73. Vicente de Herrera to Gálvez, México, May 27, 1785, AGI, México 1416. See also Relación de un Sargento que tiene esta compañía acreedora a la gracia de retiro con expresión de su edad, años de servicios, campañas, y destino de solícita, signed by Pedro Alberni, Real de Monte, February 18, 1785, AGI, México 1416.

74. Extracto de la Revista pasada por los Ministros Principales de la Real Hacienda de esta capital con intervención del Theniente Veterano Don Nicolás García (hereinafter cited as Extracto de la Revista), Guadalajara, December 11, 1787, AGI, México 1515.

75. Extracto de la Revista, Guadalajara, December 11, 1787, AGI, México 1515.

76. Ibid.

77. Alberni to Flores, Guadalajara, December 31, 1787, AGI, México 1515.

78. Extracto de la Revista, Guadalajara, February 11, 1788, AGI, México 1515.

79. Revista de Comisario, signed by Pedro de Alberni, Guadalajara, March 15, 1793, AGI, Guadalajara 509. See also Pedro Gorostiza to Revillagigedo, México, March 30, 1793, HLM 327. Gorostiza commented that Alberni's force had been sixty-four troops upon the return from Nootka.

80. Gorostiza to Revillagigedo, México, February 16, 1793, HLM 327.

81. Pedro de Alberni, Hoja de Servicios, December 1800, AGS, Guerra Moderna 7277, c:8. Pedro de Alberni, Hoja de Servicios, July 1798, AGI, Guadalajara 509. Viceroy Miguel de Azanza to Juan Manuel Alvaner, México, October 27, 1798, AGI, Guadalajara 509.

82. José Font de Bermudes, Hoja de Servicios, December 1800, AGS, Guerra Moderna 7277, c:8. See also José Font y Bermudes, Hoja de Servicios, December 1798, AGS, Guerra Moderna 7275, c:7.

83. Simón Suárez, Hoja de Servicios, December 1800, AGS, Guerra Moderna 7277, c:8. See also Simón Suárez, Hoja de Servicios, December 1798, AGS, Guerra Moderna 7275, c:7.

84. Joaquín Tico, Hoja de Servicios, December 1800, AGA, Guerra Moderna 7277, c:8; and, Joaquín Tico, Hoja de Servicios, December 1798, AGS, Guerra Moderna 7275, c:7.

85. Pablo Avila, "Naming of the Elector-Designate, Santa Bárbara, 1830," *CHSQ*, 27, 337. See also Bancroft, *History of California*, II:5, n. 8.

86. Félix Berenguer de Marquina to José Antonio Caballero, México, July 27, 1802, AGI, México 1464.

87. Berenguer to Caballero, México, July 27, 1802, AGI, México 1464.

88. Berenguer to Caballero, México, July 27, 1802, AGI, México 1464. Berenguer's words were: No propongo para subteniente al sargento de la expresada, Joaquín Tico que sirve a S.M. de veinte anos, diez meses y quatro

dias a esta parte con buenas notas, porque es casado, y no me constan las circunstancias de su mujer.

89. Braulio Otalora to the Commander of Navy and Arms of the Station of San Blas, On board the Frigate *Princesa,* anchored in the port of Monterey, September 2, 1803, MN, Ms. 575 bis.

90. Signed statement by Braulio Otalora, On board the Frigate *Princesa,* anchored in the Port of Monterey, August 31, 1803, MN, Ms. 575 bis.

91. Bancroft, *History of California,* II:16.

92. Braulio Otalora to the Commander of Navy and Arms of the Station of San Blas, On board the Frigate *Princesa,* anchored in the port of Monterey, September 2, 1803, MN, Ms 575 bis.

93. Bancroft, *History of California,* II:17, n. 26.

94. Braulio Otalora to the Commander of Navy and Arms of the Station of San Blas, On board the Frigate *Princesa,* anchored in the port of Monterey, September 2, 1803, MN, Ms. 575 bis.

95. Bancroft, *History of California,* II:18.

96. Ibid.

97. Extracto de carta por un G.D.D. a otro D.J., September 2, 1778, AGI, Indiferente General 1632b.

98. Signed statement by Pedro Fages, November 4, 1774, AGS, Títulos de Indias 2°–58–307.

99. Extracto de carta por un G.D.D., September 2, 1778, AGI, Indiferente General 1632b.

100. Ibid.

101. Additional correspondence regarding Arnold are numerous in the Spanish archives. See AGI, Indiferente General 1632b.

102. Relación por antiguidad de los oficiales, December 1794, AGI, Audiencia de México 1438.

CHAPTER 9

1. Navarro García, *El Marqués de Croix,* 195.

2. Gálvez to Marqués de Croix, México, January 23, 1768, AGN, Provincias Internas 154. English translation of this letter may be found in Richman, *California under Spain and Mexico, 1535–1847* (New York: Houghton Mifflin Company, 1911), 503–13.

3. Signed statement by Antonio de Pol, México, May 23, 1772, AGI, México 1392.

4. Ynstancia de don Juan Puyol comisionado al descubrimiento de las minas de Sonora sobre various ausilios que pide para pasar al Puerto de San

Blas y de ahi a su destino (hereinafter cited as Instancia de Juan Puyol), signed by Francisco Manron, Cádiz, August 26, 1778, AGN, Provincias Internas 258.

5.   Ibid. Another list of Puyol's colonists is given in Mario Hernández y Sánchez-Barba, "Frontera, población y milicia," *Revista de Indias* (Enero–Marzo 1956), 16, no. 63, 29, n. 12.

6.   Puyol to Bucareli, México, December 3, 1778, AGN, Provincias Internas 258. Puyol reiterated the plan of travel and his responsibility of locating and caring for the families.

7.   Noticia que manifesta los hombres, apellidos, estado y destinos, de familias que vinieron de España al cargo de Don Juan Puyol (hereinafter cited as Noticia que manifiesta los hombres), signed by Pedro Fages, México, September 20, 1778, AGN, Provincias Internas 258.

8.   Ibid.

9.   Puyol to Excelentísimo Señor, no date, AGN, Provincias Internas 258.

10.   Teodoro de Croix to Martín de Mayoraga, Arispe, October 12, 1780, AGN, Provincias Internas 258.

11.   Resumen general de las hostilidades cometidas por indios enemigos . . . signed report by Don Felipe Barry, Durango, June 30, 1777, in Velasco, "La Administración de Bucareli," *PAGN*, 29, 376. The same document may be found in AGI, México 1380.

12.   Mario Hernández y Sánchez-Barba, "Frontera, población y milicia," *Revista de Indias* (Enero–Marzo 1956), 165, no. 63, 37.

13.   Bolton, *Palou's New California*, III:230.

14.   Serra to Bucareli, San Carlos de Monterey, August 24, 1774, in Tibesar, *Writings of Serra*, III:149.

15.   Serra to Bucareli, San Carlos de Monterey, August 24, 1774, in Tibesar, *Writings of Serra*, III:149.

16.   Serra to Bucareli, Apostolic College of San Fernando of the Franciscan Missionaries of this court of México, March 13, 1773, in Tibesar, *Writings of Serra*, I:235.

17.   Bancroft, *History of California*, I:565.

18.   Ibid.

19.   Florian Guest, O.F.M., "The Establishment of the Villa de Branciforte," *California Historical Society Quarterly* (hereinafter Guest, "The Establishment of Branciforte," *CHSQ*) 41 (1962), 32. See also Expediente sobre erección de la villa de Branciforte en la Nueva California, 1796–1803, University of Texas Library, Austin, W. B. Stephens Collection (hereinafter cited as Expediente sobre erección, 1796–1803, UT-WBS) Californias 9.

20.   Copia de los informes del Real Tribunal de Quentas y Ministro encargo de la segunda mesa de marina de una nueva Poblazon en Californias con el

título de Branciforte in Expediente sobre erección, 1796–1803, UT-WBS, Californias 9. Guest, "The Establishment of Branciforte," *CHSQ*, 41, 32.

21. Borica to Branciforte, Monterey, August 4, 1976, in Expediente sobre erección, 1796–1803, UT-WBS, Californias 9. Bancroft, *History of California*, I:565.

22. Ynstrucción aprovada por S.M. que se formó para el establecimiento de la nueba villa del Pitic en la Provincia de Sonora mandada adaptar a las demas nuevas Poblaciones proyectadas y que se establecieren en el dentro de esta comandancia general, November 14, 1789, in Expediente sobre erección, 1796–1803, UT-WBS, Californias 9.

23. Borica to Branciforte, Monterey, September 23, 1796, in Expediente sobre erección, 1796–1803, UT-WBS, Californias 9.

24. Bancroft, *History of California*, I:565.

25. Guest, "The Establishment of Branciforte," *CHSQ*, 41, 33–34.

26. Ibid., 38.

27. Borica to Alberni, Monterey, June 16, 1796; and Borica to Córdoba, Monterey, June 16, 1796, both in Expediente sobre erección, 1796–1803, UT-WBS, Californias 9.

28. Alberni to Borica, San Francisco de California, July 1, 1796, in Expediente sobre erección, 1796–1803, UT-WBS, Californias 9.

29. Alberni to Borica, San Francisco de California, July 1, 1796; and Córdoba to Borica, Presidio de San Francisco, July 20, 1796; both in Expediente sobre erección, 1796–1803, UT-WBS, Californias 9.

30. Alberni to Borica, San Francisco de California, July 1, 1796, in Expediente sobre erección, 1796–1803, UT-WBS, Californias 9.

31. Alberni to Borica, San Francisco de California, July 1, 1798, in Expediente sobre erección, 1796–1803, UT-WBS, Californias 9. Alberni noted that San Francisco was thirty leagues away from his suggested site, and that Monterey was twenty-two leagues distant by land and twelve by sea.

32. Alberni to Borica, San Francisco de California, July 1, 1796, in Expediente sobre erección, 1796–1803, UT-WBS, Californias 9.

33. Alberni to Borica, San Francisco de California, July 1, 1796, in Expediente sobre erección, 1796–1803, UT-WBS, Californias 9.

34. Alberni to Borica, San Francisco de California, July 1, 1796, in Expediente sobre erección, 1796–1803, UT-WBS, Californias 9.

35. Alberni to Borica, San Francisco de California, July 1, 1796, in Expediente sobre erección, 1796–1803, UT-WBS, Californias 9.

36. Córdoba to Borica, Presidio de San Francisco, July 1, 1796, in Expediente sobre erección, 1796–1803, UT-WBS, Californias 9.

37. Signed statement by El Fiscal de Real Hacienda, México, December 29, 1796 (con sello) in Expediente sobre erección, 1796–1803, UT-WBS, Californias 9.

38. Father Pedro Callejas to Branciforte, México, January 27, 1797, in Expediente sobre erección, 1796–1803, UT-WBS, Californias 9.

39. Borica to Branciforte, Monterey, August 21, 1797, in Expediente sobre erección, 1796–1803, UT-WBS, Californias 9.

40. Borica to Branciforte, Monterey, August 21, 1791, in Expediente sobbre erección, 1796–1803, UT-WBS, Californias 9.

41. Plan que Manifiesta la idea de una Poblacion Nueva en la alta California con el Distingidismo nombre de Branciforte cituada en la Latitud Norte de 37°, 0', 00" y en la longitud-oeste de 16°, 43', 0" del Meridiano de San Blas, signed by Alberto de Córdoba, Misión de Santa Cruz, September 28, 1797, in Expediente sobre erección, 1796–1803, UT-WBS, Californias 9.

42. Guest, "Establishment of Branciforte," *CHSQ*, 41, 35.

43. Ibid.

44. Ibid., 44.

45. Ibid., 45.

46. Ibid., 47.

47. Ibid.

48. Pablo Avila, "Naming of the Elector-Designate, Santa Bárbara, 1830," *CHSQ*, 27, 333–37, is analytical of Fernando Tico's role in California politics during the Mexican Period.

CHAPTER 10

1. Vilaseca to Viceroy Flores, San Blas, February 16, 1788, AGN, Marina 77.

2. Signed statement by Domingo Elizondo, Pitic, April 28, 1771 (con sello), AGN, Marina 77.

3. Ibid.

4. Signed statement by Agustín Callis, Real del Monte, June 14, 1774 (con sello), AGN, Marina 77.

5. Ibid.

6. Signed statement by Pedro de Alberni, Guadalajara, August 20, 1787 (con sello), AGN, Marina 77.

7. Pié de la lista de la Compañía que de orden de S.M. se ha formado con destino al Virreynato de México por saca voluntaria en la tropa de el Segundo Regimiento de Infantería Ligera de Cataluña, signed by Alonso Cavallero, Sevilla, May 13, 1767, AGI, México 2455.

8. Marqués de Croix to Juan Gregorio Muniain, México, September 24, 1767, AGI, México 2429.

9. Libro de Servicios de las Compañía Franca de Volunterios de Cataluña

. . . hasta Diciembre de 1776, AGI, México 1379. No *hoja de servicios* was included for Vilaseca, probably because of his retirement from the Catalonian company. Earlier records of Vilaseca's military service have not been located.

10. Vilaseca to Viceroy Flores, San Blas, February 16, 1788 (con sello), AGN, Marina 77.

11. Pié de la lista de la Compañía que de orden de S.M. se ha formado con destino al Virreynato de México por saca voluntaria en la tropa de el Regimiento de Infantería Ligera de Cataluña, Sevilla, May 13, 1767, AGI, México 2455.

12. Signed statement by Francisco Hixosa, San Blas, July 8, 1788 (con sello), AGN, Marina 77.

13. José María de Monterde signed statement, San Blas, Febraury 28, 1787 (con sello), AGN, Marina 77.

14. Vilaseca to Viceroy Flores, San Blas, February 16, 1788, AGN, Marina 77.

15. Unsigned letter to Señor Comisario de San Blas ¿222. April 13, 1790. Francisco Hixosa was the *comisario* at San Blas. AGN, Marina 78.

16. Signed statement by José María Monterde contador proprietorio de la Real Caja del Departamento de San Blas, San Blas, February 28, 1787, AGN, Marina 77.

17. Signed statement by Francisco Trillo y Vermudes and Nicolás Carrión de Velasco, comisario y contador de la Real Hacienda y Caja del Departamento de San Blas, San Blas, December 20, 1782, AGN, Marina 77.

18. Signed statement by José María Monterde, San Blas, February 28, 1787, AGN, Marina 78.

19. Los Ministros de la Real Hacienda y Caja del Departamiento de San Blas . . . signed by Francisco Hixosa, Estavan de Vilaseca, and Juan Francisco Rosales, August 31, 1788 (con sello), AGN, Marina 78.

20. Real Tribunal de la Contaduría Mayor y Audiencia de Cuentas, August 9, 1788 (con sello), AGN, Marina 77.

21. Vilaseca to Flores, San Blas, February 16, 1788, AGN, Marina 77.

22. Signed by Vilaseca, San Blas, May 8, 1788, AGN, Marina 77.

23. Signed statement by Don Pedro Carbajal, Don Dionicio de la Mota, Don Juan Camamalle cirujanos de la embarcación de S.M. en el Departamento de San Blas, February 1788 (con sello), AGN, Marina 77.

CHAPTER 11

1. Juan Antonio de Viruega, Hoja de Servicios, December 1800, AGS, Guèrra Moderna 7277, c:8. Agustin Yslas, Hoja de Servicios, December 1800,

AGS, Guerra Moderna 7277, c:8. Agustín Malavar, Hoja de Servicios, December 1800, AGS, Guerra Moderna 7277, c:8.

2. Signed statement by José Ruiz, Francisco Servando Muñóz, Juan de los Rios y Piedras, Pedro Analla, Santo Lazarín, Bartolomé Beyo and Juan de Viruega, December 16, 1810, AGN, Operaciones de Guerra 1019.

3. Estado que manifiesta la fuerza que tiene dicho Batallón con expresión de ausentes, Queretaro, August 13, 1815, AGN, Operaciones de Guerra 1019.

4. San Diego, Piquete de Voluntarios de Cataluña y sus familias, 1796–1817, AGN, Provincias Internas, tomo 17.

5. General Félix María Calleja to Viceroy Francisco Xavier Venegas, Campo sobre Cuautla, April 5, 1812, AGN, Operaciones de Guerra de Realistas, tomo 32.

6. El Conde de Colombini to Viceroy Francisco Xavier Venegas, Mexico City. February 9, 1812, AGN, Causas de Infidencias, tomo 101. See also report of Interrogation signed by Matías González, AGN, Causas de Infidencias, tomo 101.

7. Parte del General Calleja al Virrey, con la notica de muertos y heridos habidos en el ataque de Cuautla, Campo de Cuautla, February 20, 1812, AGN, Operaciones de Guerra de Realistas, tomo 30. See also summaries of the attack on Cuautla in Operaciones de Guerra de Realistas, tomo 32.

8. Calleja to Venegas, Campo sobre Cuautla, April 5, 1812, AGN, Operaciones de Guerra de Realistas, tomo 32.

9. Ibid.

10. Parte de José Antonio Andrade . . . dandole cuenta del ataque, AGN, Operaciones de Guerra de Realistas, tomo 32.

11. Calleja to Venegas, Campo sobre Cuautla, April 5, 1812, AGN, Operaciones de Guerra de Realistas, tomo 32.

12. Parte de José Andrade, AGN, Operaciones de Guerra de Realistas, tomo 32.

13. For reports on the referred to actions against insurgents see AGN, Operaciones de Guerra de Realistas, tomos 7, 32, and 101.

Bibliography

MANUSCRIPT MATERIALS

Documents used in Archivo General de Indias, Sevilla, Spain, may be found in the following sections and legajos:

Audiencia de México		Audiencia de Guadalajara
1366	1464	276
1379	2429	416
1380	2455	506
1382	2458	509
1383	2459	515
1394	2477	
1405	1515	Papeles Procedentes de Cuba
		338

Indiferente General
1632b

Documents used in the Museo Naval, Madrid, Spain, may be found in the following volumes of manuscript collections:

Manuscript	Volume Numbers
Ms. 143	Ms. 334
Ms. 271	Ms. 468
Ms. 330	Ms. 575
Ms. 331	Ms. 575 bis
Ms. 332	Ms. 2305

Sección Cartografía
Be III, Ce B-No-3
Be III, Ce B-No-1

Bibliography

Documents used in the Archivo Histórico Nacional, Madrid, Spain, may be found in the following sections and legajos:

Estado	Diversos Documentos de Indias
3883	464

Maps and illustrations used in the Archivo del Servico Histórico Militar, Madrid, Spain, may be located as follows:

Mapa de la Provincia de Sonora, Opatas, Pimas altos y Pimas bajos, o-b-7-18.
Mapa de la Provincia de Sonora, o-b-7-7.
Carta Reducida del Océano Asiatico, drawn by Miguel Costansó, 1770, n-b-1-9.
Mapa de la Nueva California, o-b-6-22.
Carta Esferica de los reconocimientos hechos en 1792, p-b-2-3.
Carta Esferica de los reconocimientos hechos . . . de la Entrada de Juan de Fuca, 1793, k-b-4-22.
Uniform of Catalonian soldier in *Album de la Infantería Española*.

Documents used in the Archivo General de Simancas, Simancas, Spain, may be found in the following section and numbers:

Guerra Moderna
2811
7275
7277

Documents used in the Archivo General de la Nación, México, D.F., may be found in the following sections:

Marina	Historia	Californias	Provincias Internas
77	24	9	246
78		17	258
		31	266
		66	

Operaciones de Guerra de Realistas
32, 101, 1019

Causas de Infidencias
101

Documents used in the Huntington Library, San Marino, California, may be found in the following manuscript collection:

Bibliography

Huntington Library Manuscript 327

Documents used in the University of Texas Library, Austin, may be found in:

The W. B. Stephens Collection:
Californias 9

PRINTED SOURCES

Bolton, Herbert E., ed. *Historical Memoirs of New California by Fray Francisco Palou, O.F.M.* Berkeley: University of California Press, 1926. 4 vols.

———, ed. *Fray Juan Crespi: Missionary Explorer on the Pacific Coast, 1769–1774.* Berkeley: University of California Press, 1927.

Documentos Históricos Obra Conmemorative del Primer Centenario de la Independencia de México. México: Museo de Arqueología, Historia y Etnologia, 1910. 7 vols.

Documentos para la Historia de México. México, 1853–1857.

Gaceta de México, Compendio de Noticias de Nueva España. México, 1784–1808. 15 vols.

Geiger, Maynard, O.F.M., ed. *Francisco Palou's Life of Fray Junípero Serra.* Washington, D.C.: Academy of American Franciscan History, 1955.

Gómez Canedo, Lino. *De México a la Alta California: Una Gran Epopeya Misional.* México, 1969.

Hoyo, Eugenio del, and Malcolm D. McLean, eds. *Diario y Derrotero (1777–1781) por Fray Juan Agustín de Morfi.* Monterrey, 1969.

Keneally, Finbar, O.F.M., ed. *Writings of Fermín de Lasuén.* Washington, D.C.: Academy of American Franciscan History, 1965. 2 vols.

Priestley, Herbert I., ed. *A Historical, Political and Natural Description of California by Pedro Fages, Soldier of Spain.* Berkeley: University of California Press, 1937.

Salva, Miguel, and Pedro Sainz de Baranda, eds. *Colección de Documentos Inéditos para la Historia de España.* Madrid, 1842–1895. 113 vols.

Temple, II, Thomas Workman, trans. and ed. "Three Early California Letters," *Publications of the Historical Society of Southern California Quarterly,* 15 (1931), 28–64.

Thomas, Alfred B., ed. *Teodoro de Croix and the Northern Frontier of New Spain, 1776–1783.* Norman: University of Oklahoma Press, 1941.

Bibliography

Tibesar, Antonine, O.F.M., ed. *The Writings of Fray Junípero Serra.* Washington, D.C.: Academy of American Franciscan History, 1955—. 4 vols.

Velasco Ceballos, Rómulo, ed. *La Administración de D. Frey Antonio María de Bucareli y Ursúa.* Publicación del Archivo General de la Nación, tomos 29–30. México, 1936. 2 vols.

Wagner, Henry R., ed. *Spanish Explorations in the Strait of Juan de Fuca.* New York: AMS Press, 1971 edition. Originally published in 1933.

BOOKS

Alessio Robles, Vito, ed. *Alejandro de Humboldt, Ensayo Político Sobre el Reino de Nueva España.* México, D.F., 1941. 4 vols.

Archer, Christon I. *The Army in Bourbon Mexico, 1760–1810.* Albuquerque: University of New Mexico Press, 1977.

Bancroft, Hubert H. *History of California.* San Francisco: A. L. Bancroft and Company, 1884–1890. 7 vols.

Brinckerhoff, Sidney B., and Pierce A. Chamberlain. *Spanish Military Weapons in Colonial America, 1700–1821.* Pennsylvania: Stackpole Books, 1972.

Carrillo y Gariel, Abelardo. *El Traje en la Nueva España.* México: Instituto Nacional de Antropología e Historia, 1959.

Cook, Warren. *Flood Tide of Empire, Spain and the Pacific Northwest, 1543–1819.* New Haven: Yale University Press, 1973.

Eldridge, Zoeth Z., and E. J. Molera. *The March of Portolá and the Log of the San Carlos.* San Francisco: The California Promotion Committee, 1909.

Geiger, Maynard, O.F.M. *The Life and Times of Fray Junípero Serra, O.F.M.* Washington, D.C.: Academy of American Franciscan History, 1959. 2 vols.

Hernández Sánchez-Barba, Mario. *La Ultima Expansión Española en América.* Madrid, 1957.

Ives, Ronald L. *José Velásquez: Saga of a Borderland Soldier.* Tucson: Southwestern Mission Research Center, 1984.

Navarro García, Luis. *Don José de Gálvez y la Comandancia General de las Provincias Internas del Norte de Nueva España.* Sevilla, 1964.

———. *El Marques de Croix, 1766–1771.* Sevilla, 1967.

Priestley, Herbert I. *José de Gálvez, Visitor-General of New Spain, 1765–1771.* Berkeley: University of California Press, 1916.

Richman, Irving B. *California Under Spain and Mexico, 1537–1847.* Boston and New York: Houghton-Mifflin Company, 1911.

Velásquez, María del Carmen. *El Estado de Guerra en Nueva España, 1760–1808.* Mexico: El Colegio de México, 1950.

DISSERTATIONS

Cutter, Donald C. "Spanish Exploration of California's Central Valley." Ph.D. diss. University of California, 1950.

Nuttall, Donald A. "Pedro Fages and the Advance of the Northern Frontier of New Spain, 1767–1782." Ph.D. diss. University of Southern California, Los Angeles, 1964.

Rowland, Donald W. "The Elizondo Expedition against the Indian Rebels of Sonora, 1765–1771." Ph.D. diss. University of California, Berkeley, 1930.

THESIS

Jones, Oakah L. "The Spanish Occupation of Nootka Sound, 1790–1795." Master's thesis. University of Oklahoma, Norman, 1960.

ARTICLES

Aiton, Arthur. "Spanish Colonial Reorganization Under the Family Compact," *The Hispanic American Historical Review,* 12 (August 1932), 269–80.

Avila, Pablo. "Naming of the Elector-Designate, Santa Barbara, 1830." *The California Historical Society Quarterly,* 27, 333–38.

Bolton, Herbert E. "In the South San Joaquín Ahead of Garcés," *The California Historical Society Quarterly,* 10 (September 1931), 211–19.

Bibliography

Cutter, Donald C. "Pedro Alberni and the First Scientific Agriculture Experiments in the Northwest," unpublished article, 1973.

Finke, Detmar H. "La Organización del Ejército en Nueva España," *Boletin del Archivo General de la Nación,* 11 (1940), 617–63.

Guest, Florian, O.F.M. "The Establishment of the Villa de Branciforte," *The California Historical Society Quarterly,* 41 (1962), 29–50.

Hernández y Sánchez-Barba, Mario. "Frontera, poblacion y milicia," *Revista de Indias,* 16 (Enero–Marzo 1956), 9–49.

Ives, Ronald L. "From Pitic to San Gabriel in 1782: The Journey of Don Pedro Fages," *The Journal of Arizona History,* 9 (Winter 1968), 222–44.

———. "Retracing the Route of the Fages Expedition of 1781," *Arizona and the West,* 7 (1966), 49–70, 157–70.

McAlister, Lyle. "The Reorganization of the Army of New Spain, 1763–1766," *Hispanic American Historical Review,* 33 (February 1953), 1–32.

Nuttall, Donald A. "The Governantes of Spanish Upper California: A Profile," *The California Historical Society Quarterly,* 51 (Fall 1972), 253–80.

Park, Joseph F. "Spanish Indian Policy in Northern Mexico, 1765–1819," *Arizona and the West,* 4 (Winter 1962), 325–44.

Rensch, Hero Eugene. "Fages' Crossing of the Cuyamacs," *The California Historical Society Quarterly,* 24 (June 1955), 193–208.

Index

Index